THE END OF
CORPORATE SOCIAL
RESPONSIBILITY

SAGE has been part of the global academic community since 1965, supporting high quality research and learning that transforms society and our understanding of individuals, groups and cultures. SAGE is the independent, innovative, natural home for authors, editors and societies who share our commitment and passion for the social sciences.

Find out more at: **www.sagepublications.com**

PETER FLEMING & MARC T. JONES

THE END OF CORPORATE SOCIAL RESPONSIBILITY

CRISIS & CRITIQUE

Los Angeles | London | New Delhi
Singapore | Washington DC

Los Angeles | London | New Delhi
Singapore | Washington DC

SAGE Publications Ltd
1 Oliver's Yard
55 City Road
London EC1Y 1SP

SAGE Publications Inc.
2455 Teller Road
Thousand Oaks, California 91320

SAGE Publications India Pvt Ltd
B 1/I 1 Mohan Cooperative Industrial Area
Mathura Road
New Delhi 110 044

SAGE Publications Asia-Pacific Pte Ltd
3 Church Street
#10-04 Samsung Hub
Singapore 049483

Editor: Kirsty Smy
Editorial assistant: Ruth Stitt
Production editor: Rachel Eley
Marketing manager: Alison Borg
Cover design: Wendy Scott
Typeset by: C&M Digitals (P) Ltd, Chennai, India
Printed by MPG Books Group, Bodmin, Cornwall

Library of Congress Control Number: 2012939653

British Library Cataloguing in Publication data

A catalogue record for this book is available from
the British Library

MIX
Paper from
responsible sources
FSC
www.fsc.org   FSC® C018575

ISBN 978-1-84920-515-3
ISBN 978-1-84920-516-0 (pbk)

For Mandy and Mary

CONTENTS

About the Authors   ix

Preface   xi

Introduction: Why the End of Corporate Social Responsibility?   1

1 Welcome to the House of the Blind: What CSR Does Not See   18

2 The MNC to the Rescue? Corporate Citizenship Theory   33

3 Stakeholder Theory and Other Fantasies of the 'Ethical Corporation'   50

4 The New Opium of the People: CSR and the Employee   67

5 From Propaganda to Parasite? Towards a Critical Political Economy of CSR   80

Conclusion: The Beginning of (Non) Corporate Social Responsibility?   96

References   108

Index   120

ABOUT THE AUTHORS

Peter Fleming is Professor of Work and Organization at Queen Mary College, University of London. His research focuses on the political economy of corporations and the relations of power that underlie them. One line of investigation explores the way in which conflict and resistance constitute the formal corporate form currently dominating Western economies. Another area of interest is the cultural politics of work organizations, and the modes of ideological control that operate to enlist the participation of labour, including corporate social responsibility. His books include *Authenticity and the Cultural Politics of Work* (2009, Oxford University Press), *Charting Corporate Corruption* (2009, Edward Elgar), *Contesting the Corporation* (2007, Cambridge University Press) and *Dead Man Working* (2012, Zero Books).

Marc T. Jones has a PhD in Strategic Management from the University of California. He curently holds positions at the Maastricht School of Management (where he is Professor of Strategy), the University of Sydney and the Ashridge Business School in England. He has taught and conducted research on six continents, publishing over 50 articles and co-authoring three books on subjects ranging from corporate social responsibility and business ethics to business strategy, cultural studies, international political economy and business education. His current research interests focus on investigating the institutional requirements for sustainable business ecosystems and exploring the impacts of long-term 'gigatrends' on economy and society.

If one searches for a Google image of *corporate social responsibility* or *sustainability* hundreds of pictures appear. But the most frequent, and for us most disturbing, pictorial representation is that of a pair of giant hands holding a globe, planet earth. Sometimes the hands are white, sometimes brown, feminine or masculine. The visible part of the globe might be the United States, but we found more often it was India or Africa. The intended meaning of the image is clear, as we discovered when presenting it to students in university business ethics and political economy classes. The answers were predictable but telling. Some said it represented humankind finally handling earth in a tender manner or that our future well-being was 'in our hands'. It was strange how many identified with the entity holding the globe rather than with the globe itself. Other interpretations pointed to the softness of the hands, as if they were holding a fragile egg or a newborn kitten. The protector motif was primary, as if the planet was on the brink of some savage attack from an alien invader. The position of the hands was deemed significant: palms open, welcoming and passive, a well-known gesture of peace. All underlined the singularity of the earth and human palms – it denoted *one* humanity and *one* earth, a global togetherness and a standing tall to the dangers that are out there. The colours of blue (*water*), white clouds (the *dove*) and the dark background (the *alien*) were also rendered from the many images. The pictorial conveyance of corporate social responsibility (or CSR) was an admixture of fear, hope and a low-down sense that ultimately someone will save us. But who?

It is then that we share with our students an alternative interpretation, one that makes them smile and sometimes frown. It is clear, to us at least, that there is something obviously (and humorously) ridiculous about the image. First, the idea of giant hands around the world is creepy. They clasp the earth like some alien god that is omnipresent, evincing an image of total control. The hands are apparently human, but we never see a face or body, and one could imagine an abrupt change of mind as the giant nonchalantly squeezes the globe until it bursts like an overripe tomato. The hands also protrude from a dark jacket that strongly resembles a business suit. They hold the globe close (especially when poor India or Africa is visible), conveying a Promethean dominion over the planet. It is almost as if a meddling humanity has won (even if we know it never does when it has a face-off with Gaia). Only in its failure does it desire to call the shots and make right the havoc and destruction it has wreaked over the last 200 years. Yes, a chilling image – something reminiscent of Charlie Chaplin's *Great Dictator* when the tyrant sadistically enjoys his play with the inflated replica of planet earth. Lying on a plush and spacious oak desk, Chaplin hits (with various parts of his anatomy) the hapless sphere into the air, toying with it like a cruel child. Earth gently flies across the room only to be met with another wry knock, fired off with unmistakable satisfaction.

Despite the striking similarity between Charlie Chaplin's rendering and those designed by in-house and external advertising agencies, it is clear that the intention behind these images is very different. Chaplin's portrayal of the great dictator seeks to reveal the humorous yet fatal hubris associated with the belief that humankind might 'own' the world. The advertising agencies, however, do not exhibit the same natural proclivity to comic irony. In a stunningly uncritical manner they present an image of the earth, the human and the corporation existing side by side, in complete harmony.

That corporations wish to produce this beguiling symbiosis is far from surprising. As long as the corporation comes across as a player with good intentions (though routinely failing to live up to them) it evades fatal criticism from the public. But why academics would like to be complicit in this mendacity is harder to fathom. As we will argue in the course of this book, the soft-toned façade of social well-being observed in CSR discourse belies a more disconcerting institutional logic. The reader may tell that this book will be critical of CSR and its correlates of sustainability, the 'triple bottom line' and business ethics. We are so not because we are against ethics in business. Paraphrasing Gandhi's wonderful rebuff when asked what he thought about Western civilization, we would say that *business ethics might be a good idea*. This would require taking seriously the question of ethics, which is much harder than it often seems. CSR is a discursive system that would like us to see it as a step towards correcting the woes of a world system on the brink of social, economic and financial disaster. We plan to demonstrate that it is part and parcel of a structure that perpetuates the atrophy it sought to cure. The reasons for this assertion are varied, sometimes simple and at other times complex. But the position stems from a number of presuppositions that we will defend, elaborate and refine during the course of the book.

First, the institutional matrix of multinational capitalism prioritizes economic rationality primarily. That is its 'nature'. Second, much of the basic axiomatic aspirations of CSR (industrial democracy, sustainability and the so-called 'triple bottom line') are at serious odds with the general tendencies of global capitalism. Third, this disconnect, contradiction and tension are not an aberration (good ethics meeting some 'bad apples'), but symptomatic of the anti-social operating code of the world economic system, especially in its neo-liberal manifestation. Fourth, this preponderant institutional logic invariably subordinates CSR to its own ends, thus relegating it to an empty gesture – like the open palms holding the globe – that garners some legitimacy, bides time with critics and even provides a number of avenues for extending market rationality deeper into society (e.g. carbon emissions trading). Fifth, CSR therefore represents a specific development in neo-liberal ideology that is more of a *step backwards* from progressive socio-political change rather than a way forward. And finally, this conclusion demands critical scholarship and political interventions outside the obstruction that is now CSR (theory and practice) if our grandchildren are not to inherit a dead world writ large with so many lost opportunities.

At the time of writing, Wikileaks – founded by Julian Assange – has been front-page news for a number of weeks. The leaked governmental memos and reports are noteworthy for their brutal realism regarding the nature of contemporary international geo-politics. When it comes to the things that really matter to the power elite, we find very little in the confidential reports about climate change, reforming the exploitative practices of large companies and governments around the world or anything remotely connected with business ethics. Instead, we gain a glimpse of the cold reality of the global political hegemony – especially its rampant irrationalism and flagrant dismissal of democracy. What really matters is the protection of key resource providers, military arms factories, strategic communication lines – all of those concrete institutional supports of an untenable world economic system, one that is in serious decline and crisis. Take this example that conveys the reality of late capitalism: a confidential cable indicates that the petroleum firm, Shell, has allegedly infiltrated local governmental authorities in Nigeria, the scene of one its most controversial moments (in the 1990s the petroleum firm was accused of supporting local thugs who murdered and tortured people protesting about the company's exploitation of the country's natural resources). As a major newspaper reported:

> The oil giant Shell claimed it had inserted staff into all the main ministries of the Nigerian government, giving it access to politicians' every move in the oil-rich Niger Delta, according to a leaked US diplomatic cable. The company's top executive in Nigeria told US diplomats that Shell had seconded employees to every relevant department and so knew 'everything that was being done in those ministries'. She boasted that the Nigerian government had 'forgotten' about the extent of Shell's infiltration and was unaware of how much the company knew about its deliberations.
> (*Guardian*, 2010d: 1)

All of this from a company apparently committed to sustainable development, dialogue with local stakeholders, bio-diversity and indigenous social justice? The leaked cable tells us that, in reality, it is the ruthless 'cold world' (Fox, 2009) of economic influence and control that is the guiding principle of large multinational firms. And this is the backdrop upon which we should view the espoused CSR policies and discourse of the business world more generally. In this sense, CSR practice is often not about addressing or correcting the negative side of enterprise. On the contrary, we feel that it is intimately linked to the continuing systemic aggression of the corporation, as we hope to demonstrate in this book.

But why be so critical of the corporation, given the wealth and well-being it enables? Would we not still be in the 'dark ages' without it? Would not society fall apart, go hungry and suffer disease and servitude? This is what the ideology of big business would have us believe, something we feel inverts the truth of the matter. Is it not *because* of capitalism that we continue to languish in these dark times, that society is falling apart, and more people are hungry now than ever? Indeed, it is the paradoxical *anti-social* essence of this social logic that we find so troubling, especially when we step back and scrutinize it as a global entity. For it makes economic sense to overfish the seas of tuna to the brink of extinction (and when the end of the supply looks inevitable, continue to overfish and simply stockpile frozen supplies so that a higher price can be sought after extinction). It makes economic sense to purchase public infrastructural assets (such as transport) and 'sweat' them so that commuters have no choice but to pay for overpriced tickets for substandard services. It makes economic sense to lobby governments to free up protected nature reserves for oil prospecting. It makes economic sense to locate factories in countries that condone hyper-exploitation and child labour. It makes economic sense to keep defective automobiles on the road since a cost/benefit analysis clearly reveals that it is cheaper to pay court settlements to bereaved loved ones. Of course, from a broader social point of view (what the recent Occupy movement calls 'the 99 per cent') this 'economic sense' is often entirely irrational and self-destructive, often even from its own economic vantage point – the ultimate contradiction of capitalism. But it is an irrationality that is largely ruling the globe to enrich a fraction of humanity at the expense of most, even as the polar ice caps melt and species become extinct before our very eyes. Because conventional CSR theory and practice gives this intrinsically *anti-social* formation an air of ethicality (or potential ethicality), we have become very suspicious of it. It is this conventional or mainstream current of CSR that we find problematic since it often renders ethics into a strategic management issue. As indicated in the introduction and contributing articles in a recent special issue of the *Journal of Management Studies* on CSR (McWilliams et al., 2006), the overarching question is: does it enhance profitability or not?

Having said this, we might also say that much of the literature on CSR in academic scholarship has its heart in the right place. It sees the terrible social effects of the global economic system and is rightly concerned. However, we feel that much of it, even if insightful and relevant, does get bogged down in the liberal precept that capitalism and social ethics might finally be reconciled. Given the recent track record of the corporation over the last 15 years – from Enron and the current finance crisis to the Gulf of Mexico oil spill, and outlandish executive bonuses to the Wikileaks revelations mentioned above – it is amazing that scholars can still have faith in the idea that capitalism can save anything. We would wager that not even the intelligent (but opportunistic) CEOs in these world-spanning firms believe this. So, our book sets out to challenge these liberal assumptions and make some suggestions about how the discussion might develop in a productive manner. In doing so, it offers a more thorough and critical understanding of the interchange between the social expectations placed upon business, the ensuing CSR response in the corporation, and the underlying structural dynamics of late capitalism within the international socio-political economy.

It is easy and sometimes rather facile to be negative about the way business can take up the parlance of ethics as it stridently kicks the globe à la Chaplin's tyrant. Pointing out the hypocrisy, double standards and contradictions of any discourse can often foster a smug self-righteousness that exempts one from the travesty being presented. This is the ugly side of socio-political critique. We are aware of this and are at pains to avoid such an attitude (we are all implicated to some extent). Moreover, in this book we make an effort to move the discussion forward beyond merely criticizing corporate hegemony (which includes an abiding and increasingly punitive state apparatus). First, our analysis of the political economy of CSR positions it within current permutations in late capitalist or post-industrial societies. This is important for recognizing that we need to go further than simply dismiss CSR as a piece of harmless propaganda. Matters are more serious since it is also a concrete corporate practice interconnected with marketization, corporate coercion and commodification. In other words, it has material effects. As such, it requires relatively sophisticated theoretical means to unpack it. We are not boasting to have succeeded in this task, but we do build upon the important critical work of others to make inroads into this problem. Second, as the forthcoming discussions develop towards our overarching theory about what CSR is and how it works (explicated in the final chapter), we also put forward some suggestions on how we might make some positive interventions about how business and society might be improved. Neither of the authors are moralists – we see ourselves as the object of criticism, much as the theories and ideas we challenge in this book. We put forward our ideas not in the hubristic manner of saving the globe from Chaplin's sadistic toying, but instead make some modest theoretical offerings, criticisms and suggestions about advancing the field and practice of CSR and business ethics. In this sense, we are emphasizing the *affirmative* dimension of criticism, as something positive and constructive.

The book is structured as follows. The introduction gives an overview of our argument, especially pertaining to the end of CSR. We suggest that much CSR discourse is about perpetuating the myth that business firms might still pursue their narrow profit-seeking objectives *and* be socially responsible. We demonstrate how this 'win–win' scenario is more than just optimistic: it is a fundamental feature of neo-liberal ideology. It is the deafening silence in CSR discourse and practice regarding the systemic features of global capitalism that we then discuss in Chapter 1. Much of the CSR research and corporate discourse of ethics is blind to some fundamentally destructive processes inherent in the global capitalist system. The reason for this blindness is understandable, since mentioning the glaringly obvious would seriously undermine the cultural legitimacy of 'business as usual'. In Chapters 2 and 3 we engage with some of the key concepts in CSR to further our argument that it is part of the problem rather than the solution. Chapter 2 discusses the recent popularity of corporate citizenship as a way of guaranteeing citizen and human rights in the wake of a receding social welfare state. The chapter argues that in light of the continuing domination of a socially unfriendly neo-liberal discourse that underlies much corporate activity (and the unwillingness to jeopardize profits and short-term returns), the idea that the transnational firm might go out of its way to become a bastion for democratic rights seems far fetched. In Chapter 3 we deal with another pivotal area in CSR, the stakeholder theory of the firm. This approach argues that the organization ought to view its business activities strategically in the context of a network of stakeholders. Best practice dictates dialogue, compromise and conversation with stakeholders to enhance value across the board. Again, our argument stems from the empirical evidence that indicates the indomitable logic of economic gain in the corporate sphere. The assumption that a powerful petroleum firm prospecting in Africa might also be a warm, communitarian forum for mutual exchange is somewhat fantastical.

Chapter 4 discusses an important driver of CSR that is hardly mentioned in research – employees and their changing values and expectations. Workers as much as anyone else are more cynical, anti-business and disappointed following the post-Enron era of unregulated markets, the Occupy movement and the prevalent financial crisis. The contemporary firm is attentive to the problem of enticing and motivating the emergent Generation Y sector of employees who might otherwise find capitalism and the world of business antithetical to their own values. Increasingly, business ethics and CSR consulting firms are selling the programmes to companies as a way to ameliorate classic human resource problems in the face of changing employee demographics, especially in light of a pervasive anti-corporate cynicism in the popular imagination. CSR becomes not only an external branding exercise to appease the consumer, but a way of tapping into and addressing the otherwise counter-corporate concerns of workers, smoothing over any dissonance that could arise from participating in enterprises that harm the community (petroleum, arms, alcohol and tobacco companies are good examples here).

Chapter 5 develops a framework to situate CSR practice within a broader political economy of capitalism in crisis and change. To do this, we survey the various political economies of CSR presented in the literature, and place our approach within a research field that views it as a kind of ideological smokescreen. Rather than changing business practice, it provides a cloak of ethicality so that conditions remain unchanged. It is clear that in many cases CSR represents a pre-emptive or reactionary public relations exercise for consumers, the state, workers and so forth. However, our approach in this chapter suggests that the typical dismissal of CSR as mere propaganda (to soften the image of an otherwise uncaring profit-seeking enterprise) needs to be contextualized within the changing nature of capitalism more broadly. Once we do this, we then can demonstrate how CSR is becoming a predatory corporate practice, in which firms prospect and appropriate aspects of the non-corporate (and even anti-corporate) world in order to enhance their own interests.

In our concluding chapter, we present an overview of the argument and then begin to posit some solutions. With the end of CSR comes a new beginning, one in which the debate around the overwhelming force of global business is conducted on a platform that is not predefined by an unwavering interest in its maintenance. And following the insight of the German philosopher Walter Benjamin, we ought not to view our aspiration for a future free of corporate domination as some kind of unpredictable runaway train. No, it is the world of unbridled neo-liberalism that is truly extreme, speeding away uncontrollably (with us in it) towards oblivion. The critic's intervention, therefore, is more akin to pulling the emergency brake.

This book is the result of long discussions between the authors over the last five years. Sometimes the debate has been heated, but always enlightening and inspired by the mutual feeling that contemporary business and society are extremely problematic, and that the discourse that had the most to say about this – CSR – was riddled with some major misunderstandings regarding the nature and logic of capitalism, often involving hypocritical gestures and even ideological attachments to the very structures it sought to redress. The discussions have also been honed and enhanced from the support of great colleagues and friends who have commented on the text and helped us clarify our arguments. Peter would like to express his gratitude to his colleagues at Queen Mary College, University of London, who have been immensely supportive in this and other projects, especially Gerard Hanlon, Stefano Harney, Matteo Mandarini and Arianna Bove. They have all pressed issues, enriched the concepts and given much food for thought. Conversations with Ger in Chicago and Lisbon, and with Stefano in Rome, were particularly important for some of the propositions we develop here. And the wonderful discussion with Dirk Matten (in Montreal) is memorable for its generosity and intellectual inspiration. Parts of the book were prepared while Peter was a Visiting Professor at Lund University, Sweden. He would like to thank Mats Alvesson, Dan Kärreman, Stephan Schaefer and other colleagues at Lund University for their hospitality, critical engagement and support. Carl Cederström at Cardiff University (but previously of Lund University) read many parts of the text too, and gave some extremely helpful advice that we are grateful for. And Carl, Sally Tally and 'Professor Esther' were such generous hosts during Peter's visit to Lund, which undoubtedly hastened completion of the book. Also, 'Café Ariman' in Lund is a haven for reading and writing (among other things), from which this book benefited very much.

Marc would like to thank the Ashridge Business School for giving him the opportunity to spend five stimulating years working with senior executives from all over the globe. This experience yielded many valuable insights on the reality of CSR from the perspective of corporate 'insiders'. He would also like to acknowledge the support of the Maastricht School of Management, which enabled him to spend considerable time in developing countries in Asia, Africa and the Middle East, where CSR takes on a somewhat different glean – in terms of both theory and practice – compared with its 'home' regions in North America and Europe. Elements of Marc's earlier work with Matthew Haigh of the School of Oriental and Asian Studies, University of London, have been formative to some of the arguments advanced in this text. Finally, the city of Barcelona merits mention due to the January refuge from the British winter it furnished Marc throughout his five years at Ashridge. It was during the January 2009 sojourn that the authors' long-standing conversations on CSR were finally formalized into a book proposal. Several chapters were also written in Barcelona over the summer of 2010.

INTRODUCTION: WHY THE END OF CORPORATE SOCIAL RESPONSIBILITY?

Why *the end* of corporate social responsibility? Why would we entitle a book with such a bold statement when today companies are spending more on their corporate responsibility budget than ever, when it is one of the most prominent aspects of their websites, frequently mandatory in business school curriculums and the daily topic of conversation in the business press? Why would we claim that corporate social responsibility has ended, moreover, at a time when it is needed in business now more than ever (just think of the 2010 oil spill in the Gulf of Mexico and the ecological catastrophe that ensued). Furthermore, when the financial sector is in a state of disarray following the rampant profiteering of the sub-prime era, should we not be championing the adoption of CSR rather than heralding its demise? In this sense, our proclamation might seem misleading and somewhat provocative. Could it not be for these reasons that some might argue the opposite – corporate social responsibility is really only beginning? No; if the title of our book is misleading, it is because we feel that *corporate social responsibility never really began*.

It is true that almost every large corporation in the West today makes some effort to communicate how it is committed to social issues that ostensibly lie beyond its basic business objectives (i.e. increasing profits). One need only take a cursory glance at the websites of large multinationals like BP, Shell, British American Tobacco and BT to notice that firms in many industries and sectors create much fanfare around their corporate responsibility initiatives. Indeed, what has come to be called corporate social responsibility (or CSR) is now a key marketing and branding exercise for most large and medium-sized corporations. This trend extends beyond controversial industries that invest in CSR policies such as those producing petroleum or tobacco products. For example, there is a large industry built around ethical business (with the Body Shop and Fair Trade being early examples). This corporate stratum claims to make profits while avoiding the exploitation of people and natural resources, minimizing what economists call 'negative externalities'. Moreover, today CSR is also an academic growth industry. It is increasingly written about in business and management journals. Prestigious ones like the *Academy of Management Review* are devoting more space to CSR, and the *Harvard Business Review* increasingly features articles on the socially embedded nature of business (which would be almost unimaginable 20 years ago). The United Nations even runs a university network for responsible management.

For us, however, the key starting point for making sense of CSR is the context (i.e. capitalism) in which the discourse and practice is set. The institutional forces propelling business, the corporate form and the ideological matrix of economic rationality forward (some would say into oblivion) immediately transposes most gestures of responsibility – including sustainability and stakeholder dialogue – into something of a farce. Indeed, the idea that the logic of the neo-corporate enterprise might be reformed to consider social issues beyond economic rationality misunderstands how capitalism functions. There is a deep tension between what we might expect to be ethical organizational citizenship and the general sense that businesses follow (increasing profits, control, reducing costs, increasing consumer dependence, widening commodification, privatization, etc.). And it is this code of business that will always take precedence over all other considerations (Heilbroner, 1985), not because the people who manage corporations are 'bad', but because that is how corporations were designed to operate. In this context, much of what CSR proclaims begins to look like either wishful thinking (i.e. a projected ideal regarding how the firm could behave in some future state) or simply propaganda (or what Bansal and Clelland (2004) wonderfully call 'talking trash'), designed to pull the wool over the eyes of consumers, environmental protection groups and society more generally.

This does not mean that we cannot find instances of businesses pursuing profits in an ethical manner (however one might want to define that). Of course, it is easy to find such cases, but as an institutional totality, many commentators argue that the system is largely antithetical to the moral assertions large firms make about themselves via the discourse of CSR (see Korten, 2001). When a multinational oil company or pro-green government professes a desire to be sustainable and environmentally friendly (while prospecting the Arctic), a pharmaceutical enterprise makes 'world health' its key philosophical aim (while embarking on restrictive intellectual property strategies) or an arms manufacturer invests in bio-diversity (while thousands needlessly die in Iraq and elsewhere), then we must wonder what exactly is going on.

When we abstract away from particular instances to the level of totality (see Hardt and Negri, 1999), we are able to conceptualize the rather *extreme* nature of this institutional configuration. With the multinational corporation as the leading manifestation of late capitalism, we can easily distil its drivers (i.e. growth, surplus, exploitation, commoditization, marketization, rationalization, class control, etc.). But how this connects with broader social values is the real issue. For us, the observable tension, disconnect or gap between society (or 'the 99 per cent') and the axiomatic operating principles of modern business is not an aberration, but a defining feature of current corporate hegemony. Was this not revealed starkly when the superpowers of Western capitalism were unable to agree to a modest change in carbon emissions at the 2009 Copenhagen Climate Change Conference or the 'failure of epic proportions' that was the 2012 Rio+20 Earth Summit? This is the intransigent 'capitalist realism' (Fisher, 2009) that lies behind the airbrushed tones of a firm's annual CSR report. The very notion of social value (what we evaluate as right or wrong, worthless or worthwhile, indeed our ability to choose) is completely subordinated to the dictates of economic rationality, a subordination that eliminates or erases rather than provides ethical co-ordinates. Fisher defines 'capitalist realism' in the following manner:

> What counts as 'realistic', what seems possible at any point in the social field, is defined by a series of political determinations. An ideological position can never be really successful until it is naturalized, and it cannot be naturalized while it is still thought of as a value rather than a fact ... over the last thirty years, capitalist realism has successfully installed a 'business ontology' in which it is *simply obvious* that everything in society, including healthcare and education, should be run as a business. (2009: 17)

We think this realism functions in two ways in relation to recent elaborations of CSR, especially in the context of neo-liberal societies. First, it is the backdrop against which we need to evaluate business ethics aspirations, in which the very logic of the corporation has become metabolized into an *ontology* that eliminates questions regarding its desirability. For example, many of the scholarly debates in CSR could never imagine a world without capitalism. And second, when it perpetuates the myth that social justice can co-exist alongside this totalizing 'business ontology', CSR also trades in the ideology that we have really found the best society we could ever hope for: capitalism. This is where the deep conservatism of CSR lies.

We will maintain in the following pages that the concept of CSR is embedded in the political shifts of the contemporary business model and its intersection with the state, contemporary culture and the socio-economic demands of late capitalism more generally. These permutations in economic rationality are intimately related to the discourse of ethics and 'giving back to society' currently espoused by the business sector. We are thus highly critical of the concept of CSR not because we feel that business corporations should not be more responsible to societal stakeholders (such as workers, the environment, governments and consumers). Of course, they should. But the way most CSR policies (and scholarship) view business and society is a little bit like 'having one's cake and eating it too'. Given the intrinsic violence of neo-corporate regulation, it must bar any meaningful adherence to the ethical protocols announced by business ethics pundits. For such adherence would be tantamount to a major transformation of the current status quo, in which the corporation would cease to exist. In this sense, CSR is particularly problematic because it conceals the very source of the ills it claims to address. That is to say, CSR is frequently a tokenistic gesture when one observes the broad structures of the global capitalist system, providing yet another alibi for business as usual, extending market forces even deeper into a social body that is already in seizure.

CSR AND CAPITALISM

This book aims to deal with two basic dimensions of CSR and its related correlates (i.e. business ethics, sustainability, stakeholder theory and so forth). First, we deal with the *practice* of CSR in the large enterprises that now dominate the global economic scene. The practice of CSR is set against the backdrop of the corporate economic system that functions as an excessive expression of unbridled capitalism. It is for this reason that we call for caution when evaluating the meaning and efficacy of CSR initiatives. While there are a growing number of 'ethical companies' that brand themselves and their products as sustainable (the Body Shop etc.) we are more concerned here with the majority of firms that use CSR for reputational purposes. This is because they make up the greater part of the present corporate forays into business ethics – the petroleum company that is worried about bio-diversity, the retail chain that claims it is defending workers' well-being, and so on.

The second dimension of this topic concerns the way in which it is treated in research and scholarship. CSR in the discipline of management studies and organization theory has largely been co-opted by strategic management. Here, the key research problem is to link CSR to performance outcomes and vital economic indicators. In other words, does CSR make money for the firm? And, if so, how can it be strategically leveraged in relation to brand reputation, customer loyalty, employee motivation and competitive advantage? In the business ethics field, we are sympathetic with a growing number of critical views that aim to politicize CSR and the firm along with it. These studies are very sceptical about CSR because of the blatant hypocrisy that it frequently entails. Critical analyses of stakeholder theory, sustainability and 'the triple bottom line' have similarly pointed out the double standards that are a defining feature of CSR when practised in the corporate sector (see Dunne, 2007).

But before we proceed to our stance on CSR, what exactly do we mean by the concept? While various forms of CSR initiatives have been a keen aspect of industrial capitalism for many years (especially in the form of charities, philanthropy and so forth), today CSR has developed into a prominent and cogent corporate discourse involving marketing, recruitment, employee motivation, governmental policy and a keen awareness of shifting consumer values. In its contemporary guise, CSR is defined in consistent ways in various quarters of the business world. For example, these are some of the definitions used to capture the phenomenon (from Blowfield and Murray, 2008: 13):

> CSR is a concept whereby companies integrate social and environmental concerns in their business operations and in their interactions with their stakeholders on a voluntary basis. (European Commission, Directorate General on Employment and Social Affairs)

> CSR is the proposition that companies are responsible not only for maximising profits, but also for recognising the needs of such stakeholders as employees, customers, demographic groups and even the regions they serve. (PricewaterhouseCoopers)

CSR in business practice has today moved well beyond mere philanthropy. It includes a multifaceted set of corporate activities that attempt to attend to the ethical implications of the firm. This may include recruitment initiatives (whereby the corporation is considered a more 'progressive' employer), social accounting and reporting (where firms publish reports on their environmental impact, etc.), corporate culture (e.g. using fair trade coffee in the office) and, most importantly, reputation management (Hanlon and Fleming, 2009). One of the assumptions that we have much trouble with, amply displayed in the quotations above, is that ethics and capitalism can find a happy overlap, a unison in which both corporate hegemony might grow, make money and exercise control *and* co-exist in a liveable social landscape. It is this liberalist notion of a 'win–win' (e.g. Elkington, 1994) outcome that will be a major objection in this book. As Banerjee (2007) has also noted, only a cursory glance at the facts pertaining to climate change, social exploitation, the homogenization of culture (one language dies every 14 days), and the discernible link between orthodox economics and war tells us that, in practice, the fantasy world of an 'ethical capitalism' is built upon a misunderstanding of the kind of society that history has bequeathed us.

THE CSR FIELD

We might find three general perspectives in the literature regarding what CSR means for business today. The first concerns *why business should adopt CSR*. Normative arguments acknowledging a need for CSR are based on ethical or instrumental rationales, while those against are based on institutional function or property rights perspectives (Jones, 1996). Ethical rationales are derived from religious principles, philosophical frameworks or prevailing social norms. Ethicists argue that firms are compelled to behave in a socially responsible manner because it is the morally correct thing to do (Frederick, 2006). In its extreme form, ethics-based advocates of

CSR would support such behaviour even when it involves an unproductive resource expenditure for the firm. The more commonly invoked instrumental arguments in favour of social responsibility are based on a rational calculation that CSR actions will benefit the individual firm over time. Such arguments rely on organizational legitimation. By appearing responsible, a firm can proactively anticipate objections to its activities, postpone governmental scrutiny, exploit opportunities arising from increasing levels of cultural, environmental and sexual awareness, differentiate its products from those of less proactive competitors, and continue to privilege economic rationality. The perspective is illustrated by Jones:

> [B]ehaviour that is trusting, trustworthy, and cooperative, not opportunistic, will give the firm a competitive advantage. In the process it may help explain why certain 'irrational' or altruistic behaviours turn out to be productive and why firms that engage in these behaviours survive and often thrive. (1995: 422)

The second perspective concerns *why business should not adopt CSR*. It is interesting to note that CSR was originally a term of disdain. For free market zealots like Levitt (1958) the very thought of business ethics was equated with some socialist conspiracy. The argument was popularized in Milton Friedman's (1970) classic statement that the corporation's only responsibility is to increase profits for its owners. The case against social responsibility is based on corporate function and property rights. The institutional function argument asserts that non-corporate institutions like governments, labour unions and civic and religious organizations are the proper vehicles to pursue social responsibility; that business managers have neither the skills nor the time to implement public policy; and that an empowered business sector would not be accountable for its actions, unlike governmental bodies held accountable through the electorate. Allowing or encouraging business to expand its institutional role by way of social responsibility is dangerous in that it allocates tremendous authority without accountability (Levitt, 1958).

The property rights argument against social responsibility has its roots in neoclassical capitalism and continues to be influential due to its simplicity and resonance with the views of many in the business community, particularly those in financial services. This perspective maintains that management has no right to do anything other than act in ways that increase shareholder value (Benston, 1982). To do otherwise constitutes a violation of management's legal, moral and fiduciary responsibilities. The rationale for all managerial action is the primacy of stockholder rights over those of auxiliary stakeholders and management's corresponding duty to maximize economic performance.

The third perspective concerns why we must be *critical of CSR*, and this is where we locate our book. The integration of ethics into the institution of modern business is theoretically a good idea. One only has to look around today to see that things are not going well – that we are living in a kind of 'end times' as Žižek (2010a) recently put it. But the current use of business ethics – including intimations towards sustainability, responsibility and 'the triple bottom line' – is something of a misnomer since it does very little to modify the systemic negativities of a world that it is supposedly remedying. In some cases, CSR appears even to be capitalizing on some of these negativities. For example a large multinational food company that is well known for its highly exploitative supply chains might carry a certified fair trade product in order to have its brand visible in the ethical area of the supermarket. There is a growing and, we suggest, promising stream of scholarship that is critical of CSR as both a practice in the business world and a theoretical concept in academic research. It claims that much CSR discourse in corporations performs an ideological function by lending a tokenistic element of ethicality to an inherently unethical institutional form. According to Roberts (2003), for example, CSR can often be dismissed as a cynical ploy to enhance reputational value. For Banerjee (2007), CSR is frequently disingenuous and diversionary. He demonstrates how the international activities of multinational capitalism dwarf in priority and significance corporate aspirations to be ethical. And Hanlon (2007) and Shamir (2008) argue that CSR may even be a way of extending market rationality into the social world. With the rise of neo-liberalism and the privatization of vast parts of society, CSR becomes a vehicle for corporatizing non (or even anti) business ways of life, with eco-innovation, human resource management and ethical branding gaining powerful leverage over activities that might have once been performed outside of business.

TOWARDS A CRITIQUE OF CSR

This critical view of CSR is useful since it positions it in the context of an international political economy. Like Jones et al. (2005), we are not against ethics but *for ethics*, only in a more thoroughgoing manner. For, at one level, the ideological proclamations of CSR, including industrial democracy and sustainability, are very progressive. The nub of the problem is that these latent dreams of 'socializing the firm' are not really meant to be taken seriously. If they were, it would signify a major transformation (or even revolution) in business and society. Like many other aspects of liberalist discourse, the trouble is not its aspirations but the obligatory *distance* we are meant to take from their full realization (e.g. real democracy would obliterate the current joke that is parliamentary democracy). An inbuilt cynical distance is operating here that quietly sustains a hypocritical tension between what one claims and what actually happens. Moreover, as we slowly build towards a robust theoretical political economy of CSR (explicated in Chapter 5), it will be suggested that the discourse of corporate ethics should not be simply dismissed as harmless 'window dressing' or 'talking trash'. It may be this and much more, but it is also a concrete business practice that has real effects – that of partially sustaining the structures of late capitalism, of an environmentally unfriendly hegemony governed by the corporation.

Some may say, 'Well, even if it is all talk, at least it is a topic of discussion in boardrooms and at annual general meetings. That is better than nothing, and something might come of it.' Roberts (2003), for example, makes an interesting case that while it is easy to demonstrate the double standards of much CSR in practice, the discourse of ethics nevertheless opens a space for a different kind of mentality in which one is in dialogue with 'the Other' (be it workers, environmental campaigners or consumers). He draws upon a phenomenological philosophy of responsibility to argue that ethics is about exposing oneself through the language of others, precipitating a leap into the void of the 'social relation'. The talk of business ethics might be very important for at least creating the potential for this to occur – indeed, has not this very book benefited from CSR talk to begin our criticism? This is a thoughtful way of approaching the myriad of political possibilities that the very presence of an ethical discourse in the firm might broach. But it is the power effects of such talk that we are interested in. From that standpoint, *CSR is actually a step backwards*, rather than a primary move forward to some future state of social justice. A step backwards because it has the consequence of actually solidifying the myth that large corporations (and the consumer culture that goes along with it) can exist in a world where glaciers do not melt or species extinction is not a common occurrence. By entrenching this untenable 'win–win' ideology, we will argue in this book, CSR must be viewed as an obstruction to genuine progressive change rather than its harbinger.

It is in this sense that we feel CSR, more than anything else, represents a failure, a retreat from politics. What might have once been a critical stance towards multinational capitalism has been effectively mainstreamed so that its contours, the assumptions and the political parameters are preset before one enters the language game. So, the provocative title of our book has a number of interlaced meanings that we think are important for current and future research in this area. CSR has ended because it never began – it was always linked, we think, to a failure to deal seriously with the task of politicizing the firm in business studies and beyond. What once might have been a meaningful social movement many years ago to counter the inimical externalities of capitalism has weirdly become a pro-business position. If CSR ever had a modicum of radicality (which we see as a synonym for reasonableness rather than extremism), then as a project, it never really got off the ground. The language of ethics has been appropriated to become the servant of the very institutional gridlock it sought to reform. But, CSR has ended in other ways. If we accept that to take seriously the ideological claims of CSR would be tantamount to a revolutionary dislodgment of corporate hegemony, then it behoves us to speak about it only if we want to take its underlying message *to the very end*. That is to say, to remain stubbornly true to the tenets of stakeholder theory, sustainability and the 'triple bottom line'. For sure, if a radical socialization of the corporation is latent here, then it must be put at the forefront of the discussion. If we are not willing to do this, then we ought to remain silent, at least within this framework.

The final way in which we feel that CSR has ended regards the major socio-political events over the last 15 years that have sobered even the most ardent champion of neo-liberal capitalism. The atrocious reality of this socio-economic paradigm has been exposed for what it really is to such an extent that we suspect even the most gleeful CSR consultant feels slightly embarrassed as he or she delivers yet another PowerPoint presentation on the competitive advantages of sustainable business practices. The corporatization of war following 9/11; major ecological catastrophes such as the melting of glaciers in Chile within a generation or the 2010 Gulf of Mexico oil spill; the failed 2012 Rio+20 Earth Summit; firms fighting over the spoils pending the disintegrating of the polar ice caps; the global decline of workers' 'rights'; the state flagrantly supporting a banking and finance sector that has not only handcuffed most of us to a volatile economic model, but which is also perversely greedy and religiously supported even when in crisis; the predatory exploitation of the human genome by bio-genetics firms transforming the human body and its reproductive capacities into a 'for-profit' zone; the continuing mass slaughter of non-human animals under increasingly cruel and unforgiving conditions; the … . Well, the list continues indefinitely. This is certainly the right time to herald the end of CSR.

If the above propositions are correct – and we will endeavour to give credence to these arguments over the course of the forthcoming chapters – then perhaps we need to think about two courses of action in the realm of theory and politics. The first is to link CSR to neo-capitalism in a manner that positions it as a political project of ruling elite interests. The radical message that might have once been the raw material of the CSR intervention is long gone. We now live in an age where even management consultants and popular business writers are evoking the language of emancipation, counter-culture rebellion and anti-hierarchical values. This is what Žižek (2009) has recently chided as 'liberal communism' in that a pro-business mentality seeks legitimation through the cultural motifs of ethics, radicalism and social well-being. Bob Geldof and Bono might be seen as prime examples of the liberalist communist. All of these intimations to remedying the broken world of modern global capitalism are, of course, made to chime with the advance of business. Bob Geldof has even highlighted the social justice benefits of 'private equity' in relation to his plans for investing in Africa. This mindset seeks to enjoy both the rewards of rampant profiteering and the euphoric afterglow of 'caring for society'.

And second, perhaps we need to change the co-ordinates of the discussion since the discourse of business ethics and CSR is now so shot through with the values of economic rationality that it has been rendered virtually useless. Maybe the only way that an honestly ethical position on the current corporate-led crisis might be possible is precisely outside the realm of CSR practice and theory. This is not to say that we should no longer speak of ethics in relation to the business world. Indeed, we are calling for the very opposite, a more candid political engagement with the realities of the corporation, something that is missing in much orthodox CSR scholarship found in journals like the *Academy of Management Review*, *Organization Science* and elsewhere.

THE DRIVERS OF CSR

Big business has endeavoured to justify itself as a 'social good' in the past through philanthropy and so forth, but the sheer prevalence and discussion around this latest iteration in the guise of CSR appears to make it something quite unique. So what has changed? This is a complex question since the reasons why the vast majority of large multinational firms might now include 'social responsibility' in their branding are probably varied and complex. A common way to view CSR in the scholarship we have consulted is to make a distinction between drivers that are *reactive* on the one hand and *proactive* on the other. Sometimes CSR initiatives might be foisted upon firms – pressure from unions, the government or consumers – and the other is where an enterprise takes the initiative and seeks profitability, reputational value-added opportunities and kudos through a business ethics campaign. Today, however, we argue that distinction is no longer useful. The discourse of CSR is now only proactive since it represents a move to foreclose political engagement that might truly challenge the firm, making CSR as mandatory now as the balance sheet or planning strategy. For sure, what we might have called external pressure (from, say, social movements, environmental agencies and so-forth) is now transfigured into a business opportunity to deepen the logic of the firm either through legitimation strategies (e.g. CSR as instrument for accumulating cultural capital that deflects critical scrutiny) or through socio-political capture, a capitalization on the growing ethos of dissent among consumers, workers and popular culture more generally. Again, this does not mean that we result in a 'win–win' situation since this capture of criticism is designed to extend rent-seeking behaviour rather than eliminate it. The irony, as we have mentioned above, is that this economic rationality obeys a set of principles that CSR is ostensibly attempting to overcome. Having said that, we would still doubt that the corporation would have put such emphasis on CSR issues on its own accord. So again, we ask, what has changed?

The drivers of CSR practice tend to overlap or interact in quite complex ways. Yet, they are analytically distinct in terms of their internal logics and immediate empirical referents. We proceed by identifying six areas where CSR is articulated through the needs of capitalist economic rationality. To reiterate our earlier point, what looks to be a pressure to curb the excesses of unbridled profiteering should more realistically be depicted as a strategic opportunity firms use to extend their influence via a 'discourse of sociality'. CSR becomes a tool for enhancing value via markets, shareholder activism and the financial system. We also identify consumer tastes, the state and non-governmental organizations (NGOs) as important components of the CSR discourse in corporations today. The justification for depicting these forces and not others is threefold: their close relation to the capital accumulation process generates the externalization dynamic; the nature of consumer identity in capitalist social formations affects whether 'enlightened consumption' can be a substantial force; and the direct access to firms demanded and sought by the state and popular mobilizations. Other voices would include the media, 'ecosystem' consultants, business schools and the general public. For the sake of cogency, we note their potential influence and point to the work of others (Freeman and Gilbert, 1992; Neimark, 1995).

CSR AS PROFIT-SEEKING BEHAVIOUR

Most instrumental arguments for CSR centre on market efficiency and risk management. By adopting a set of practices whose expected initial benefits are directed away from stockholders (while, at the same time, following those that are), the firm is arguably positioned to take advantages of previously unforeseen business opportunities, counter the risk of losing presence in existing markets and establish a presence in emerging ones. Such arguments ignore how managers are generally not provided compelling incentives to follow CSR objectives (Jones, 1996). Assuming (bounded) economic rationality, a firm can only be expected to undertake and sustain so-called social responsibility initiatives under certain conditions. If the governance structure of a European–American firm (or that of another firm seeking exposure in European–American markets) is functioning 'properly' (with respect to prioritizing the interests of stockholders/owners) then management generally pursues only those strategies/projects designed to enhance or protect the firm's position across its relevant markets (Jensen and Meckling, 1976; McWilliams and Siegel, 2001a).

Researchers note that business managers charged with operationalizing CSR in their firms filter such initiatives through an economic lens. O'Dwyer (2003: 535), after presenting the findings of interviews of senior executives in a number of Irish public-listed corporations, points at 'structural pressures' and 'perceived barriers' to a more integrated application of CSR. An interview-based study of German and UK managers in chemical and pharmaceutical firms finds that managers view CSR initiatives as ancillary to the main game of economic performance (Adams, 2002). Reflecting this priority, personnel charged with the task of producing CSR reports were functionally separated from accounting departments. The separation of CSR from core operations is commented on in other contexts. Dick-Forde (2005), interviewing managers in a partly nationalized Caribbean corporation, notes the ghettoization of environmental management/reporting functions and their isolation from strategic management and management accounting processes.

Organizational relegation of the CSR reporting function to public relations departments (rather than to cost/revenue centres under the scrutiny of accountants) would explain its observed ineffectiveness to date. Despite the widespread promotion of the 'business case' for CSR and its internal funding by boards of directors, the line of research linking CSR projects to concrete practice has produced inconsistent results. And it cannot be said that the choice and amount of a CSR initiative reflects the extent of practical enactment or performance (King and Lenox, 2001). Business managers are faced with the performative equation of maximizing the gap between revenues and specific costs. Managers might give CSR more attention if they could expect CSR-inspired actions to help maximize that gap. Captured by this short-termism, most managers are reluctant to accept the cost of CSR implementation if they cannot readily determine the likelihood of an economic return (Adams, 2002).

CSR AND THE HEGEMONY OF THE MARKET

Continuing this trend of instrumentalization, we see CSR closely linked to the principles of market rationality. For example, firms may be compelled to react to the first-mover CSR strategies of their competitors where they believe that failing to do so would disadvantage them vis-à-vis market positioning. Strong isomorphic effects are observable across industry and strategic group levels where a particular first-mover's CSR efforts gain wide positive publicity among dominant stakeholders (Bansal and Roth, 2000). In these cases, even where the CSR strategy has not been proven a 'winner' (in terms of net payback), other firms will imitate it because they perceive the costs of not doing so as prohibitive. An entire industry sector can thus behaviourally migrate to the position where it adopts non-rational responsibilities that transfer wealth to non-vested stakeholders. For example, in Australia during the 1970s, most employers in the waste collection industry held generous family leave provisions significantly in excess of statutory mandates and irrespective of labour market conditions (Brooks, 2005).

The marketization of CSR is also reflected in the way the discourse creates a second 'market of stakeholders' that then competes for attention within the orbit of the firms' activities. Take for example the wide variety of definitions and orientations in the corporate discourse of responsibility. Definitions are declarative and based on experience, convenience and observed practice. Moreover, priorities of firms vary with respect to determining which stakeholders benefit and to what extent. For example, the Body Shop's CSR activities famously focus on promoting the human rights and environmental sustainability of its suppliers, while those of Starbucks more narrowly target employee welfare. A firm can be responsive towards one stakeholder group and simultaneously exploitative of another. Indeed, the corporate responsibility research from the management field, in the main, leaves unquestioned the definitions of responsibility and sustainability adopted by an organization based on the appropriation of surplus value, cost minimization (and thus the maximum generation of negative economic externalities) and the production of unnecessary products and services. By overlooking the basic dynamic of business rationality, the research encourages practitioners to engage in ethical activity only as long as it does not alter the priority of business first (profit and market share) and society second (other stakeholders in line after stockholders).

In sum, the momentum of CSR within the firm is unlikely to change systematically the logic of neo-liberal economic rationality in any broad sense (growth, accumulation, return to shareholders). Structural and legal environments admit only instrumental variants of CSR practice. Unless and until managers' remuneration packages force them to recognize negative economic externalities generated by their firms, accounting models will not be modified to take into account such 'environmental' and 'social' costs. Fundamentally, while some CSR initiatives might generate positive or mitigating effects on externalities, they cannot fundamentally alter the externalizing engine that powers every business firm and is the primary source of capitalist pathologies.

CSR AS THE FINANCIALIZATION OF BUSINESS ETHICS

The recent global financial crisis has renewed interest in the potential viability of 'ethical' and 'social' investment funds. Practitioners use various terms to describe managed investment products offering portfolios screened against social considerations. We use the term 'social fund' to denote a unit trust that markets itself on the basis of social and environmental policies in its portfolio construction. At first blush, the concept of social investment enlarges the customary conception of stockholder value by expressing retail investors' ethical values (Gray, 1992). In practice, social funds use the instrumental argument as a marketing tool. They claim that by incorporating all externalities and pricing goods and services accordingly, invested corporations will benefit by positioning themselves to take advantage of market opportunities and avoid imposts from the state. Such benefits are expected to flow through to the investor in the form of increased capital gains and strong dividend policies (Statman, 2000): a win–win–win result for investors, invested corporations and stakeholder groups.

Belief in the potency of this argument is found in Bruyn (1987) and Cowton (2004). On closer scrutiny, the evidence at hand suggests that most institutional investors do not exert direct or indirect pressure on invested corporations to practise CSR. Some large pension funds – the California Public Employees' Retirement System and the UK-based Hermes are examples – have on occasion exercised or threatened to exercise proxy-voting rights to force management to discontinue or adopt certain actions. Such practices, while not trite, are isolated. To judge from investment mandates, most institutional investors are yet to be convinced that social responsibility is an instrumental argument for wealth generation. And this is no more true than at the present juncture defined by wasting finance markets following the 2008 economic crisis. In this context, it is unsurprising that social funds accept unaudited corporate self-reports as evidence of practised CSR (Banerjee, 2007). Moreover, social funds have accounted for a very small proportion of funds under management (no more than four-tenths of 1 per cent) since inception (Haigh and Hazelton, 2004). Small market shares limit the ability of social funds to exert pressure directly on share prices or to gain access to executive managers (and so influence corporate behaviour).

The second part of the argument made by 'social investment' advocates contends that social funds will outperform managed investments that do not explicitly take into account social considerations. Studies neither confirm nor disconfirm systematic differences between social and mainstream investment products. Any other expectation, as pointed out by Gray, Owen and Maunders (1988), defies economic rationality. The majority of social fund portfolios are modelled on mainstream stock market indexes or tailored variants (see Haigh and Jones, 2010). Obviously, social mutual funds are constrained by pressures to maintain economically competitive portfolios. To survive, institutional investors must sustain a focus on continuously maximizing economic performance earned on investments in large corporations. Studies of retail investors find mixed levels of commitment. Milne and Chan (1999) use an experiment to measure the positive impact of corporate social disclosures on subjects' purchasing decisions, finding limited support. The survey study of Mackenzie and Lewis (1999) notes that social investors had invested most of their discretionary investable wealth in mainstream investment products. Studies of institutional investor demand for CSR reports also present mixed and inconclusive results (Freedman and Stagliano, 1991; Patten, 1990).

Ultimately, the contention that social funds might promote CSR-type outcomes across industrial sectors is questionable. The outperformance argument relies on a social fund distinguishing itself in the pack. Most mainstream financial institutions have offered social investment products for a number of years; as such, managers of social funds compete for market share and view investment criteria as providing a competitive advantage, much as might any fund manager (Patten, 1990). Manufacturing differences between portfolio screens negate the potential that social funds might exert collective pressure on invested corporations and produce observable outcomes in industrial sectors. Coupled with low market share, the influence that publicly mandated social funds might exert over the operations of corporations is negligible (Haigh and Hazelton, 2004). In sum, research and practice suggest that corporations with stock held by social funds are more likely to ignore than to heed calls for social responsibility actions.

THE ETHICAL CONSUMER?

Has not the rise the 'ethical consumer' fundamentally changed the business model of many corporations, especially those concerned with brand reputation and consumer loyalty? Since the 1970s, studies have focused on the demand characteristics of consumers of products and services to which are attached green characteristics: 'natural' cosmetics, recycled paper, eco-vacations and suchlike (Crane, 2001; Davis, 1994; Drumwright, 1994; Marks and Mayo, 1991). For some analysts, such as Prothero (1990) and Smith (1990: 88), eco-consumerism can be viewed as a strategy of capturing new markets, and is thus inherently linked to the overall logic of capitalist production/consumption cycles more generally. Conceptually, consumers can promote CSR practice through their purchase decisions in certain product markets. If consumers are consistently willing to pay some form of premium for CSR-affiliated products (or brands or reputations), firms will gain a competitive advantage, thus forcing non-CSR firms to migrate to similar positions. This is, of course, an extension of the basic concept of consumer sovereignty, which has been applied elsewhere in modelling citizenry behaviour in political 'markets' (Crane and Matten, 2010).

For us, the argument that eco-consumerism can promote social justice is flawed in three respects. One, the practice of purchasing consumer goods and services to pursue social and environmental goals necessarily accepts the assumptions of neoclassical economics. The inability of that model to address allocative equity within and without economic markets is evident. Two, treating social and environmental questions as ancillary to the purchasing act valorizes consumption and reifies the legitimating myth of consumer sovereignty, when an informed assessment of retail industries would show that consumers have very little say over what they buy, and even less over the means of production. Echoing Galbraith's (1958) adage of 'Render unto Caesar that which is Caesar's', Dugger (1989) demonstrates how monetarist policies underlying corporate mergers actually created rather than responded to market and consumer preferences. Such behaviour suggests that corporations do not adjust operations to meet the demands of consumers (Dugger, 1989: xi). And three, the idea of a key capitalist pathology – consumerism – being addressed by the pathogen, as it were, is highly problematic. As Heilbroner (1985) notes, capitalism is not only about producing goods and services, but also about producing people, in the sense of certain and particular forms of dominant consciousness. The contemporary individual may be inconsistent, alienated and so forth, but he or she still contributes to the reproduction of capitalist institutional structures and social relations through obligatory acts of consumption and labour.

Moreover, it is very difficult to correlate empirical relationships between firms' CSR behaviour, consumers' perceptions of that behaviour, and consumers' purchasing behaviour. As an example, Bhattacharya and Sankar (2004) found that despite indications that eight in ten Fortune 500 corporations address CSR issues and that eight in ten survey respondents stated they considered CSR when making purchasing decisions, robust linkages between corporate CSR initiatives and actual consumer purchasing patterns did not appear. Most subjects in the study were unaware of corporate CSR activity per se and those that were aware were unwilling to pay premium prices for CSR-embedded goods (Wicks et al., 2010).

To sum up, the proposition that a moneyed echelon treating itself to ethical luxury could somehow serve to alter basic capitalist dynamics seems unjustifiable. The literature on consumer boycotts does little to contest our argument (John and Klein, 2003; Tyran and Engelmann, 2005). From the perspective of encouraging corporations to practise CSR, both eco-products and social investment products offer little promise of radical change except as a palliative to individuals' consciences (Fleming, 2009a). We do not believe consumers can be counted on to promote CSR outcomes. Indeterminate associations between consumers' perceptions, attitudes, values and behaviours would bar CSR from the cost/benefit deliberations of most manufacturing firms. Moreover, as firms' overall competitive approaches and differentiation strategies increasingly integrate CSR initiatives, the quality of information transmitted to consumers becomes captured by the marketing function, leading to confusion, cynicism and exit choices (Biddle, 2000). Green consumers, perhaps more susceptible than other consumer groups to focused emotional advertising (Dacin and Brown, 1997), might suspect opportunism on the part of manufacturers and suppliers (Kulkarni, 2000). Such perceptions, if held, might account for relatively muted consumer demand for such products and services (Schwartz, 2003).

THE ETHICAL STATE OR THE CAPTURED STATE?

Jurisdictions are yet to require substantive legislation requiring sustainability reporting of all large organizations, and no benchmark of government responsiveness to CSR has emerged even following large environmental incidents and corruption scandals. Governments have tended to tax negative externalities since the 1970s by using shifting mixes of tradable permits, direct regulation and corrective market mechanisms such as emission standards (Abelson, 2002: 155). In the United States, the Toxics Release Inventory and other environmental legislation is administered through the Environmental Protection Agency and supplemented through a very decentralized state-by-state process. Moreover, several European Union governments have introduced legislation to make environmental reporting mandatory for corporations. Since 1995, the Dutch government has offered personal income taxation exemptions to retail investors in a reportedly successful attempt to stimulate environmentally sensitive energy, agriculture and technology projects. Debentures issued to fund projects certified by the government environmental agency carry concessional taxation benefits for debenture holders (Richardson, 2002). Other governmental environmental initiatives emanate at the EU level. The Restriction of Hazardous Substances (ROHS) legislation bans all products containing any more than trace amounts of dangerous substances like lead or mercury. The Waste Electrical and Electronic Equipment Act commenced in the EU zone in 2004, mandating that electronics manufacturers accept and recycle used electrical products. The Registration, Evaluation, Authorisation and

Restriction of Chemicals Directive requires that EU-registered firms register chemicals used in manufacturing processes.

Lehman argues that critical evaluation of the state is necessary if reformist research agendas are to 'tackle the entrenched interests of corporate power and prestige' (1999: 236). We would agree, and further add that the resurgence of what Harney (2009) calls 'extreme neo-liberalism' in the governmental sector (extreme because it's entirely untenable even on its own terms) has profound implications for the way business and society interface. In light of the overreliance on capital as illustrated in the financial crisis 'bailout' of private firms, the state seems to have been captured by business interests rather than becoming an organ for democratic voice. And for this reason, it is unlikely that governmental regulatory pressures can be counted upon to promote CSR outcomes at the industry and firm levels, for four basic reasons.

First, a major focus of corporate lobbying in Europe over recent years relates to the perceived costs of ensuring compliance, which lobbyists argue are prohibitive either for large firms employing high levels of outsourcing, such as Dell, or with respect to new layers of governmental inspectors, adding to what many observers already perceive as a bloated EU central bureaucracy. In the United States, lobbying groups have been successful in curtailing US commitment to CSR on economic grounds. Indeed, many governments now agree that imposing regulatory compliance costs on the business sector increases firms' non-productive overheads and negatively impacts competitiveness in international markets wherever such regulations are not in force. Second, lobbying activities of business groups and the reluctance of business to recognize the costs of its negative externalities lead to superficial treatments of environmental reporting legislation, by both the regulators and the regulated (see Haigh and Jones (2010) for examples of this). Lobbying around the Copenhagen Climate Change Conference and the 2012 Rio+20 Earth Summit similarly revealed how powerful business interests were aligned with the nation-state (*Guardian*, 2012; Jowit, 2010). Proposed regulation then becomes subordinated by the lobbying efforts of practitioners' associations; consequently, investment managers are permitted to define the scope, terms and content of relevant disclosures. As the requirements are silent on audited disclosures, investors have little reason to expect that the quality of information will improve (Banerjee, 2007).

Third, the hegemony of economic rationality (Deetz, 1992; Gorz, 1989) and its colonization of non-corporate institutions (Hardt and Negri, 2009) means that the corporate sector has already won the discursive battle, although not necessarily through the Trojan horse of CSR itself. The extent to which governments have adopted national economic competitiveness as their *raison d'être* has led to capital and the state becoming almost indistinguishable from each other with respect to public policy making, for example, environmental taxation (Chomsky, 1999). And fourth, to impose more aggressive environmental and social regulations on business would require that states enjoy a significant degree of autonomy from corporate and finance capital. The global financial crisis and the massive corporate 'bailout' (involving one of the largest transfers of public funds to the private sector) disabuse us of any such notion as governmental autonomy. Moreover, globalization has empowered capital as the level of institutional pluralism has decreased. Individual states are currently much more dependent on capital than is capital on any individual state. Bourdieu (2001: 14) notes that states promote market hegemony by endorsing the very policies that tend to consign them to the sidelines. To expect that the 'left hand of the state' (Bourdieu, 2001: 34) would price itself out of markets through aggressive regulations attacking negative externalities is unrealistic.

THE NGO

Organizations formed from popular mobilizations, hereafter referred to as NGOs, coalesce in various formal and informal alliances with other organizations located in capitalist markets. A useful categorization of NGOs follows Smith's (1990: 108) distinctions between sectional, promotional and anchored pressure groups. *Sectionals* protect the interests of a particular component of social systems; *promotionals* seek to address what they consider as pressing ecological or humanitarian problems; *anchoreds* present as promotionals but are grounded in sectionals.

Ethicists posit promotional NGOs as the natural facilitators of CSR based on their minority membership of corporations (Matten and Crane, 2005). For example, promotionals are known to purchase stock in corporations so as to either call special meetings to put voting resolutions on single issues or to attend general meetings to vote on matters such as those affecting board composition. As an example, the Australian Wilderness Society recently placed shareholder resolutions at the annual general meetings of two national Australian banks. The resolutions were drafted as a response to the banks' holdings in a corporation engaged in old-growth forestry and sought to change the banks' articles of association so as to prohibit those specific investments. And there are many reports of shareholder activists threatening special meetings to gain access to management (Fleming and Spicer, 2007). Promotional and anchored NGOs have also sought occasional collaborations with public corporations and institutional investors. As examples, the Interfaith Center on Corporate Responsibility, established by churches and investment managers, organizes and documents stockholder resolutions to be put to US corporations, while the US Friends of the Earth targets many of its publications and activities at mutual funds.

From a more critical perspective, however, some have convincingly argued that a number of key NGOs have been co-opted into extending the logic of corporate dominance in the context of global capitalism (see Hardt and Negri, 1999). And as such, we must remain pessimistic about the ability for these institutional forms to enforce the substantial changes on business and society that many argue is required. Let us take, for an example, the Global Reporting Initiative (GRI) to illustrate the institutional capture of NGOs. The GRI was formed in Boston in 1997 after the Coalition for Environmentally Responsible Economies secured a financial grant from the United Nations Foundation, and is designated as a UN Environment Program Collaborating Center. The GRI issued its Sustainability Reporting Guidelines in 2002, which were followed by a second edition, known as G2, in 2004. G2 lists hundreds of measures that signatories can choose. Purportedly, all derive from a 'triple bottom line' approach: the management doctrine that presents accounting profits by reference to impacts on employees and urban/non-urban environments.

It is not our intention to address the dubious contribution that a triple bottom line report might make to environmental and social justice here (see Brown et al., 2005; Gray and Milne, 2002). However, the industrial sectors represented by GRI reporters point to its increasingly limited role as a mere legitimating agency: 363 of the 429 GRI signatories, or 84 per cent, were in politically visible industrial sectors, namely retail products, financial services, health care, telecommunications, construction, mining and energy. The tobacco manufacturing industry is particularly prominent, with 17 subsidiary companies of the British American Tobacco Group counted as GRI reporters. Corporations engaged in politically sensitive operations have also been quick to proclaim their status as GRI reporters. Legitimation as a motivating factor in CSR disclosures is not new (Gelb and Strawser, 2001; Moneva et al., 2006).

While legitimation might underpin the instrumental argument for CSR, it carries certain other consequences. In the sense that the motivations of promotional NGOs are replaced with those originating in the business sector, corporate signatories contaminate the GRI memberships of less dominant promotional NGOs. In their critical analysis of GRI, Moneva et al. (2006) come to the conclusion that it has been appropriated to such an extent that one might view it as a way of camouflaging unsustainability rather than promoting it. As Moneva el al. put it:

> the understanding of the meaning of sustainable development, the three dimensions/ pillars of sustainability and their interactions has been changing as the concepts have been analysed, reinvented and operationalized for institutional purposes. The process of the development of the GRI guidelines has meant an opportunity for the different lobbies to further their own (environmental) agendas by appropriating these concepts … and more companies are adopting the GRI methodology to prepare their sustainability reports but, at the same time, the level of compromise with sustainable development assumptions is low. As a consequence, the guidelines developed by the GRI are used as a new tool for legitimizing management decisions and actions. (2006: 134)

To drive the point home, the ongoing collaboration of the GRI, the UN Environment Programme Finance Initiative (UNEPFI) and European investment banks illustrates the primacy of capitalist rationality. Among the UNEPFI's working programme of climate change, military conflict and water, the significance of a lack of available sanitary water in large areas of populated Africa is reduced to the problem of:

> an emerging risk of strategic importance to businesses and their financial backers around the world … becoming even more important with rapid globalisation within the business supply chain. Therefore, a business case for strategically addressing water challenges is getting stronger … . Water supply problems can open a window to improve operational performance and efficiency. This can give a company a competitive advantage on its peers … an investment opportunity for financial institutions to propose sustainable improvements which can benefit business. (www.unepfi.org, 2005).

The GRI, operating as the supra-representative of ecological/social activist movements but dominated by heads of industry, inverts the original relationship by hijacking (promotional) NGOs. The influence that an industrially diversified conglomerate might wield over a human rights NGO from a small European country need not be elaborated here. However, in terms of achieving outcomes consistent with social responsibility, promotional NGOs over time tend to concern themselves only with reforms likely to be accepted by business; that is, with those that can be expressed through the discourse of governance guidelines emanating from vested interests, not with those that would question the role of business in directing social progress towards its own ends.

CONCLUSION

This introductory chapter has sought to justify our provocative statement that CSR never really began in a genuine sense, and is yet another facet of the corporate justification of the capital accumulation process, this time utilizing the veneer of 'social goods', 'giving back to society' and 'sustainability'. If the capitalist system is in social, economic and environmental crisis, we do not see CSR as a way out of the current jam, but as an excuse for avoiding some inconvenient truths or, even worse, a Trojan horse designed to co-opt criticism and deepen the current paradigm of global unsustainability.

Most of the assumed causes of CSR in business posit the motivations for CSR as being outside the firm. In this view, organizations are reacting to shifting societal values and expectations. For example, in the post-Enron era of sceptical consumers and citizens alike, organizations now have to place more emphasis on how their corporate practices are actually adding to the well-being of the community at large. Consumers are now decidedly more unwilling to accept visible profiteering. The Nike and Gap cases from the 1990s are good examples (see Farzad and Boje, 2008). Child labour and sweatshops discovered within their supply chains markedly changed the marketing (if arguably not the actual material production) process. The consumer boycott of Nestlé following the powdered baby milk scandal had a major impact on the firm's operating practices (also seen in permutations in governmental regulation), but as we mentioned, this was more around the image of the company as a strategic resource than something that changed the internal business model (Crane and Matten, 2010).

However, these are isolated cases. In relation to mainstream purchasing patterns, there is indeed much debate about whether consumers really care about the CSR profile of the products or firms that they endorse (or more accurately, if ethical concerns translate into paying a high price for commodities). For sure, ethical products associated with environmental and worker-friendly businesses are often purchased by middle and upper-middle classes who are more likely to afford them. Some surveys tracking the consumption patterns in the EU indicate that the majority of consumers are concerned about the ethical status of the products, but only one in five would purchase a more expensive product on these grounds (Crane and Matten, 2010). In the grip of an economic crisis, fewer are willing to do so. The recent attempt by organic produce farmers to reform regulations to allow them to use pesticides in the face of dwindling demand reveals an increasing willingness to allow cost considerations to trump ethics.

We will now unpack our critical analysis in more depth, taking each key CSR concept into consideration. As the chapters proceed, our objective is to develop a robust and clear framework for understanding what has gone wrong with CSR theory and practice. And in doing this, we are better able to posit possible solutions, some of which might require abandoning the CSR paradigm altogether.

WELCOME TO THE HOUSE OF THE BLIND: WHAT CSR DOES NOT SEE

While the ethicality of business has long been a topic of scholarly discussion, CSR has only emerged over the last 20 years or so as a fully fledged academic field. As noted by many observers (cf. Jones, 2009a; van Oosterhout, 2005), however, the discipline has yet to constitute itself fully around core epistemological assumptions, including: an agreed-upon definition of the central construct of CSR itself; methodological issues of measuring the construct; the scope of relevant empirical enquiry; the relationship between positive and normative theory; and whether the field is intent on locating itself only within the business school or at a greater critical distance (also see Frederick, 2006).

As mentioned in the introduction, we argue that CSR research has been increasingly subordinated to the discipline of strategic management and the logic of instrumental economic rationality. This uncontested colonization has probably ended the usefulness of the CSR concept. The central question for most CSR scholars, business managers, PhD candidates and undergraduate students now is: does it create economic value for the firm? Although results of numerous investigations have been inconclusive, the research agenda takes the for-profit firm for granted and implicitly legitimates it as a social institution that is 'good' for society (especially when highlighting the so-called aberrations of Enron, Tyco, RBS, Bear Stearns, Lehman Brothers, etc.). Moreover, we would argue that much of this research unconsciously operates to obfuscate the significant political outcomes associated with the corporation by suggesting (implicitly or explicitly) that this institution (along with the market and commercialization) might also yield something *beyond* its institutional logic of profit maximization.

Our central contention is that conventional CSR fails to recognize the *systemic* damage – to workers, communities, the environment – ensuing from the activities of big business. For example, scholars have very little to say about the current global financial crisis or the crisis tendencies of capitalism in general. Instead, CSR research tends to downplay the detrimental effects of the enterprise since it only studies extreme cases, thus implying that under normal circumstances the firm is a benign social institution. The economic, environmental and social costs *constitutive of capitalism* are addressed as if we can reform the logic of capitalist enterprise when it goes astray. This chapter intends to illustrate how CSR is therefore a profoundly conservative moment of academic enquiry, particularly where the elemental assumptions of capitalism are involved. Here we see an institutional *blindness* or blinkering regarding the axiomatic operating system of the corporation, which taps into the more general liberalist misconception that, except for a few bad apples, we might make this (unsustainable) world last for ever.

In this chapter we will subject orthodox CSR to the logic of *immanent critique*. According to Harvey:

> Critical theory at its most abstract and general level … begins as a formal 'negativity.' As a dissenting motif, it selects some tradition, ideological premise, or institutionalized orthodoxy for analysis. As immanent critique, it then 'enters its object,' so to speak, 'boring from within.' Provisionally accepting the methodological presuppositions, substantive premises, and truth-claims of orthodoxy as its own, immanent critique tests the postulates of orthodoxy by the latter's own standards of proof and accuracy. Upon 'entering' the theory, orthodoxy's premises and assertions are registered and certain strategic contradictions located. These contradictions are then developed according to their own logic, and at some point in this process of internal expansion, the one-sided proclamations of orthodoxy collapse as material instances and their contradictions are allowed to develop naturally. (1990a: 5)

For example, an immanent critique of the 'free market' would expose the fallacy of corporate self-regulation by demonstrating the need for state oversight and periodic intervention in order to ensure allocative market outcomes (Preston, 1985). Our immanent critique begins with CSR's scope of enquiry and key concerns. As these are nowhere clearly and formally stated in an uncontested manner – which includes any consensus on a definition of CSR itself (see van Oosterhout and Heugens, 2008) – we instead assume they are substantially evidenced by the actual output of CSR scholars over a prolonged period. We then identify gaps which CSR research has not investigated, which we find incongruous given the field's apparent *raison d'être*. In many ways, the CSR academic field is defined by what issues and subjects it *avoids* rather than those the scholars throw themselves at – over and over again, with largely indeterminate results. We then present our explanation for why this blindness persists, which calls into question the critical autonomy, integrity and, ultimately, the rationale for the field as currently constituted. Finally, we present some thoughts on how the field might 'remake' itself in order to remain relevant in relation to the crises that the twenty-first century undoubtedly holds in store.

In conducting this task, we note that there have been several comprehensive reviews of the CSR and closely related literatures (stakeholder theory, corporate citizenship) in recent years (cf. Lee, 2008; Margolis and Walsh, 2003; Vogel, 2005). We thus see no purpose in repeating such an exercise. Instead we will draw upon the most significant findings that are useful in framing our central argument.

THE CENTRAL CONCERNS OF MAINSTREAM CSR RESEARCH

Two facts are readily evident upon reviewing the corpus of CSR research that has accumulated over the past few decades. First, scholars have focused their efforts on defining the CSR, stakeholder management and (more recently) corporate citizenships constructs, and determining the relationship between CSR and the economic performance of the firm. Second, these efforts have failed to generate anything beyond notional offerings of what CSR is; impart a general consensus that CSR's impact on performance is not clearly negative, and may in some cases be somewhat positive; and (consequently) provide a basis for a range of normative arguments in favour of CSR.

CSR AS AN ECONOMIC DISCOURSE

Despite several decades of effort, it remains correct to note that there is no agreed-upon definition of CSR among either scholars or practitioners, nor does such agreement seem in any way imminent. In a then-comprehensive review of the literature, Wood (1991: 695) defined CSR in the following manner: 'The basic idea of corporate social responsibility is that business and society are interwoven rather than distinct entities; therefore, society has certain expectations for appropriate business behaviour and outcomes.' Carroll (1998) defined CSR in terms of an ascending 'pyramid' whose base was constituted by economic considerations upon which legal, ethical and philanthropic elements were sequentially added. Schwartz and Carroll (2003) later integrated the ethical and philanthropic elements of this model. The task of defining the basic theoretical construct of CSR has not progressed further than these articulations.

In a recent review of CSR, Lee (2008) stressed the extent to which CSR research is increasingly focused on the link between CSR and financial performance, to the exclusion of wider and deeper issues that pertain to ethics, society and the capitalist institutional order. Notwithstanding this preoccupation within the field, the claims we can make from the research are circumscribed: in the aggregate, there is no mass of evidence that CSR-oriented behaviour by corporations negatively impacts economic performance. There is *some* evidence to support the notion that CSR-oriented behaviour has a positive – although not substantial – impact on firm-level economic performance, although there are strong claims for an 'industry effect' in operation here (Porter and Kramer, 2006).

The relative ambiguity of these findings is significant in terms of organizational practice. The lack of clarity in the relationship between CSR activities and corporate social performance leaves executives a significant amount of 'room to manoeuvre', as there is no clear negative impact from undertaking many CSR initiatives. Senior executives thus have some licence to embark on projects that allocate resources to benefit selected stakeholders within and beyond the boundaries of the corporation. What is primarily achieved by such initiatives is a 'feel good' factor – among employees, customers or the executives themselves – which ostensibly generates increased levels of engagement, loyalty and/or productivity to the benefit of corporate reputation and, ultimately, economic performance. This instrumental rationale is *always* the (explicit or implicit) logic behind CSR actions in the 'real world'. Yet it may often constitute a façade which conceals other, more personal motives at work which are not reducible to economic rationality.

Following Gioia (1999), we would stress the potential *existential* or what we call in Chapter 4 *ideological* drivers of such actions among the contemporary generation of CEOs and senior managers, many of whom not only want to create shareholder value, but also desperately desire to 'give something back' to the wider society – particularly where such actions have no discernibly negative impact on their firms' financial performance. CSR thus becomes a sort of 'holy grail' for some executives, helping to instil purpose in their organizations but also constituting a form of personal redemption for perceived sins. It allows the self-reflective CEO – aware to some degree of his or her alienation from other organizational actors, the wider society and even themselves (Rinehart, 2006) – to seek to attenuate that alienation through actions consistent with conceptions of the 'public good'.

THE MATRIX

Extant CSR research can be usefully depicted in the typological Business Activity Impact Matrix (BAIM) from Jones (2009a), shown in Figure 1.1, where the vertical

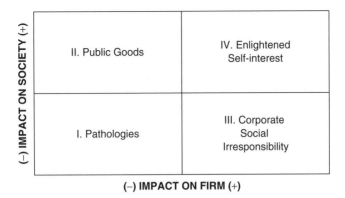

Figure 1.1

axis measures net 'impact on society' from positive to negative outcomes, and the horizontal axis measures net 'impact on firm' from positive to negative outcomes. The BAIM can be usefully employed to position practical CSR initiatives as well as theoretical perspectives with respect to both their intended effects as well as their actual empirical outcomes. We will also employ the BAIM to organize our discussion in the final section of this chapter on the question of *what is to be done*?

We begin our discussion of the BAIM with quadrant I. This quadrant is labelled 'pathologies' because it incorporates outcomes that are negative both for wider society – or at least some stakeholder groups – as well as for the firm whose actions are primarily responsible for the outcomes. Among the types of activities/outcomes that would be represented in this quadrant are cases of criminal fraud such as Enron. However, not all activities in this quadrant would necessarily be illegal; nor would all forms of illegal activities be limited to this quadrant. For example, heavy fines by the US federal government against British Airways for price fixing in its transatlantic airfreight operations represent a stark case of a corporation knowingly breaking the law in pursuit of financial advantage (*Guardian*, 2008). The *intention* of this action would thus have located it in quadrant III, while its eventual *outcome* would place it in quadrant I (assuming the fines levied on BA exceeded the benefits accruing to the firm from its errant behaviour). In addition, we would place many of the reckless banking activities underlying the current global financial crisis in this quadrant. With the gift of hindsight, it is now clear that the 2008 subprime meltdown was the outcome of some very self-destructive corporate practices.

The upper left of the matrix, quadrant II, is titled 'Public Goods' as it is a container for outcomes which benefit the wider society but represent negative returns to the sponsoring firm; that is, no net payback in terms of reputation, employee satisfaction, competitive differentiation and/or share price appreciation which offsets the time, energy and money of the firm's efforts is evident. In general, we would expect government, civic organizations and the voluntary sector to be most active in this quadrant, although there will also be a substantial presence of non-listed businesses whose owners have a preference for altruism. Importantly, representation of publically listed corporations in this quadrant would constitute a governance failure and *de facto* hijacking of shareholder wealth by management fiat (see Jensen, 2002).

On the lower right of the matrix is quadrant III, bearing the title of 'Corporate Social *Irresponsibility*' (CSI); this quadrant includes outcomes which generate some manner of payback for the firm that commits the directive actions, with damages inflicted on the wider society or given stakeholder groups. Various types of negative externalities generated by business activity are salient here, ranging from the exploitation and alienation of workers, to the degradation of the natural environment, to the commodification of culture – all in the name of profit. While some of these actions may on occasion be criminal in nature, most often they occur within legal boundaries, if not within acceptable normative codes of conduct.

Finally, on the upper right of the matrix is quadrant IV, labelled 'Enlightened Self-interest' (ESI). This quadrant is home to those actions which generate the proverbial 'win–win' situations, such as when Microsoft's donation activities function to some extent to ameliorate the reputational damage caused by its predatory competitive behaviour, at the same time unquestionably benefiting the recipients of new computer labs, IT training, tertiary scholarships, etc. Vogel (2005) notes that decades of investigation have failed to confirm (or reject) comprehensively the intuitively compelling notion that 'doing well by doing good' can serve as an important foundation for executive thinking. Nevertheless this unverified sentiment is rapidly becoming a mantra in the corporate discourse, fuelled now by the consulting industry on the one hand and 'ethical' fund analysts on the other. Clearly, quadrant IV is the normative destination for the way business *should* behave, but the rhetoric appears to be considerably ahead of the empirical reality of many business–society interventions. Indeed, it would be systemically *impossible* for all business activity to be seated in this 'win-win' quadrant given the nature of neo-liberal capitalism today.

THE IDEOLOGY OF THE 'GOOD CORPORATION'

Significantly, the vast majority of theoretical and empirical research on CSR would fall into quadrant IV ('Enlightened Self-interest') of the BAIM. This includes high-profile publications by Porter and Kramer (2006), Vogel (2005), Porter and Kramer (2011) as well as increasing output from consultancies such as McKinsey & Company (2006). Actions undertaken in the name of concepts such as 'strategic corporate philanthropy' (Porter and Kramer, 2002), social entrepreneurship (*The Economist*, 2008), 'shared value' (Porter and Kramer, 2011) and corporate citizenship (Matten and Crane, 2005) would also constitute quadrant IV activities. All are manifestations of the instrumental pursuit of enlightened self-interest of particular institutional/ organizational actors. Such actions also essentially (if not always explicitly) validate that most precious mantra of 'free market' ideology – that the 'invisible hand' truly will engender arrangements that are optimal for both firm and society.

We would not dispute the empirical existence of quadrant IV outcomes. But we *would* question its empirical magnitude relative to the other quadrants currently. Also, we would caution stakeholders in all institutional locations not to get 'carried away' with the notion that CSR activities *always* fall within this quadrant, thus mitigating the need for the formation of effective countervailing forces to corporate power in government, labour organizations, NGOs and the like. We would maintain that much normative CSR theory incorporates dangerous idealism of this type, itself rooted in a fundamental theoretical misspecification of the institutional function, capacities and *limits* of the business firm in a capitalist political economy.

ELEPHANTS IN THE ROOM

We would argue that the largely fruitless efforts which have characterized the vast majority of extant CSR research to date are particularly unfortunate given the major shifts in economy, politics, society and culture which have occurred since the field's inception. Our position is that these shifts, potentially epochal in their impact, will largely structure future organizational fields within which corporations must operate; that corporate actors are not only passive reactors to these developments, but also in many instances *active shapers* of market, industry and sector evolution operating at various geographical levels; and that, by and large, these developments have not been explored by CSR scholarship.

THE RISE OF 'GIGATREND CAPITALISM'

Despite its overwhelming salience, the fact remains that there are other, far more challenging events looming on the horizon than the current financial crisis blighting the United States and Europe. We will refer to these developments as *gigatrends*, our more dystopian rendering of the once popular notion of 'megatrend' coined by futurologist John Naisbitt (1982). These include various dislocations linked to climate change; energy depletion; the ascension of the BRIC nations; the genome revolution; and the rise of a 'surplus humanity' in (mostly) southern megacities. This constitutes the proverbial elephant in the room for much CSR research since some of these trends (especially the first two) will in the future make current CSR research concerns look rather quaint. These gigatrends are directly relevant to CSR in two ways. First, they are in some cases the result of a conspicuous *failure* of CSR and/or ethically suspect (if not illegal) business practices. Second, each challenge will require some form of effective corporate response in order to realize opportunities and/or mitigate the risks stemming from that trend. In this chapter we will review the giga-trends that will shape the future global business environment, and comment on the specific challenges they each represent for CSR theory and practice.

The first and pre-eminent gigatrend facing not only economic actors but all of humanity is that of climate change, including inexorable species extinction and the decline of bio-diversity (by 80 per cent over the last one hundred years according to some analysts). The overwhelming judgement of the scientific community is that global warming is a fact, and that human industrial activity (based on fossil fuels) is a major contributor to the process (Intergovernmental Panel on Climate Change, 2008; Stern, 2007). Sea levels are already on the rise, fostering 'climate refugees' (Klein, 2007; Welzer, 2012); weather patterns appear increasingly unstable in comparison with historical norms, undermining agricultural productivity; and some estimates of temperature increases suggest we are approaching a 'tipping point' which could be sufficient to trigger positive feedback loops driving runaway temperature increases (*Guardian*, 2009a). Scientists from the Global Carbon Project suggest that the most likely scenario is for a 6° (Fahrenheit) rise by 2100, due to the manifestation of feedback loops through the failure of natural 'carbon sinks' to absorb greenhouse gas emissions, which have increased 29 per cent over the 2000–2008 period (*Independent*, 2009). Other consequences of such a radical increase in global temperatures would include the release of methane from the Siberian tundra and sea-level rises of approximately 14 metres as the Greenland and Western Antarctic ice shelves melt completely (Lee, 2008). This combination of circumstances could trigger a 'mass extinction' event such as that which occurred 252 million years ago at the Permian-Triassic boundary, during which an estimated 95 per cent of the earth's existing fauna perished (Lynas, 2007).

The second gigatrend is that of continuing (and accelerating) energy depletion associated with 'peak oil' (see Greer, 2008; *Guardian*, 2009b), its consequences for energy security and, ultimately, the sustainability of the model of a technologically advanced, energy-intensive civilization that emerged first in the West during the nineteenth century. The International Energy Agency (IEA) has identified 2006 as the year in which we hit 'peak oil', the point at which known global petroleum reserves exceed consumed reserves (IEA, 2012). This means that we are in the early stages of an extended decline in which supplies of oil and (in time) other fossil fuels (coal and natural gas) will be unable to keep up with demand (Heinberg, 2005). Meanwhile, alternative energy sources and technologies (e.g. geothermal, hydro, solar) will not come near to offsetting the energy deficit left by fossil fuels because their *net energy yield* – the difference between the amount of energy one unit of a substance generates and the energy that has been expended in producing it – is typically only a fraction of that of fossil fuels (Greer, 2008). Moreover, progress in developing 'clean' energy is well behind the 2020 targets identified by the 28 IEA member countries a few years ago, as are efforts to increase energy efficiency (IEA, 2012).

The third gigatrend driving large-scale structural change in the world is the rise of the so-called 'BRIC' nations and the consequent (at least relative) decline of the West (and Japan) in terms of their role and status in the global economy. Inevitably, with rising economic power also comes political clout – witness the recent morphing of the G8 into the G20 as the world's most important international forum on economic affairs, along with China's major role in scuppering the recent climate negotiations in Copenhagen (Lynas, 2010). Perhaps most significant from a longer-term perspective, however, will be the eroding value of the Western narrative of development through markets and democracy so celebrated in the 'end of history' thesis (Fukuyama, 1992) and manifested in the neo-liberal policies of the Washington Consensus (see Panitch and Konigs, 2009).

The extent to which the Western (i.e. Anglo-American) development model has been discredited should not be underestimated. Some observers trace a growing conflict regarding the global 'rules of the game' back at least to the aftermath of the Asian financial crisis of 1997 (Aglietta and Berribi, 2007). Conversations within key international institutions in the future will likely take on a much more pluralistic tone where multiple varieties of capitalism with differing roles for market, state and democracy will compete for policy influence over the institutional architecture of the global system. The BRIC nations can also be expected to compete with the West for access to key global resources such as energy, strategic minerals and arable land (see Klare, 2002), a contest which is already evident in the neo-colonial 'race for Africa' between China and the United States (*Financial Times*, 2010; Moyo, 2012). Significant here is the fact that for China and many other emerging nations the benchmark development model is not the United States or Western Europe, but rather Singapore. With its effective mix of strong state, political stability, attenuated democracy and social 'harmony', its success puts into question the robustness of the Western formulation of democratic capitalism as the modal institutional framework for developing countries (Kagan, 2009).

The fourth gigatrend impacting future history relates to the potentially vast implications of the genome revolution, particularly with respect to life extension technologies. While some scientists rather humorously claim that we are within reach of living up to 1,000 years (de Grey, 2008), more widely held opinions expect a significant percentage of children born today to experience life spans considerably in excess of 100 years. Yet technological possibilities need to take into account political, social and cultural factors. The impacts on superannuation systems, labour markets and occupational structures are only the most obvious areas of disruption, but there are even more fundamental issues at stake. For example, in a world of vastly unbalanced distribution of life chances owing to chronic inequality, it is entirely likely that only those who can afford it will get to live longer – just like today, only *much* more so. A plausible scenario would depict a predatory global minority of 'elders' being serviced by masses of much younger and less healthy (due to eroding public health infrastructures, Greer, 2009) people working in factories, on farms, in retail establishments, and in retirement communities and rest homes – a kind of *Logan's Run* (Nolan and Johnson, 1967) in reverse! Already, in fact, social commentators such as the novelist Martin Amis have written of the coming generational conflict and advocated voluntary 'euthanasia booths' for seniors as one means to dissipate the rising tensions between young and old (*Guardian*, 2010a).

The final gigatrend shaping the global business environment is the rise of massive slums in the megacities of the South. This trend is largely a consequence of globalization, as rural populations are forced off their land through contemporary 'enclosure' measures aimed at opening up formally subsistence acreage for agro-industrial production of specialized crops for export. Davis (2007) notes the linkages between global neo-liberalism, the increasing urbanization of world poverty, and the rise of a 'surplus humanity' which is excluded from formal networks of production and exchange, forced to survive by any means necessary in the midst of increasing resource scarcity and environmental degradation. He argues that the state's capacity to create formal jobs and housing has been sacrificed to the goal of monetary stability imposed by neo-liberal regimes. This is consistent with a UN report which observed that: 'The collapse of formal urban employment in the developing world and the rise of the informal sector is seen as a *direct function of liberalization* [italics added] … . Urban poverty has been increasing in most countries subject to structural adjustment programs, most of which are deliberately anti-urban in nature' (UN-Habitat, 2003). *Foreign Policy* (2006) noted that by 2015 almost all of the 21 global megacities will be in developing countries (Tokyo and Seoul are the only exceptions) and will be wracked by pollution, inadequate services and crime. Significantly, the 'southern' megacities' curently emerging represent a *reversal* of the classical (and functional) labour-intensive countryside/capital-intensive industrial metropolis couplet. We now witness capital-intensive hinterlands and burgeoning de-industrialized cities with shrinking formal economies, with few linkages between the two save for a one-way flow of urban migration (Davis, 2006).

MISSING THE FOREST FOR THE TREES

We suggest that CSR is unwittingly wedded to a naturalized notion of Western neo-liberal capitalism – what Fisher (2009) calls a 'business ontology' – and that it is necessarily blind to the *systemic* (and not aberrational) crises of gigatrend capitalism, almost sleepwalking through yet another rehearsal of the story that multinational business might be redeemed. To explain, let us summarize some important points. The gigatrends associated with climate, resources and development are, to a greater or lesser extent, interlocking. So what are the fundamental institutional actors and processes driving these specific gigatrends, and what are the links to CSR? The most powerful causal driver of the gigatrends is the capital accumulation process itself as it manifests across time and space through globalization, embodied most effectively in the institutional forms of the multinational corporation (MNC) and the dense networks of financial capital. This process is not static but dynamic, not tending towards equilibrium but rather expansionary in terms of both intensive (deepening within sectors) and extensive (colonizing new sectors) aspects in addition to its geographical incorporations of China (since the late 1970s) and the ex-USSR and its satellites (since the end of the Cold War). The key actors at the international level which any MNC interacts with include other MNCs, states, trade organizations, the media and (increasingly) NGOs such as Greenpeace and Amnesty International; at the national level other entities such as local firms and labour unions may also be salient features of the MNC's organizational field.

With respect to climate change, clearly there is a direct causal connection between the globalization of the capital accumulation process and ever-increasing levels of production, consumption and waste as societies shift from subsistence to consumerism. As noted by Heilbroner (1985), capitalism is not only about producing goods and services at a profit, but also about producing *people*, by which he means forms of consciousness and worldviews dominated by instrumental economic rationality. To the extent that there is no stable 'equilibrium point' at the individual, firm or any other level of analysis *in practice*, capitalist globalization necessarily represents an increasing scale of economic activity which can only add to global warming. While the immediate environmental impacts of this economic activity have shifted in recent decades from the North to Asia and parts of the South as Western and Japanese MNCs have restructured their supply chains (Dicken, 2010), the aggregate amount of environmental degradation continues to increase with the volume of industrial activity, despite improvements in productivity which allow more outputs from fewer inputs.

To some, the notion of a 'globally sustainable capitalism' constitutes an oxymoron. This is fundamentally a question of political economy, where key institutional actors, discourses and processes interact in a complex field structured by wide power differentials and conflicting interests (a subject unpacked in more detail in Chapter 5). Clearly, a sustainable capitalism is not theoretically or practically viable under conditions of financial hegemony which privilege, reward and *require* growth. Rather, sustainability would require capitalism to be small scale and local, with largely self-contained circuits of production and exchange and only a minor role for trade between given production-exchange networks in an 'ecotechnic' economy (Greer, 2009; see also Schumacher, 1973). How we get *there* from *here* without a revolution (or cataclysm), however, is seemingly beyond CSR's ability to articulate convincingly.

THE AGE OF ENERGY WARS

The gigatrend of energy depletion most directly impacts MNCs and state-owned enterprises active in the oil, natural gas and coal segments of the energy sector, as these organizations are even now confronting the realities of 'peak oil'. Yet since industrial (and post-industrial) economies are based fundamentally on an ample supply of cheap energy from fossil fuels, the ramifications of energy depletion are *totalizing* – think, for example, of the rapidly rising levels of electricity needed to power Google's servers! Unless there occurs an as yet unforeseen technological breakthrough which leads to some alternative energy source taking up the slack as fossil fuel stocks wind down, the type of civilization which developed in Western Europe and the United States in the nineteenth century, extending itself throughout most of the world in the twentieth century, will be *literally* unsustainable. That is, available energy resources will not be able to generate levels of electrical and other forms of energy necessary to power the built environments and transportation grids integral to an advanced technological civilization.

Greer (2008) argues convincingly that existing and foreseeable alternative energy sources cannot begin to fill the vacuum created by the exhaustion of fossil fuels. Rather than expect a sudden catastrophic 'end days' scenario, Greer instead posits a long decent through a process of 'catabolic decline'. Somewhat ironically, the United States will be among the worst affected advanced nations, largely due to the fact that it was the global first-mover in terms of exploiting the energy potential of fossil fuels on a vast continental scale. The US model of development was based on an endless supply of cheap energy. As these supplies are depleted, the structural inefficiencies of the US economy are contributing to the declining status of the United States as the global hegemon. This is despite the partial and temporary alleviation achieved through 'fracking' natural gas depicted so powerfully in the documentary film *Gasland* (2010).

The gigatrend of energy depletion explains much of the geo-political activity we have witnessed over the last 15 years. In the US, securing oil supplies through any means necessary (including war) is an inevitable corollary to its current economic predicament. With Iran possibly becoming a nuclear-armed state, some have predicted dire scenarios for the Middle East region as the race for oil intensifies. The civil wars ravaging a number of African states can be linked to contested control over hugely lucrative natural mineral and oil reserves. Many commentators are now speculating on the future role that China, in particular, might play in politico-military activities linked to the global scramble for natural resources, water and food (c.f., Moyo, 2012).

AN AUTHORITARIAN FUTURE?

The rise of the BRIC nations (along with other emerging markets) is a gigatrend in which the MNC is directly implicated as the key agent behind the 'global shift' (Dicken, 2010) that has witnessed the world's manufacturing belt moving from North America, Western Europe and Japan to countries in Asia (South Korea, Malaysia), Eastern Europe (Poland), Latin America (Mexico, Brazil), Africa (South Africa) and (above all) China. And it is China that poses the greatest challenge to the hegemony of the Anglo-American development model of democratic capitalism. This is because China has managed – that is, *directly* managed – to generate faster sustained economic growth than any other country in history. It has accomplished this without in any way having the Communist Party release its grip on political power, thus falsifying the teleological 'modernization thesis' (Moore, 1967) that linked the articulation of an economic system based on market exchanges with the development of a democratic political system and the rise of a civil sphere in which ideas and information could be freely circulated (Anderson, 2010; Jacques, 2009).

As noted earlier, the development model for China is not the United States but Singapore, which has reached very high levels of development through a long period of authoritarian capitalism administered by a regime characterized by nepotism, a nationalistic orientation, and the foresight that increasing the wealth and prospects for the few depends upon achieving a degree of material improvement for the many (Jacques, 2009; Whitley, 1992). A challenge for 'democratic' countries going forward will be their structural disadvantage in dealing with chronic long-term challenges such as the gigatrends of climate change, species decline and energy depletion due to their preoccupation with short electoral cycles and reliance on market forces – both of which tend to discount the future heavily. It may well be, then, that only some form of authoritarian capitalism has any hope of surviving the twenty-first century *and* dealing effectively with the gigatrends.

BIO-POLITICAL DOMINATION

Proceeding to the next gigatrend, the most starkly apparent characteristic of the genome revolution – in great contrast to the 'open-sourced' spread of the Internet – is that it is unfolding in an overwhelmingly *privatized* organizational field composed of research labs (often spin-offs from public universities), biotech and pharmaceutical firms, medical equipment manufacturers, health care delivery providers (hospitals and clinics), insurance companies and regulatory agencies. Here we see 'life itself' or *bios* become the field for capitalist development pertaining to the body and its biological correlates (see Rose, 2007). The trajectory of technological development and commercialization of basic research will likely mean a profound skewness in the direction of treating those illnesses (e.g. diabetes, obesity) that afflict relatively well-off citizens/customers in wealthy countries, rather than dealing with age-old maladies (e.g. tuberculosis, malaria) which torment hundreds of millions of poor people across the globe. This is because a so-called functioning market requires not only that a demand exist but that potential customers have the means to pay (Banerjee, 2009). As noted by John Sulston, who led the UK branch of the Human Genome Project, 'The fact of the matter is that many human genes have patent rights on them and this is going to get in the way of treatment unless you have a lot of money' (*Guardian*, 2010b). This unequal access to life-preserving/extending technologies for the global minority, while the global majority experiences *shortening* life spans as the ravages of climate change and energy depletion undermine states' ability to fund public health initiatives (Cecchetti et al., 2010; Greer, 2008), raises issues of social justice which clash directly with the 'ethics' of property rights.

The final gigatrend (which is also closely related to the bio-politics of the rich labs and technological campuses) concerns the rise of global slums, and is directly linked to the globalization of agriculture and the integration of developing countries into global circuits of production and consumption. Formerly self-sufficient nations have become in many instances net food importers as their specialty crops fall victim to cyclical demand patterns and international competition from both developing and (heavily subsidized) advanced economies in North America, the EU and Japan. Indeed, since the food riots of 2008 across large parts of the developing world, 'food security' has become a central issue for policy makers in national and international institutions (Brown, 2005). The massive influx of rural peasants to urban areas is thus largely a consequence of the articulating global division of labour fostered by neo-liberal trade policies enforced by the World Trade Organization (WTO). The governance of this system is characterized by massive asymmetries of power between individual states, especially in cases where small states bargain with powerful blocs such as the EU or the North American Free Trade Agreement (NAFTA).

The rapid growth of megacities such as Sao Paulo, Jakarta and Lagos also catalyses the 'weaponizing' of urban space elaborated by Sassen (2006), as police and private security organizations experience similarly explosive growth to cope with the challenges of keeping the expanding underclass in check so that key flows of people, goods and information can continue to interact in a functional manner. This aspect of the phenomenon will be particularly significant in driving the institutionalization of *de facto* authoritarian capitalist regimes (justified through narratives based on 'law and order', 'border control' and the like) throughout most of what Fukuyama would have termed the democratic capitalist West over the next few decades as fears of 'barbarians at the gates' intensify.

DISASTER CAPITALISM: THE RULE, NOT THE EXCEPTION

We would argue that other actors such as 'new social movements' and NGOs, which have received increasing attention in recent years from both academics (cf. Castells, 1997; Hardt and Negri, 1999) and policy makers (cf. Anyon, 2005), do not (yet) constitute 'shapers' of these global gigatrends, although at finer-grained geographical levels they can certainly exert some influence over MNCs, states and international trade organizations. This ineffectual influence is largely due to the difference between structural processes (e.g. capital accumulation) which are embedded in the DNA of firms, becoming self-evident 'cognitive maps', and acts of resistance which by their very nature tend to be idiosyncratic (i.e. non-structural). The former generate (at least somewhat) predictable actions undertaken without 'reflection' by agents (see Friedland and Alford, 1991), while each instantiation of the latter depends on *intentional* deployments of agency in specific times and places.

Here we see a paradoxical melding of a blind 'business ontology' (Fisher, 2009) – in that we see no alternative since the cognitive maps of corporatized life are so entrenched – with a strong requisite of agency or free will. This is important for linking the idiosyncratic choices of firms to the systematic flow of corporate domination. It is not that some firms choose to act 'unethically' while others decide to be virtuous. Business ontology requires agency, but harnesses it to the unquestioned 'cause' of business. And this, in turn, allows us to dismiss the notion that 'negative cases' only occur when a firm chooses wrongdoing since (paradoxically) the decision has already been made – now it only requires retrospective ratification through the display of choice. Greenpeace International Executive Director Kumi Naidoo saw the difficulty in contesting the 'business as usual' cognitive maps of neo-liberal capitalism at the 2012 Rio+20 Earth summit. His frustration is palpable: 'We didn't get the future we want in Rio, because we do not have the leaders we need. The leaders of the most powerful countries supported 'business as usual', shamefully putting private profit before people and the planet' (*Guardian*, 2012).

THE APOCALYPSE WILL BE DISAPPOINTING

An example should suffice to illustrate this important distinction between the structural and the idiosyncratic. Take the activities of Royal Dutch Shell. This firm scans the globe for new deposits of fossil fuels, as well as managing ongoing relations with various national regimes such as those of Nigeria, where its role in contributing to human rights violations and environmental destruction have been well documented (cf. BBC News, 2010; Hahn, 2010). The key decision makers at Shell do not daily – or perhaps, ever – consider why Shell exists or what criteria beyond profit seeking should drive their strategic choices. Rather, these considerations are sublimated in cognitive maps constituted by economic rationality and the structuring power of financial hegemony. These maps explain how the world works and define appropriate decisional parameters within organizational fields, as well as appropriate executive *responsibilities*. Thus, one might say that the Shell machine grinds away in pursuit of its *raison d'être* – to make money for the interests that own it. Meanwhile, Greenpeace or Amnesty International must allocate their limited resources for maximum impact in monitoring, publicizing and (hopefully) curtailing these acts of environmental degradation on a case-by-case basis. They cannot count on any automatic mechanism like the 'cognitive maps' mentioned above to fulfil this role, but must instead 'reinvent' themselves through continual organizational acts of wilful cognition in order to keep fighting selected battles across a global front.

A useful metaphor to capture structural versus idiosyncratic properties is that of a fire control team (Greenpeace) amidst an uncontained 'wildfire' (global capitalism). The fire expands of its own volition depending on temperature, wind and the supply of consumable materials; its growth is structurally determined by these variables. The fire control team, conversely, must decide *where* and *when* to fight the fire. Here the opportunity cost is obvious, for the team cannot be in two places at once. Meanwhile, the fire is *everywhere* that conditions for combustion exist. As we know, even the largest fires eventually burn themselves out, but rarely due (primarily) to fire control efforts; rather the underlying conditions which sustained them must expire. Until and unless the institutional mechanics which support global capitalism are altered and subordinated to more socially oriented priorities, we can expect organizations such as Greenpeace (and perhaps nation-states and their regional conglomerates like the crisis ridden Eurozone) to continue to behave like fire control teams – unable to prevent the next 'corporate wildfire' from happening, only able to attend to its aftermath and, by publicizing why the event occurred, perhaps to subject particular firms, industries and government regulators to the media spotlight for a time.

Commenting on these large-scale shifts for the worst, Žižek (2009) observes that we live in 'apocalyptic times' driven by ecological breakdown, the bio-genetic revolution and total social regulation through digitization. He builds on Ayres' (1999) description that: 'We are being confronted by something so completely outside our collective experience that we really don't see it, even when the evidence is overwhelming. For us, that "something" is a blitz of enormous biological and physical alterations in the world that has been sustaining us' (Ayres, 1999: 584–585). Ayres writes of four 'spikes' (or accelerated developments) approaching a convergence at which a qualitative change will completely reconfigure our physical and social lifeworlds: population growth, the depletion of finite resources, carbon gas emissions and the mass extinction of species. According to Žižek (2009), the dominant ideology (neo-liberalism) increasingly mobilizes mechanisms of dissimulation and self-deception which include a 'will to ignorance' – a general pattern of behaviour among threatened human societies to become more blinkered, rather than more focused on the crisis, as they fail (also see Banerjee, 2009; Diamond, 2006). And as Greer (2008) has convincingly demonstrated, the descent will not be sudden, but 'catabolic', a slow down-shift of the capitalist oil-reliant civilization. Following Blanchot's (1997) paraphrasing of Eliot's lyrical lament that the world will end not with a bang but a whimper, the apocalypse will undoubtedly be disappointing.

CSR AS THE 'NEW OPIATE OF THE MASSES'

So where does CSR fit into all of this? Žižek (2009) argues that the form of hegemony that is emerging out of the present crisis is that of a 'socially responsible eco-capitalism'. This is where collaboration with employees, dialogue with customers, respect for the environment and transparency are held as key success factors of a model that aligns business goals with positive outcomes for the broader society. He writes:

> The new ethos of global responsibility is thus able to put capitalism to work as the most efficient instrument of the common good. The basic ideological dispositive of capitalism – we can call it 'instrumental reason', 'technological exploitation', 'individualist greed' or whatever we like – is separated from its concrete socio-economic conditions (capitalist relations of production) and conceived of as an autonomous life or 'existential' attitude which should (and can) be overcome by a new more 'spiritual' outlook, leaving *those very capitalist relations intact*. (Žižek, 2009: 35, original italics)

We would maintain that the effect, if not the intent, of orthodox CSR scholarship supports the 'will to ignorance' referred to by Žižek by avoiding almost completely the gigatrends unfolding in the capitalist political economy. The vast majority of extant CSR research effectively avoids examining these 'elephants in the room'; that is, tackling the major topics relevant to corporate–society interactions. For example, CSR theory fails to provide a coherent analysis of power and interests (of the MNC, the state), and how these interact to generate distributional outcomes (see Jones and Fleming, 2003). Issues of the social and economic efficiency and justice of capitalism, the corporate form, hierarchy and managerialism are all marginalized (if not entirely ignored) because these are reified in much mainstream CSR discourse – literally part of the conceptual landscape – and thus outside the realm of analysis.

CONCLUSIONS

The purpose of this chapter has been to point out the blindness of recent CSR discourse and practice when it comes to the tectonic shifts in global capitalism that ought to undermine any confidence in it as a tenable project. But strangely, it is exactly this confidence we find gushing in a good deal of current CSR research. This might be harmless at one level, but it does play into a broader ideological project of valorizing the new world order of economic rule. It is for this reason that we see CSR as indirectly in the service of neo-liberal capitalism, as a retreat from politics rather than a politicization. Moreover, we have posited the Business Activity Impact Matrix (or BAIM) to assist in mapping the relationship between the corporation and society (we will return to this matrix in the concluding chapter).

In our wide-ranging discussion in this chapter, we offer some thoughts on a fundamental question that has been lost in the CSR discourse, or, more accurately, which never properly entered it: *what are the limits of business?* Many of the works of orthodox CSR bombard us with discussions of what business *is* doing, what business *could* do or what business *should* do. Conspicuously absent from this oeuvre are thoughtful examinations of what business *cannot* do given its intrinsic anti-social nature (this is why it is such a troubling social institution). Instead, we have what amounts to the orthodox CSR discourse at least implicitly supporting a notion of Adam Smith's 'invisible hand' in which voluntary CSR activities prove the point that laissez-faire works in practice.

This last point is significant and merits a little more elaboration. The work of the Frankfurt School of Critical Theory notably developed the linkages between the hegemony of scientific–technical rationality, the notion of material progress and the role of the 'culture industries' in securing a stable environment for capital accumulation in the Western nations and in the several decades following the Second World War (see Jay, 1984; Marcuse, 1964). Since the 1970s, however, it has become increasingly clear that material progress has significantly stalled for many people, including those who would be termed 'middle' class, as noted earlier. This has consequently undermined confidence in universal notions of progress, as well as in 'science' (Feyerabend, 1993).

Vitally, these developments have occurred largely outside of the political sphere and have, for the most part, not translated into organized political movements complete with coherent counter-hegemonic narratives. Instead, we have witnessed an expansion of the politics of 'denial' and/or 'know-nothingism' in the United States but also elsewhere – most of which have at least implicitly translated into support for right-wing parties. Rather than the dissatisfaction of the 'multitude' becoming a trigger for progressive action, many wait and hold onto the unreasonable fantasy that things might hopefully turn out for the best (Watkins, 2010; Žižek, 2009; but see also the Invisible Committee, 2009).

To the extent that the most recent orthodox literature in the field suggests that CSR is 'smart business', it underwrites the ultimate triumph of enlightened self-interest and the Smithian 'invisible hand'; that is, that large corporations have matured and finally 'got it' with respect to understanding their appropriate role as 'good corporate citizens'. Since the corporate form is (increasingly) the most articulated expression of scientific-technical rationality (*In Our Times*, 2010), the CSR discourse also perpetuates the fundamentally historicist notion that evolutionary leaps in the form of technological breakthroughs will arise to deal with the critical gigatrends discussed above (see Greer, 2009). Thus actual or potential countervailing forces and alternative narratives of economic or political organization simply have no *raison d'être*. This constitutes a mystification of certain objective realities. It also promotes an anaesthetization of thought and action on the part of stakeholders who are, in fact, not benefiting from the Smithian 'rising tide which lifts all boats' but, rather, are experiencing first hand *real* rising tides on their coastlines.

The following excerpt is from a recent call for papers issued by a popular business studies conference:

> Over the last few decades, the heretofor neat separation between the political and economic spheres has become blurred. In the process of globalization, the national context of governance is eroding. In many cases the state system fails in regulating the economy, dealing with transnational social and environmental problems, providing public goods, administering citizenship rights and serving the public interest. This is particularly true when public institutions lack the necessary resources or enforcement mechanisms. Under these conditions, civil society groups and private actors often step in and fill the void … Today, many multinational business firms have started voluntarily to regulate their activities or produce global public goods. As the widespread participation in the UN Global Compact shows, these firms assume political responsibilities that once were regarded as belonging to government. They contribute to public health, education, social security and the protection of human rights, or engage in self-regulation to fill gaps in legal regulation and to promote societal peace and stability … Distinct changes in political ideology since the 1970s have led to massive changes in most industrialized countries. Substantial reforms of the post-war Keynesian welfare state – often commonly referred to as 'neo-liberal' reforms – have led to massive privatization of formerly government-provided services (e.g. health care, basic shelter, education, telecommunications, public transport, utilities). These developments have put corporations in charge of the provision of goods whose nature in terms of quality, accessibility and affordability have an intricately political character. (From the 'European Group for Organization Studies Conference', 2009 call for papers.)

This statement highlights how significant the concept of corporate citizenship has become for understanding the evolving relationship between business and society. Like CSR and stakeholder theory, the notion of citizenship links the capitalist firm to broader ethical and moral questions about how organizations ought to behave in society and the effects they have on their surrounding communities. Citizenship itself is a concept derived from classical political discourse, whereby individuals enjoy certain rights and must bear certain responsibilities. As it has been adopted in business research and practice, corporate citizenship highlights how such rights and responsibilities are achieved and influenced by corporations (Maignan et al., 1999). Indeed, a basic legal frame of reference for private firms is the 'imaginary' corporate citizen.

Law treats the organization *as if* it was an individual, which has special significance with respect to limited liability status as well as enabling the institution to pursue its interests directly in the political process.

In this chapter we build on our initial arguments regarding CSR by turning to one of its most popular sub-themes, that of corporate citizenship. This area of research (and practice) argues that in the wake of the withdrawal of the state from many sectors of society, the private corporation must become involved in the provision of legal, economic and civil rights. Some of these observers even conclude that the distinction between public and private spheres has become effectively obsolete (see Ronit and Schneider, 1999). Rather than think of corporate citizenship in terms of conventional CSR or philanthropy, McIntosh et al. (1998), for example, suggest we view the corporation as a conduit and provider of citizenship rights. Scherer et al. (2006; see also Scherer and Palazzo, 2008a) argue that the 'new situation' driven by gaps in global regulation, the erosion of national-level governance and a loss of moral and cultural homogeneity in the corporate sector creates conditions for a 'politically enlarged' concept of CSR in which the role of the corporation is extended beyond instrumental activity into the realm of socially responsible political actions in society. These lines of thought are consistent with the World Bank's recent interest in civil society following the failure of many of its 'structural adjustment programmes' during the 1980s and 1990s (see Stiglitz, 2003; Wood, 2009), and they have significant implications for how we study the political and ethical consequences of the corporate form (as manifested in the MNC) in an age of globalization.

Perhaps the most significant recent developments in corporate citizenship scholarship are the contributions by Matten, Crane and their colleagues (most clearly articulated in Matten and Crane, 2005; but see also see Matten et al., 2003; Moon et al., 2005). We will refer to this body of work as 'new corporate citizenship' theory or NCC. In this chapter, we will analyse NCC theory as the most prominent representation of new conceptions of the corporation's expanding role in societal affairs. The aim is to highlight what we see to be the shortcomings in this approach when viewed through a critical political economy lens (see Cox et al., 1995). We argue that NCC theory must account for the continuing importance of the state (in its 'extreme neo-liberal' form as Harney (2009) puts it), recognize the highly anti-social logic of the multinational corporation (MNC) and more directly confront contradictory empirical evidence in order to be taken seriously by both scholars and practitioners. Since much of NCC theory is discussed in the context of globalization, we too will use multinational capitalism as an illustrative example for studying the problematic components of the notion that the firm might secure citizenship rights. This critical analysis will be 'deep' rather than 'broad' in terms of its focused intent. We hope to introduce a more politically aware orientation based on the ubiquity of structurally opposing stakeholder interests, discursive conflicts and asymmetrical power configurations.

In light of the theoretical and empirical developments noted above – and in the midst of the current rise of a disaster-prone 'gigatrend' capitalism discussed in Chapter 1 – this chapter addresses the simple question: how *useful* are these new conceptions of corporate citizenship for making sense of firms that are increasingly transnational in scope? Our overall conclusion is that it is simply not in the MNC's institutional DNA to provide citizenship rights under any circumstances beyond a 'business case' logic – and if it ever did, then it would do so in an unreliable, unaccountable and undemocratic manner.

There is no doubt that the notion of corporate citizenship is of fundamental importance for ascertaining the role of the business firm within society as a legal, economic and moral agent. The rise to dominance of the corporate form in the twentieth century was acknowledged – even celebrated – by orthodox observers in economics, sociology, business history and elsewhere, as being a consequence of its functional superiority over other forms of economic organization in terms of managing risk (Ansoff, 1965), lowering transaction costs (Coase, 1937; Williamson, 1975), generating economies of scale (Chandler, 1977) and/or accelerating technological innovation (Galbraith, 1967; Schumpeter, 1945). But rather than the corporation evolving 'naturally', it emerged from heated conflict, violence and political wrangling. For example, Lustig (1979) chronicled the controversies that surrounded the elevation of the corporate form in the late nineteenth century in the United States, a struggle whose outcome was in no sense inevitable (see also Perrow, 1986; and in relation to Europe, Hindess, 1993). The outcome of conflicts over the period 1890–1920 led to the establishment of a form of 'corporate liberalism' which Lustig defines in terms of a hegemonic cultural logic that structures wide-spanning institutional and organizational fields (also see Miller and O'Leary, 1989).

Considering the history of this period, Lustig (1979) identifies several battles fought between populist forces (composed of industrial workers, small-scale capitalists and family farmers) and a nexus of agricultural, industrial and financial capitalist interests. These battles coalesced around democratic participation, class and worker control and debates about whether the rights captured by the corporation could be in some way offset by the state in order to redress distributive imbalances. In Lustig's view, each of these conflicts ended in the defeat of populist forces, though their failures were not inevitable but due to historically specific sets of circumstances. Extending his analysis into the late twentieth century, Lustig questioned whether it was possible to 'elicit good behaviour and continuing effort from people who are gathered in associations [corporations] that lack common purpose and fail to provide meaningful work' (1979: 32). He referred to the contemporary institutional order as 'corporativism'.

FROM CORPORATIVISM TO CITIZEN

Reich (1997) revisited this debate, concluding that the corporation's citizenship right to participate as a political actor should be withdrawn in order to revitalize US democracy. In his more recent work (see Reich, 2007) he continues this theme, arguing that companies cannot be socially responsible, at least not to any significant extent beyond obvious 'win–win' situations where profitable activities intersect with the public good. Reich argues that misunderstanding the nature of the corporation and the limits of its ability to 'do good' has resulted in CSR activists being diverted from the more realistic and important task of getting governments to solve social problems. He observes that debating whether Walmart or Monsanto is good or evil misses the larger point, which is that governments are responsible for setting rules that ensure that profit-maximizing firms do not act against the interests of society. His long-standing position in support of removing direct corporate participation in the political process follows clearly from this position.

Reich's work effectively highlights a conspicuous weakness characterizing the totality of mainstream CSR/Corporate Citizenship scholarship – the failure to grapple theoretically with the relationship between business and government or, more specifically, the area of state theory (cf. Hay et al., 2005; Weiss, 1998). This is not to suggest that some scholars do not come close to dealing with this important area of enquiry. For example, Moon and Vogel (2008: 318) note that:

> The boundaries between business and government do not take place in a vacuum; they are strongly influenced by corporate political preferences and their lobbying activities. For all the increasing importance of CSR, public policy remains the most important vehicle by which private business purposes and broader social objectives can be reconciled.

But Moon and Vogel fail to conceptualize the relationship between business, the state and other key stakeholders as anything more than an implicit pluralism of competing rational actors. Exempted from sustained consideration are the more complex structural linkages between the state and capital which frame 'interest group politics', as well as any nuanced exploration of the extent and implications of various state bureaucracies acting as self-conscious agents in pursuit of agendas which are aligned neither with 'capital' nor with external interest groups (see Alford and Friedland, 1985).

Once one recognizes that there are empirical categories wherein corporate activities impact society in negative ways (e.g. through generating and socializing negative externalities), it becomes critical to limit the ability of corporations to penetrate government agencies and bureaucracies in order to influence and shape regulatory frameworks and compliance mechanisms (also see Gond et al., 2009). But what if the state is unable or unwilling to act as an 'honest broker' because it has been penetrated by particular interests, or perhaps simply due to a lack of critical resources? Are there conditions under which the corporation *can* or *should* redefine its role to fill the vacuum created by the absent state?

NCC THEORY

As noted by Edward and Willmott (2008), corporate citizenship is anything but a new concept. They cite references to corporate citizenship going back to the late 1950s (cf. Gossett, 1957; Johnson, 1958). However, academic work on corporate citizenship commenced only during the late 1990s (cf. McIntosh et al., 1998; Tichy et al., 1997; Wood and Logsdon, 2001). More recently, a novel conceptualization of corporate citizenship has been elaborated by Dirk Matten, Andrew Crane and their colleagues (see Crane and Matten, 2010; Matten et al., 2003; Moon et al., 2005) to position the firm within a changing business and society context. Matten and Crane (2005) develop a perspective which focuses not on the corporation as a *fictitious* citizen, but rather the empirical conditions under which the corporation might be expected to engage in administering the political, legal and civil rights of *real* citizens. This expanded corporate role is depicted as filling an institutional vacuum resulting from the withdrawal (or complete absence) of the state from significant areas in society.

THE WITHERING OF THE STATE?

There is no doubt that globalization has significantly reshaped the demands placed on corporations by wider communities of stakeholders. According to Matten and

Crane (2005: 170), this has led to a shift of the responsibility for protecting individ-ual citizenship rights from governments to corporations as the latter influence more areas of peoples' lives on a daily basis:

> [the NCC concept] is not simply about corporate social policies and programs that might (or might not) be adopted in the same vein as CSR. Rather, we argue that the effective functioning of [individual] liberal citizenship has been sufficiently affected by the corporate uptake of government functions to render corporate involvement in 'citizenship' a largely unavoidable occurrence.

The authors identify three ways in which governmental and corporate roles in the administration of individual citizenship rights are changing. The first is with respect to cases in which government withdraws from the administration of citizenship rights, through mechanisms such as privatization or welfare reform. The degree of such withdrawal will be context specific. In the West, for example, the neo-liberal era experienced a fundamental transformation as the provision of social goods was increasingly conducted by the private sector (with government oversight). The sec-ond is with respect to cases in which government has never administered citizenship rights, as with some developing or underdeveloped countries where rights to health care, education and the like have yet to be secured. In extreme cases, such as dur-ing the occupation of Iraq, private contracting firms such as Halliburton took full control of the administration and provision of security, tax collection and other basic infrastructural functions – sometimes at exorbitant prices (*New York Times*, 2005). The third is with respect to cases in which the administration of citizenship rights is beyond the reach of the nation-state, as with effectively dealing with the impact of the globalization of markets or global environmental issues.

THE CORPORATION AS PROVIDER?

A key aspect in Matten and Crane's (2005) analysis is a discussion around the way big business might be standing in for governmental services following the retraction of the state in many aspects of society. As such, they define their project as going 'further in exploring how corporations might play an *active role* in reconfiguring the whole notion of citizenship itself' (Crane and Matten, 2008: 27, italics added). We argue that there are some central weaknesses with the NCC concept. It seems to have been developed without reference to any theory of the business firm and its institutional function in contemporary capitalist society – especially pertaining to those trends dis-cussed in the preceding chapters (also see Hanlon, 2007; Jones, 2009a). As we have already indicated, this disconnect is typical of research in CSR, business ethics and related areas. As such, the kinds of organizational attitudes and actions necessary for the NCC concept to be operationally relevant quickly break down in light of long-existing legal and fiduciary obligations in which the corporate form is embedded.

A good example of this problem might be found in Matten and Crane's (2005) refer-ence to Shell in Nigeria as a case example of NCC theory in action. They point out that Shell had the opportunity to 'step in' when the Nigerian state failed to maintain the Ogoni people's civil rights, and that the corporation was itself implicated in this failure.

But let us look at the case from a simple critical political economy perspective: was Shell's failure to act a strategic mistake, a moral lapse, or both? If Shell *had* acted, why would this have supported the contentions of NCC theory rather than simply constitute a case of the organization behaving more 'strategically' in terms of pursuing its economic interests in a more enlightened manner? The crux of the matter here is whether or not Shell *should* have acted because (1) there was something 'in it' for the company in terms of payback, and/or (2) that acting was the morally 'correct' thing to do. Considering this from a corporate citizenship perspective risks missing these crucial features regarding the realpolitik of the MNC.

THE PREDATORY NATURE OF THE FIRM

Another weakness with NCC theory is that its genesis seems to have occurred in a vacuum, in that its central construct – the empowered corporation as provider of citizenship rights to individuals – is clearly inconsistent with some of the more significant developments of the last several decades in the global political economy. As discussed earlier, corporations have, if anything, been moving *away* from rather than towards an expanded notion of corporate citizenship (for themselves) in terms of maximizing rights and minimizing responsibilities to most stakeholders, at least among many OECD countries. The de-industrialization of many North American and European manufacturing sectors in the 1970s and 1980s is one example of this trend (see Harrison and Bluestone, 1988). The (successful) corporate flight from tax liability since the 1960s is another (Dicken, 2010; *Guardian*, 2010c). And the recent financial crisis has witnessed so-called laissez-faire governments intervene to rescue large banks from ruin in the name of social justice rights for its citizens (protecting personal savings, etc.), thus restating a certain role for government.

Although the development of NCC theory has taken note of certain aspects of citizenship theory, important insights about the evolution of citizenship by analysts such as Lasch (1996) and Held (1996) are not considered. Lasch examines how previously universalistic notions of material progress have been displaced by much narrower – sometimes zero-sum – conceptions contingent upon an individual's or group's particular locational co-ordinates in the socio-economic hierarchy. Citizenship now means different things to different people within diverse and fractured late-capitalist societies. By emphasizing the ideological nature of the citizenship discourse, Held develops the theme of the transformation of citizenship rights from a universalistic political construct to an increasingly economistic construct accessible on a user-pays basis – that is, the commodification of citizenship.

Both Lasch and Held are addressing developments that have unfolded during a period of increasing hegemony of the discourse of economic rationality (Foucault, 2008; Gorz, 1989); the encroachment of this discourse into previously non-economic spheres (cf. Becker, 1981) and its consequent impact on identity formation (Deetz, 1992; Sandel, 2009; Sennet, 1998); its macro manifestation in terms of the domination of neo-liberalism and the 'Washington Consensus' in international affairs (Gowan, 2009); and its organizational manifestation in the discourse of managerialism (Burawoy, 1979). NCC scholars' failure to consider these redefinitions and restrictions of individual citizenship is a curious oversight, as the development of such a line of argument actually serves to strengthen their case, at least in those situations where services can be provided under profitable circumstances.

GLOBALIZATION AND THE RECONFIGURED STATE

Although NCC theory does rightly point out that the role of the nation-state has changed, it misses the political context of such a reconfiguration, especially in the context of neo-liberal globalization. Permutations in the state have been driven by the prominence of 'New Right' ideology, first in the UK and the United States in the late 1970s, then onto the other Anglo-Saxon countries (Canada, Australia, New Zealand) in the 1980s, and subsequently further dispersed (although in considerably modified form) to many Western European nations along with Japan in the 1990s (see Gray, 1998; Mittelman, 1996).

A typical New Right policy mix incorporated the internationalizing of national economies through the lowering of barriers to foreign trade and investment; the deregulation and privatization of most sectors which had formally been state controlled or owned; a shift away from Keynesian macroeconomic management to a focus on controlling inflation through monetary policy, leaving articulation of supply and demand to market forces; changes to industrial relations systems which marginalized unions and individuated employment contracts; contraction of welfare programmes and the lowering of the social wage; and a shift in tax policy towards lowering taxes on corporate profits, capital gains and high incomes while increasing (regressive) taxes on property and consumption, as well as raising fees for basic services through 'user-pays' schemes. In the aggregate, such measures served to shift socio-economic patterns of income, wealth and life chances from a diamond shape (with a bulge in the middle signifying a large middle class) to an hourglass shape (representing growing segments of haves and have-nots and a shrinking middle class) (Galbraith, 2008).

A rather different set of issues concerns the role of the state within the circuits of globalized capitalism. This leads us to observe another basic weakness of NCC theory. States have obviously lost some of their powers of economic management to both supra- and sub-national bodies over the past couple of decades. For example, Sassen (1998) notes that within states, bureaucracies concerned with social equity have lost influence to those that are financially oriented and promote globalization with the support of powerful interests in the business sector (see also Weiss, 1998). Yet states retain an essential monopoly over *enforcing the conditions of marketization within their territories* (often by coercion). This point is omitted in the NCC approach, as it seems to accept the empirical salience of neo-liberal rhetoric (e.g. the state withdrawing from the provision of public goods). Furthermore, it would seem that massive state intervention throughout the developed world in reaction to the global economic crisis directly undermines a fundamental assumption of NCC theory.

WHEN THE STATE AND CORPORATION BECOME ONE

In fact the power of the nation-state has not disappeared, but been reconfigured in a more market-oriented and disciplinary manner. Brenner (1998; 1999), Guillén (2001) and Held et al. (1999) all demonstrate how the state apparatus is pivotal in translating flows of neo-liberal marketization. Meanwhile, most advanced states have in the post-September 11 'war on terror' period substantially increased the information they collect on individuals, expanded police powers and rescinded various civil liberties and protections afforded to citizens and employees. An argument can be made that 'the state' is evolving in a post-democratic direction (Sandel, 2009), or possibly devolving around a set of early modernist functions focusing on maintaining social order through force as described by Foucault (1979).

The shift to 'extreme neo-liberalism' in the statecraft of not only Western economies but also those in Asia and the South means that the classic distinction between government and the corporation has become tenuous. Not only has the corporate form been streamlined by a myopic economic rationality, but the state too has been transformed, whereby it is both the support and servant for multi-national capital (Stiglitz, 2010). In the UK, the university system provides a good example, whereby student numbers and funding are dictated by the market, and internal performance measures are as strident as (if not more than) those found in the business sector. In any case, the so-called 'coming to the rescue' of states every-where on behalf of their financial sectors and wider economies has put to rest two long-standing questions of critical social theory: that of the relative autonomy of the state (from capital); and the Althusserian question of what institutional com-plex (e.g. political, cultural, economic) was determinate 'in the last instance' with respect to shaping the social formation (Althusser, 1969). To the former question we have a clear and definitive answer: in crisis situations there is an essential iden-tity of interest between the core ruling elements of advanced capitalist states and their financial sectors. To the latter question we observe that the 'last instance' actually arrived in September 2008, and that (to cite the well-known expression) 'it's the economy, stupid'.

IS THE MNC A GOOD CITIZEN?

We have proposed that the MNC and the state are not mutually exclusive since the state has been reconfigured in alliance with private firms to assume a more disciplin-ary role to facilitate the market forces unleashed by globalization. But if we provi-sionally accept the NCC proposition that the firm is – in some places, under certain conditions – supplanting the state in providing citizenship rights, is this something we would want to endorse?

As mentioned earlier, NCC scholars largely avoid this question, preferring a posi-tive (theoretical) rather than normative analysis. The distinction, of course, is dubi-ous. Values are inscribed in even the most ostensibly objective analysis. A critical political economy of the MNC, while certainly normative in some respects, reveals important descriptive facts absent in NCC theory. This is the generative and unmask-ing nature of 'critical' enquiry (Habermas, 1973).

IS CAPITAL INTERESTED IN YOUR CIVIL RIGHTS?

The crucial question here is the difference between the generic business firm and the MNC, since the latter 'plays by different rules' in relation to its role in society and thus its potential to provide citizenship rights as per NCC theory. The generic busi-ness firm (we focus here on the Anglo-Saxon variant) is a hierarchical organization, incorporating both co-operative and conflictual social relations, which exists primar-ily to produce goods and services at a profit, those profits being the private property of its owners. The co-operative social aspect of the business firm emanates from the mutual interest of major stakeholders (e.g. owners, creditors, management, employ-ees, the state) that the firm generates an adequate income stream so as to survive and continue to transfer resources to these groups. The conflictual aspect arises over how the income stream is distributed among them.

With respect to the possibility of corporations attempting to fill 'institutional vacu-ums' when such actions generate a net resource and performance drain, we should expect corporate governance (if functioning properly) to prohibit such initiatives. Further, substantial organizational structures and bureaucratic procedures exist in large corporations to try to ensure that non-instrumental activity is minimized. As Herman some time ago insightfully noted:

> Bureaucratic pressures and the disciplined pursuit of overall corporate objectives tend to be greater in large organizations. Community pressures and interests are less personally felt and tend to be lost in bureaucratic processes dominated by a market-based profit-loss calculus … . With profit motive and competitive pressure intact, market forces should produce organizations that are better structured to abandon individual plants and communities in the interests of company profits as a whole. In an important sense, *the success of large organizations follows in part from their being designed to be less 'responsible' than smaller local enterprises* [italics added]. (1981: 259–260)

An additional element – absent from the NCC conceptualization – constraining and directing the activities of large corporations is the reality that the organizational fields in which they operate are themselves structured by, and through, financial hegemony. Since the 1970s, the pace of financial market integration has increased, the composition of equity holders has shifted from individual to institutional investors, and financial (as opposed to industrial) capital has become a dominant (and destabilizing) force in the global economy. Mintz and Schwartz (1990) conceived of financial hegemony in terms of high concentration levels of investment capital and structural interdependencies among major financial institutions. And as we have seen with the recent financial crisis, the logic of finance is frequently deeply at odds with general social goods around citizenship rights.

FINANCE, VIOLENCE AND CITIZENSHIP

More recently, Gowan (2009) writes of the extent to which even ostensibly industrial firms such as General Electric (through GE Capital) and General Motors (through GMAC) have become 'financialized', and thus increased their exposure to the current (financially driven) economic crisis. In fact, until the advent of the current crisis, the structuring power of financial capital was increased further in recent years through the heightened activities of private equity funds and the emergence of sovereign wealth funds as actors in the global system (Barber and Goold, 2007). Their preferences for narrowly diversified, focused firms as investment targets drove rounds of restructuring in the corporate sector as more broadly diversified organizations strove to exhibit their 'parenting value' (Goold et al., 1998) and avoid the financial market penalty of the 'conglomerate discount'. Johnson (2009) identifies financial hegemony as a direct cause of the 'made in the USA' crisis. He notes that:

> financiers – in the case of the U.S. – played a central role in creating the crisis, making ever-larger gambles, with the implicit backing of the government, until the inevitable collapse. More alarming, they are now using their influence to prevent precisely the sorts of reforms that are needed, and fast, to pull the economy out of its nosedive. The government seems helpless, or unwilling, to act against them.

In addition to the external reality of the structuring power of financial hegemony, corporations also operate internally under the conditioning influence of the financial conception of control as elaborated by Fligstein:

> The finance conception of the modern corporation, which currently dominates, emphasizes control through the use of financial tools which measure performance

according to profit rates ... . Firms are viewed as collections of assets earning different rates of return, not as producers of given goods ... the organizational fields of the finance driven firms are no longer industrial based. Once large firms began to pay more attention to one another than to industries or products, strategic innovations that reflected the finance conception of control spread more rapidly across the population of large firms. (1990: 15–16)

Therefore, although the corporation constitutes the primary organizational manifestation of contemporary capitalism, it is finance capital and a financially oriented discourse that generate the driving force behind corporate behaviour and sectoral investment patterns. The likelihood of an MNC being interested in delivering citizenship rights must thus be seen within a context structured by financial hegemony, the finance conception of control and the evolving dynamics of the international political economy. We can expect MNCs to be similarly constrained and oriented as the generic corporation which was the focal point of the preceding discussion, with one additional critical aspect: because MNCs by definition operate in multiple host countries, they have the opportunity to enhance their structural bargaining power against workers and states, and thus reduce claims by these stakeholders on their income streams.

And this logic is exacerbated in the context of globalization. The end of the Cold War, the continuing economic progress of the BRIC countries, and technological developments which enhance command and control capabilities have vastly expanded the universe of potential sites for MNCs to locate particular value- and supply-chain activities (the former are within the boundaries of the firm, the latter are not). These firms are now able to pursue *absolute advantage* by articulating their specific resources and capabilities with country-specific locational factors. As a result, the entry barriers to core segments of key industries have considerably increased in recent years (Dicken, 2010). Contemporary megamergers occurring within (and at the intersection of) key industries further the concentration of ownership and control. These developments have substantially altered the bargaining position (or leverage) between MNCs, states and workers in favour of the former, as well as directly impacting industry structures, employment patterns and government policies. Given this increasingly asymmetrical power landscape, the prospects for MNCs *voluntarily* attending to the rights of citizens in host countries in a manner inconsistent with the logic of economic rationality would seem extremely remote, even fanciful.

The fundamental point here is that MNCs are neither democratic in their decision-making structures, transparent with respect to their internal activities, or accountable for most of the negative externalities they generate (in most geographies), nor are their interests aligned with those of the wider societies in which they operate, but rather with a much narrower group of owners, core employees, business partners, key customers and other 'patrons' or 'clients' in particular localities. They lack the aligned (material) interests, experience and 'staying power' to be given open slather in the provisioning of individual citizenship goods – unless the only alternative is no supply of those goods at all.

THE PRODUCTION OF 'SURPLUS HUMANITY'

Yet another shortcoming of the NCC approach is its failure to theorize the larger context in which 'institutional vacuums' that invite MNC intervention appear. In particular, we point to the intersection of interests between MNCs, neo-liberalism and the 'Washington Consensus', and also the numerous 'structural adjustment programmes' (SAPs) driven by the World Standard Bank–IMF nexus throughout the decades of the 1980s and 1990s. MNCs were key agents in this hegemonic project; vitally, they were also in most cases key beneficiaries (see Charkiewicz, 2005; Stiglitz, 2010), hovering around state-owned railroads and hospitals waiting for them to be sold off at bargain-bin prices. Thus, MNCs must take some degree of collective responsibility for the general failure of SAPs, the creation or extension of 'institutional vacuums', and the regressive consequences on host country populations.

For example, Davis (2007) notes the linkages between global neo-liberalism, the increasing urbanization of world poverty and the rise of a *surplus humanity* which cannot be incorporated into formal networks of production and exchange. He agrees with UN-Habitat's (2003) view that the state's capacity to create formal jobs and housing has been sacrificed to the goal of monetary stability imposed by neo-liberal regimes. According to the UN-Habitat report, 'The collapse of formal urban employment in the developing world and the rise of the informal sector is seen as a direct function of liberalization … . Urban poverty has been increasing in most countries subject to structural adjustment programs, most of which are deliberately anti-urban in nature.' Similarly, Žižek (2009) cites a 2008 research group studying longitudinal trends in tuberculosis epidemics in 20 Eastern European countries which found a clear and strong positive correlation between the incidence of IMF loans and increases in infection rates. These loans were 'tied' to savage cuts in public spending, which included public health services, fostering the ironic situation that the physical (and mental) health of citizens was seconded to externally imposed considerations of 'financial health'.

ADJUST ... OR ELSE! THE REAL MESSAGE OF CORPORATE CITIZENSHIP

A widely noted dysfunctional impact of SAPs has been in the area of water provision in some Latin American countries, where MNCs have been observed behaving in highly exploitative and parasitical ways rather than in accordance with forms of behaviour anticipated by NCC theory. For example, Wood (2009) notes the impact of Washington Consensus policies on Bolivia, where the US-based Bechtel Corporation raised water charges by 43 per cent post-privatization, forcing the poorest segments of the population to pay up to one-third of their income for access to clean water. Baer and Montes-Rojas (2008) review the corrupt neo-liberal privatization projects in Argentina during the 1990s in the rail, postal and water sectors, where the impact of extortionate price rises was hugely regressive, leading to subsequent renationalizations a decade later. De Medeiros (2009), taking a broad Latin American perspective, argues that these restructuring programmes were often primarily driven by ideology rather than efficiency, as many of the targeted state enterprises were by no means obvious drains on public resources. The cabal of interests between domestic comprador elites and the Washington Consensus institutions served to foster spaces and 'vacuums' which were subsequently filled by MNCs and their local affiliates, often under circumstances which yielded hyper-profit rates of return. These behaviours seem more akin to the 'corporate psychopath' depicted in the film *The Corporation* (Bakan, 2004) than they do to the provider of citizenship rights envisioned by the NCC perspective.

Cast in this light, the question of whether the evolutionary path of the MNC as discussed in this section is consistent with conventional notions of 'good corporate citizenship' is contentious to say the least. The political economy of the MNC is redolent of structural power relations in which the provision of rights in many host economies is either an avoidable expense (e.g. a 'just' wage in Indonesian sweatshops) or directly antithetical to its interests (e.g. an expansion of workers' democratic rights in Mexico). In this sense, NCC theory's so-called 'vacuum' created by an absent state often remains unfilled, sometimes as a result of intentional activities undertaken by MNCs themselves as key agents in shaping the neo-liberal discourse which has dominated the globalization process – and of which they are the primary beneficiaries. Moreover, as we noted in the previous section, in both developed and developing countries the state is still of utmost importance for securing the basic institutional conditions required for MNCs to operate.

DEMOCRACY ... OR A MISSED OPPORTUNITY

While on the topic of the international system, we must acknowledge the important contributions of Scherer et al. (2006; see also Scherer and Palazzo, 2007; 2008a, b, c; 2010), who take a more institutionally embedded approach to corporate citizenship, specifically with respect to the role of the MNC in shaping global governance structures. They develop the concept of 'political CSR', which they define 'as a movement of the corporation into the political sphere in order to respond to environmental and social challenges such as human rights, global warming, or deforestation' (Scherer and Palazzo, 2010: 914). We find many points of congruence between the analysis of these authors and ourselves, as for instance when they observe: 'It could be argued that corporate citizenship may not be the solution but the problem. This is especially the case when corporations exert their power to define global rules in a way that best serves their own economic interests' (Scherer et al., 2006: 522). However, it seems to us that the unquestionable desirability of their normative agenda serves to somewhat occlude their theoretical specification of the MNC in a capitalist political economy – a case of the 'tail' of normative theory wagging the 'dog' of positive theory.

For example, we would disagree with their interpretation of some empirical examples which they use to illustrate their concept of 'political CSR' as part of their larger project of 'democratizing' the MNC. Specifically, they characterize Nike's evolving stance towards CSR and NGOs since the 1990s as evidence of a 'democratic move that implies proactive sensitivity for ethical challenges'. We would rather see Nike's evolving posture much more through the lenses of risk management and instrumental CSR – or even resource dependency theory (Pfeffer and Salancik, 1979) – all of which are subordinate aspects of economic rationality. The criticisms advanced by van Oosterhout and Heugens (2008) referred to earlier are also equally valid here.

Elsewhere in the same paper, Scherer and his colleagues depict the corporation's provision of healthcare and wages as constituting the maintenance of workers' social and economic rights, respectively. This treatment is consistent with Moon et al. (2005: 440), who argue that 'corporations increasingly administer the citizenship rights of their employees and their families, such as in the case of pay and working conditions, health, and education'. Again, for us, this sits uneasily with our understanding of how capitalism works in reality. It tends to add a patina of paternalistic civility on what are fundamentally calculated transactional relations between principles and agents that are formalized through contracts. To suggest that corporations are providing citizenship rights by paying compensation for contracted labour power obfuscates the dynamics of power and interest that determine the relationship between capital, management and labour in work organizations. More plainly, if corporate citizenship theory is moving in a direction which celebrates firms as 'good citizens' when they pay wages on time and meet other contractual obligations with respect to the workforce – during an era of 'off-shoring', stagnant real incomes and reductions in healthcare and pension obligations for workers in most OECD nations since the 1970s (Armstrong et al., 1985; Galbraith, 2008; Harrison and Bluestone, 1988) – we really are in an increasingly Orwellian world where 'less is more', 'abandonment is liberation' and 'unemployment is opportunity'.

Scherer and Palazzo's (2010) claim that there is something qualitatively 'new' in the notion that corporations are political actors (or that that the 'asymmetrical' character of the contemporary international political economy somehow imposes new normative criteria to which MNCs must adhere in order to maintain their legitimacy) is not unproblematic. In particular, their favourable treatment of the notion of 'self-regulation by soft law' we find highly idealistic in light of the role 'light-handed' regulation played in creating some formative conditions of the current global crisis (Gowan, 2009). We would, rather, subscribe to the old adage that 'self-regulation = no regulation'. Interestingly, Scherer and Palazzo (2007, 2010) forcefully state their concerns as to the potential threat to democracy that corporate political activities represent. Yet their solution – strengthening political communities and making business firms democratically accountable – and the prominent role they give to communication and discourse in the process of forming and transforming preferences seem to us to limit their project to the realm of idealism. The combination of a degree of critical awareness of the 'dark side' of MNC political activities, the idealism of the proposed solution and the normative thrust of NCC theory for corporations to fill 'institutional vacuums' lends a certain 'bipolar' character to much of the theorizing.

Our disagreement with the impressive stream of work generated by Scherer and Palazzo's project is not over theoretical issues, but rather over practical concerns. Fundamentally, they have not (yet) articulated a convincing explanation of how we get 'there' (i.e. corporations acting in accordance with 'political CSR' principles) from 'here' without *material* changes in law and also in the subjectivity of key institutional actors. Such changes would have to occur against a backdrop of: (1) the 'global shift' (Dicken, 2010) in power favouring financial capital and MNCs over other stakeholders; and (2) the expanding hegemony of the neo-liberal discourse of economic rationality (Berardi, 2009; *Guardian*, 2010d). We find the notion that a private, hierarchical, authoritarian institution such as the MNC would have an interest in furthering democracy to be deeply problematic. To crystallize our argument, let us take the contemporary example of 'outsourcing' in the context of global capitalism.

NEW CORPORATE CITIZEN IN ACTION? THE EXAMPLE OF 'OUTSOURCING'

The contemporary debate on 'outsourcing' of information technology (IT) jobs from countries such as the United States, the UK and Australia to (most conspicuously) India provides a useful empirical referent for how the economic rationality of the MNC collides with the rationalities of other stakeholder groups such as workers and (sometimes) governments in their home countries. It is also an effective illustration of the plausibility of the NCC concept in such circumstances.

THE PRESSURE TO OUTSOURCE

In general, most forms of outsourcing draw upon local providers or markets (Dicken, 2010). This is essentially because outsourcing firms have strong local preferences in order to enhance communication and simplify logistics management. Other stakeholders such as workers and government would also prefer the local option, as this would mean that employment and economic activity might shift outside the boundaries of the outsourcing firm but still be captured at a local/regional level. Under some circumstances, however, foreign providers may have such an advantage (usually based on cost) that the outsourcing firm has little choice but to engage their services and cope with the opposition of local stakeholders.

This would seem to be the case with the 'outsourcing' of IT jobs to India and elsewhere in recent years. This is not exactly correct, however, for many US firms are not reducing their level of vertical integration but rather spatially restructuring (or 'off-shoring') some of their value-chain activities from the United States to other countries that offer a combination of reliable supply, reasonable quality and substantial cost savings. Like outsourcing, spatial restructuring can occur at a domestic level, as when a firm shifts activities and jobs from Ohio to Alabama in pursuit of cheaper labour in non-union environments. But spatial restructuring becomes much more visible and politicized when it occurs internationally, fuelled by globalization. It is this spatial restructuring – not outsourcing – followed en masse in the IT industry in recent years, which is at the heart of the (so-called) 'outsourcing' debate.

Interestingly, massive spatial restructuring and the type of debate it engenders are not new. In the United States (and other OECD economies) a very similar situation unfolded through the 1970s and 1980s in the manufacturing sector, where activities and employment shifted from the 'rust belt' states to the 'sun belt' states and then, in many cases, to overseas affiliates of core-based MNCs. The major differences between the two spatial restructuring waves were the types of jobs lost (i.e. 'blue-collar' versus 'white-collar') and the modal political affinity of displaced employees.

OUTSOURCING AND CITIZENSHIP

Following the logic of NCC theory, MNCs would be expected in some cases to provide citizenship rights given that the state has withdrawn from various sectors of society. *But this is not the way outsourcing firms behave.* Evidence suggests that they often do the bare minimum as required by law with respect to issues such as worker health and safety or redundancy provisions when layoffs occur (Galbraith, 2008; Jones, 2002). This sentiment is clearly evident in Craig Barret's (CEO of Intel) contribution to the outsourcing debate (*USA Today*, 2004): 'Life is tough. Life is not fair. You have to compete. It takes hard work to compete, so let's figure out how to compete.' Intel has about 40 per cent of its employees outside the United States and is focusing on both China and India as important future markets and bases for its operations. It is estimated that Intel saves up to 70 per cent on labour costs (versus Silicon Valley) by shifting activities to locations such as Bangalore (*Electronic Engineering Times*, 2001). It can save even more in countries such as Bangladesh or Ghana, where IT workers are paid less than $3 a day for data processing activities (*Austin-American Statesman*, 2002) and endure punitive management and state policing. In China, the lack of certain fundamental human rights is a *condition* of the efficiency of outsourcing since it keeps wages low, maintains labour discipline and thus increases productivity. Moreover, the Chinese state is complicit in maintaining a brutal market discipline and is far from 'absent' as NCC theory might suggest.

According to James Breyer (*Fortune*, 2004), managing partner in venture capital firm Accel Partners in Silicon Valley, 'If a company is not actively investing in China or India, they need to provide a very compelling case to board members as to why they are not.' In a very real sense, then, the decision to relocate activities and employment to India *is* socially responsible (from the perspective of the decision makers) with respect to key stakeholders, owners and customers. The central task of a firm-centred stakeholder management strategy (Freeman, 1984; Jones, 1995) in this context is effectively to communicate the advantages, the necessity and the *inevitability* (e.g. 'a natural effect of the global economic system …') of spatial restructuring to central internal and external stakeholders in order to co-opt willing parties and nullify the interest and ability of potential blockers to undermine the strategy. In relation to NCC theory, the instrumental nature of the MNC is completely missed here, since the 'business case' for providing citizenship rights to communities in Africa or Indonesia simply defies the rationale for locating activities there in the first place; that is, it is the very *absence* of these rights which can make such locations attractive bases for low-cost operations. The NCC approach thus theoretically misspecifies these empirical situations in terms of their causal logic, effectively placing the cart before the horse.

The stakeholder dynamics associated with the spatial restructuring of US IT activities and employment to India are relatively transparent. If these dynamics are implemented successfully, firms should become more competitive through substantial cost savings – or at least maintain their relative level of competitiveness – which should enhance shareholder value. Some of these savings may be passed on to customers, while (somewhat ironically) a certain level of core activity and employment could actually be made more secure back in the United States as firms would be able to redirect some cost savings into research and development and other value-adding activities at home base. Negatively impacted stakeholders would include redundant employees and the communities where the job loss is centred through a process of negative multiplier effects cascading through local service businesses, reduced local government revenues, increased crime, etc. – as depicted in the groundbreaking 1991 documentary *Roger & Me* by Michael Moore and, more recently, in Julian Temple's 2010 film *Requiem for Detroit*.

The preceding discussion of stakeholder dynamics (a concept we will discuss in more detail in the following chapter) starkly illustrates the diverse interests at play in the outsourcing debate. Clearly, in this continuing process there are both winners and losers with widely asymmetrical levels of power and voice. It also throws into question the continuing overall social utility of a corporate form unleashed by globalization to operate in an increasingly unrestricted manner. For the contemporary corporation – manifested most fully in the institutional form of the MNC – is a superbly effective mechanism for creating wealth for its owners, their senior representatives in management and a relatively small group of core employees, as well as value for its primary customers and business partners. This is the main purpose of outsourcing, as many commentators have argued. And stakeholders outside of this tight orbit will increasingly be excluded from accessing the wealth and value-creating activities of these organizations (see Jones, 2003).

INSTITUTIONAL VACUUM AS MARKET OPPORTUNITY

These developments are clearly consistent with the insights offered by Lash and Held as discussed earlier. For Lasch (1996), the massive and regressive corporate restructurings he observed during the 1980s – of which contemporary restructurings are the latest echo – epitomized the 'revolt of the elites' (see also Galbraith, 2008). To Lasch, the fragmentation of society and appropriation of increasing proportions of wealth, income and political influence by those located in the upper regions of the socio-economic hierarchy constituted betrayals of core democratic and progressive US values. Similarly for Held (1996), the asymmetrical impact of corporate restructurings on key stakeholders such as workers, owners, managers and communities entailed that those groups with the greatest economic 'voice' would capture the bulk of the benefits of globalization and be able to steer the evolution of the citizenship discourse in their direction.

The distributional impacts associated with corporate outsourcing are clearly at odds with a conception of the corporation that voluntarily assumes additional obligations irrespective of their economic consequences. There are numerous other recent examples of MNCs effecting similar or larger negative impacts on broad groups of stakeholders in order to benefit much narrower interests. Clearly, the fact that corporations largely fail to meet the basic citizenship criteria of paying income tax (*Guardian*, 2010c) should serve as obvious caution for any more ambitious schema for a voluntary expansion of corporate citizenship responsibilities.

The reality, rather, is that despite whatever need or demand there may be for MNCs to act in filling institutional vacuums with respect to the provision of individual citizenship rights, they may be expected to do so only under a particular and simple condition: that such behaviour is consistent with the norms of economic rationality operating at the level of the firm. The NCC approach thus needs to be reassessed in order to account for the undeniable structural contradictions in interests between major MNC stakeholders and the dynamic distributional effects associated with the shifting sources of MNC competitive advantage. The assumption of corporate voluntarism at the core of NCC theory withers when subjected to even cursory scrutiny. *To a significant extent, the logic of the MNC is more oriented to creating and/or exploiting institutional vacuums than it is to filling them.*

CONCLUSIONS

Corporate citizenship, or what we have labelled New Corporate Citizenship, is an extremely popular subset in the CSR discipline. We are told to expect corporations to provide for basic rights that were once taken for granted under the Keynesian welfare state. Matten and Crane posit that if private firms are now responsible for providing fundamental rights to citizens, then perhaps they ought to be democratically accountable: 'if corporations take over vital functions of governments, one could argue that they should take over exactly the type of accountability which modern societies demand from government as a facilitator of citizen rights' (2005: 118). We remain sceptical. The state has not receded, but merely reconfigured into a putative 'policeman' to shore up corporate rule. Moreover, the 'institutional vacuums' that are certainly present are, given the logic of the corporation, deemed to be opportunities for making money more than anything else.

In business practice, the discourse of corporate citizenship lends itself to an instrumental variant of CSR in which corporations merely give lip-service to community input apropos their policies (e.g. supermarket chain Tesco's policy of 'consulting' local businesses before establishing a new supermarket in the UK). This is because it is simply not in the interests of corporations to be democratically accountable to all stakeholders.

Such corporate citizenship initiatives reveal themselves as public relations campaigns designed primarily to enhance or protect the market value of the firm. By being 'good corporate citizens', firms can proactively anticipate and deter government regulations, exploit opportunities arising from increasing levels of cultural, environmental and sexual awareness, and differentiate their products from their less socially responsible competitors. We would argue that such an instrumental version of CSR is hegemonic in both the theoretical and normative domains of mainstream research.

Where does all this leave the NCC approach? Given what we consider to be a more realistic political economy of the MNC as provided in our discussion of 'outsourcing', an organization's willingness to engage in the provision of citizenship rights would fall within its instrumental discourse. The provision of citizenship rights within a specific community would consist of those activities that directly or indirectly (e.g. through enhancing corporate reputation, stabilizing a local business environment) positively impacted the economic performance of the firm in some manner. Such instrumentalism would also pervade any attempt to become 'accountable' to the citizens involved. Of course, such generalities may take different forms depending on the specific national institutional context (see Whitley, 1992; 2007). In summary, then, the political economy of the MNC highlights some significant limitations with NCC theory. The MNC to the rescue? We do not think so.

In this chapter we turn to another defining subset of CSR, that of the 'stakeholder theory of the firm' and its practical companion 'stakeholder management'. Put simply, managers should view their organizations as part of a broad network of groups such as workers, the environment, interest groups and so forth who have a 'stake' in the firm (i.e., can either benefit or be harmed by its operations). Dialogue, compromise and consultation are the key virtues of stakeholder theory. This approach to business management is considered to sit in stark contrast to the traditional model of the corporation. Indeed, much of the stakeholder literature defines itself with reference to what it is not; that is, the 'take no prisoners', utility-maximizing model of enterprise in which making a healthy return for shareholders or owners is its single-minded goal. The usual suspect identified as representative of this neo-liberal ideology of the corporation is Milton Friedman (1970). Interestingly enough, his arguments were a response to the growing trend in business schools and corporate boardrooms of considering the broader social and ethical consequences of a pure bottom line rationality. As is well known, Friedman averred in his famous essay that the only social responsibility of business is to increase profits. All other considerations relating to ethics, morality, negative externalities or the welfare of weaker groups in society were outside the purview of business management. In other words, managers were trained to administer the business operation in terms of a precise economic-efficiency model, and it would be wise to leave all other 'social issues' to the state, NGOs and the voluntary sector. Those who manage the business should focus only on making profits for owners. Any consideration of pollution, workers' rights or stakeholders who may potentially undermine or stymie this imperative should only be raised in a manner that serves profit maximization (what Friedman would later dub 'enlightened self-interest'). As Friedman writes, 'the key point is that, in his [*sic*] capacity as corporate executive, the manager is an agent of the individuals who own the corporate or establish the eleemosynary institution, and his primary responsibility is to them' (1970: 33). Of course, following Friedman's logic brings us to the bizarre conclusion that a manager is actually *irresponsible* if he or she becomes concerned about how his or her firm might damage the environment or exploit child labour.

As Roberts (2003) rightly notes, the argument becomes paradoxical when the state itself is then mesmerized by neo-classical economics and ostensibly withdraws from the public sector, subjecting society and itself to the discipline of market forces. While it is then tempting to see this sudden social lacuna following the receding state as a pressure on multinational firms to become concerned with citizen and humanitarian rights, we feel that this is not only wishful thinking but also a somewhat misleading picture of what the corporation is. As we mentioned in Chapter 2, even if we thoroughly disagree with his right-wing agenda, the 'capitalist realism' (see Fisher, 2009) underly-ing Friedman's understanding of business is by and large accurate. It generates profits by exploiting the value of resources, and this is what it was designed to do. Friedman's ideological – and thoroughly questionable – vision, however, is that this cold rationality is a cause for celebration since it signals a path to freedom and democracy. In fact, this is when we feel Friedman moves into the realm of fantasy: 'The businessmen believe that they are defending free enterprise when they declaim that business is not con-cerned "merely" with profit but also with promoting desirable "social" ends ... In fact they are – or would be if they or anyone else took them seriously – preaching pure and unadulterated socialism' (Friedman, 1970: 33). While Friedman's political candour and appreciation of the cold calculability of the for-profit business may ironically be a useful antidote to the hypocritical clichés that pervade contemporary CSR discourse (such as the one noted by Roberts (2003: 256) in a large firm: 'Profits and Principles: Does There Have to Be a Difference?'), we see the overall drift of his argument as politically dubious, indeed something to be very worried about given the inequali-ties that an unleashed capitalist system – coupled with what Harney (2009) calls the *extreme neo-liberalist* state – is shoring up.

So should we not then celebrate the rise of stakeholder theory and its diffusion into the operating principles of the contemporary firm? In this chapter we want to convey our deep ambivalence about the real efficacy of stakeholder theory as a vehicle for ushering in a socially just society. Building on the arguments made in the book so far, we will claim that there is a profound naivety in much of the discussion around this approach. Given the inbuilt myopic rationality of the contemporary corporation, the idea that stakeholders such as Third World workers, consumers and so forth might have a meaningful operational say in the objectives of a large multinational enterprise may be a laudable ideal, but ultimately trades in a misguided view of con-temporary political economy (Levy, 2008). Perhaps more worrying is the actual role stakeholder theory does have in business practices today. Using examples, especially in the context of international management within a globalizing economic environ-ment, the real utility of stakeholder management is as an instrument of *containment*. As Banerjee (2007) puts it when quoting (Tatz, 1982) in relation to mining companies 'consulting' with indigenous peoples in Australia, the Aborigines are the 'receivers of consultation, that is ... are from time to time talked to about the decision already arrived at' (Banerjee, 2007: 64).

Thus, opposed to mainstream stakeholder management, we develop the notion of *critical stakeholder analysis* (or CSA) that seeks to place the network of stakeholder interests within a critical political economy of the firm. Such a lens reveals from the very beginning, we will argue, the perversely unlevel playing field upon which so much dialogue, consultation and negotiation takes place. From this perspective, power, corporate domination and class power move to the forefront of the analysis. Two things happen when we do this. First, we begin to notice that the social structure of the business world means that corporate interests generally take priority within any stakeholder 'consultation' or 'negotiation' process. Even powerful actors such as the nation-state are often servants of the business sector, as was witnessed in the UK and United States apropos the 'bailout' following the 2008 financial crisis (Reinhardt and Rogoff, 2009). Second, and just as importantly, a critical approach to stake-holder analysis actually politicizes the corporation to the point where mainstream stakeholder analysis begins to look untenable. Would not a genuine 'stakeholder democracy' (to use Crane and Matten's (2010) phrase) actually transform the mod-ern corporation into a radically different institutional form? This line of reasoning shifts our focus to a critical political economy of the firm that is attuned to the power structures that predominate within the global economic system.

Given that mainstream or conventional stakeholder analysis is often concerned with globalization and global networks – including parties such as suppliers, labour, environmental groups and so forth – we use the example of globalization as a way of unsettling stakeholder theory and positing a more critical and (we would say) realistic understanding of life in the shadow of corporate hegemony. In particular, we will demonstrate how CSA may reveal some basic contradictions that prevail in both the globalization literature and the real world of international business. To make our case, the chapter is arranged in the following manner. First, we discuss typical approaches of stakeholder theory and management. Then we propose a more critical orientation, or what we call CSA. The case of globalization and its contradictions is used to demonstrate the utility of our approach vis-à-vis more conventional frameworks inspired by the stakeholder theory of the firm. We conclude by evaluating the overall usefulness of the stakeholder management discourse in the context of our findings.

STAKEHOLDER ANALYSIS AND ITS DISCONTENTS

As mentioned in the introduction to this chapter, a stakeholder approach to CSR often defines itself in contradistinction to the neo-classical model of the firm. Instead of the business operation competing alone in the open market driven purely by self-interest (and thus externalizing any negative costs – waste, poverty, pollution, etc. – onto other parties in the community), the organization should instead visualize itself as co-existing in a network of interested parties or 'stakeholders'. As one of the founding scholars of this idea, Freeman (1984), has suggested, the very term 'stakeholder' indicates a major departure from the conventional business model. All of a sudden, groups ostensibly outside of the managing or owning elite have a 'stake' in the activities of the business. This conceptually 'breaks open' the isolated enterprise and connects it to a myriad of groups who might affect or be affected by the business. In most texts on the subject, the typical stakeholder is the worker, the consumer, the environment, the state, civil society organizations and NGOs and so forth. Whereas previous management frameworks were based on a military metaphor of commanding and controlling external variables, this approach implies some kind of bond with interested parties that is more conciliatory, consultative and communicative.

WHAT IS A STAKEHOLDER?

Understood conventionally, the value of a stakeholder-based approach is that it sensitizes an organization to actors in its external environment that, although perhaps less salient than competitors, customers or governmental regulators, may still have the power (acting alone or in concert with other parties) to aid or impede the ability of the organization to accomplish its market and/or non-market goals (Clarkson, 1995; Freeman and Phillips, 2002). In many definitions of stakeholder theories of the firm, of most importance are those groups that can either enhance or damage its performance. Here is a classic definition of a stakeholder:

> A stakeholder of a corporation is an individual or a group which either: is harmed by, or benefits from, the corporation; *or* whose rights can be violated, or have to be respected, by the corporation. (Crane and Matten, 2010: 62)

While this technical definition is very useful, it is worth digging a little deeper to sur-face the ideological component in the stakeholder theory message. Firms often have a *legal* obligation to stakeholders. The law often imposes mandatory obligations for business regarding, say, the health and safety of workers, protecting the environment and so forth (and, of course, these legislative requirements will differ widely across the globe, which is why international business is pivotal to capitalism). But now we enter into the misty ideological realm of the concept because much of the literature suggests there is an *ethical* or *moral* obligation for consulting and negotiating with stakeholders above and beyond minimum compliance. Here the firm ought to deal with stakeholders because it then positions the corporation as a moral agent, as a vehicle for a more just society in a context where the state seems to have substantially contracted (Matten and Crane, 2005).

In a great feat of imaginative theorizing that morally legitimates the capitalist firm while appearing to be critical of it, Freeman (1984) ameliorates any nervous portfolio manager at this point by suggesting there are economic benefits to accrue with this approach. As Freeman et al. explicitly argue:

> business can be understood as a set of relationships among groups that have a stake in the activities that make up the business. Business is about how customers, suppliers, employees, financiers, communities and managers interact and create value. To understand business is to know how these relationships work. And, the executive's or entrepreneur's job is to manage and shape these relationships. (2007: 3)

The technique of stakeholder analysis involves identifying the relevant stakeholders involved in specific situations, whereas the practice of stakeholder management is concerned with incorporating the interests and anticipated reactions of these stake-holders into the decision-making process of the organization at the centre of the situation (Freeman et al., 2007). Thus, the essence of stakeholder theory (and its applications in stakeholder analysis and management) is found in its instrumental utility to management; that is, it provides useful tools for improving organizational performance (sometimes including social and environmental performance).

So why would we call this ideological? Because stakeholder theory tells us that it is by no means restricted to an instrumental concern with the pursuit of ratio-nal objectives (defined in whatever manner). For instance, Donaldson and Preston (1995) have argued that stakeholder theory also incorporates a normative dimension regarding how managers (and other actors) should act in relation to the environment and other stakeholders as well as a more descriptive aspect that aims to delineate the concrete connections between stakeholders without making overt value judgements (also see Trevino and Weaver, 1999). In this respect, Reed (1999) has employed German critical theory to distinguish further between legitimacy, morality and ethics as components of the normative dimension. In the guise of criticality, two important issues are implied here. Business and society might be idealized as a pluralist play-ing field in which institutions (potentially) co-exist, interacting and communicating with each other. Second, it pays to do good unto others – such as speaking nicely to Nigerian desert-dwellers who are about to have their village cleared to make room for an oil pipeline – because keeping the peace with stakeholders ultimately leads to economic growth. Notice the subtle ideological move here: if we can make money by 'doing good', then it stands to reason that *making money is itself a path to goodness* and may be harnessed to remedy some pressing social problems. Morality and the pursuit of profit are thus reconciled; capitalism is an ethically virtuous endeavour bar a number of rogue firms and greedy fund managers.

TOWARDS A CSA

It is here that the critics begin to raise their eyebrows about the credibility of stakeholder theory. Although stakeholder theory provides a much needed corrective to disturbingly narrow neo-liberal theories of the firm, we feel that the vast majority of the literature still omits broader structural forces related to power, capitalism, class, access to resources and so forth (also see Calton and Kurland, 1996; Daboub and Calton, 2002; Levy, 2008). That is to say, organizations and their stakeholders are often treated as autonomous actors that negotiate the conditions of their relationship in a pluralistic fashion. Moreover, much contemporary stakeholder management theory attempts to promote 'enlightened' behaviour among corporations, claiming that such behaviour inevitably generates 'win–win' outcomes for all relevant stakeholders although there are rarely attempts to examine the relative magnitude of corporate versus non-corporate 'wins'. An assumption (usually implicit) as to some semblance of resource comparability between stakeholder groups is also evident. Such a stance tends to miss the broader societal context of uneven relations of power, coercion and domination in which stakeholders are embedded, factors that are often key determinants of the configuration of stakeholder networks (Jones and Fleming, 2003).

For example, in his critical analysis of Freeman's theory of the firm, Stieb (2009) among others has persuasively argued that the specific rights of ownership are historically and socially rooted in ideas of property that must be understood in the specific context of modern capitalism. Stakeholder theory continues to treat ownership as an isolated and abstract idea divorced from this political and economic context. As a result, according to Stieb (2009), much stakeholder analysis views the ownership patterns of capitalist firms as legitimate achievements rather than the embedded result of structural conditions that are historically stacked in favour of various elites, classes and so forth. Examples of the absence of a broader critical perspective can be found in Freeman and Phillips' (2002) self-proclaimed libertarian argument that stakeholders are fundamentally 'free' and 'voluntary' actors, and in Van Buren's (2001) concept of mutual consent as the basis of a normative stakeholder approach. Indeed, this problem could also be convincingly levelled at the recent attempt to develop a more critical, Habermasian approach to CSR and related concepts by Scherer and Palazzo (2007). The very call for an 'ideal speech situation' within the confines of the corporate sector implicitly posits it as something that could happen without radically altering the corporate sector: to have one's cake and eat it too.

THE 'STAKE' OF STAKEHOLDER THEORY

We feel that conventional stakeholder theory is beset with some assumptions that ultimately legitimate the firm while appearing critical of it. Conceptually, conventional theory simply fails to consider the underlying structural linkages that may exist between various stakeholders along with complex and deeply embedded (institutionalized) processes that constitute stakeholders' materiality, identity and even forms of rationality. Echoing Levy's (2008) analysis of international production networks, the point here is that even taken on its own terms and with respect to its instrumental, actor-oriented objectives, conventional theory and its applications are often off the mark.

Indeed, from the evidence presented in this chapter, we would go so far as to argue that the stakeholder theory, and CSR literature more generally, fundamentally 'miss the forest for the trees' by failing to incorporate within their respective domains key empirical developments of the past two decades such as increasingly regressive patterns of income and wealth distribution, lowered quality-of-life and job security expectations among a significant percentage of the working population, and a massive increase in corporate power at the expense of its traditional 'checks', the state and organized labour (Harvey, 2010). In light of the stark realities of financial market control (Davis, 2009), the consequent primacy of managing to maximize shareholder value in an era of financial crisis (Lanchester, 2010), and the operational hegemony of techniques such as 'economic value added' and 'balancing the scorecard' (Chang, 2010), external pressures and internal systems will generally prohibit any but instrumentally rational forms of resource allocation in corporate hierarchies.

Normatively, stakeholder theory promotes – at best – a more 'enlightened' form of behaviour by firms (and other actors), which remains fundamentally self-serving. As a managerial tool, it implicitly sanctions actions such as the deployment of knowingly incomplete (or intentionally distorted) information (including the ideological use of the stakeholder discourse itself) to influence the behaviour of other stakeholders when necessary. It accepts existing institutional arrangements and distributional patterns as given and therefore legitimate. It ultimately fits hand in glove with the workings of 'the market', managerial prerogative and authoritarian corporate hierarchies. As Levy (2008) too argues, it is thus complicit (to the extent it influences actual practice) in problematic outcomes such as the aggregation of market power, the generation of social and environmental externalities, and the undermining of democratic and cultural institutions by those hegemonic market processes.

MAKING STAKEHOLDER THEORY CRITICAL

What we call critical stakeholder analysis or CSA thus stands opposed to the conventional stakeholder approach on both theoretical and normative grounds, holding that the latter tends towards theoretical misspecification and normative capture by (or perhaps surrender to) corporate interests. CSA is aimed at positioning organizational stakeholders within a broader context of multinational capitalism, class politics and transnational regulatory bodies in order to reveal the structural underpinnings of power and domination that invariably inform contemporary corporate behaviour and business–government relations. This framework rejects the conventional assumptions of institutional pluralism, behavioural fluidity and resource comparability, positing instead assumptions of structural conflict between various sets of institutions and stakeholder groups, embedded interests, and a fundamental imbalance in the distribution of resources and (therefore) power in society and its institutions and organizations. CSA is inspired by the insights of the radical structuralist paradigm in organizational sociology (Burrell and Morgan, 1979) and recent radical political economy (e.g. Chang, 2010; Fisher, 2009; Marazzi, 2010). The radical structuralist component of CSA entails a method of investigation in which class, group and institutional fractions bearing differing interests and resources come to the fore of an analysis rather than the isolated activities of free and consensual parties. CSA is therefore obviously related to class analysis in that all stakeholders have class coordinates (also see Banerjee, 2007).

In summary, our radical revision of stakeholder theory has two key principles. First, it recognizes that stakeholders often do not have equal power due to differentials in resource control, ownership, ability to voice interests and so forth. While some approaches to stakeholder theory posit power as an important facet (see Mitchell et al., 1997), we feel it is still inadequate because it does not connect to the wider structural backdrop of global capitalism. Therefore, and second, our approach calls for the analytical incorporation of broader social conditions related to capitalism, multinational regulatory bodies and other structural forces that consolidate the power relations identified in the first step. This is especially important in the context of the growing integration of state and society we have seen following the recent global financial crisis. Normatively, CSA calls for (1) a common understanding of key issues within the relevant organizational field, (2) the negotiated settlement of zero-sum situations that optimize collective stakeholder interests within the field, and (3) the containment and minimization of negative externalities within as well as between fields.

For example, if CSA were applied to the case of *maquiladoras* operating on the US–Mexico border today, then we would obviously need to consider the broader economic, social and cultural institutions that underscore the activities of the various stakeholders in the relevant organizational field – especially in relation to the NAFTA (see Ojeda and Hennessy, 2006). Following the relative depression of the early 2000s, the recent 30 per cent increase of workers would be observed against the background of the suppression of labour unions (Bacon, 2004), growing violence against female workers and an allegedly corrupt local government turning a blind eye to rampant exploitation (Staudt, 2008).

In this context, conventional stakeholder theory would look rather weak. A CSA, on the other hand, would begin at the level of the field itself rather than from the perspective of a focal firm as with conventional stakeholder analysis. Outcomes would also be evaluated at the field level against criteria of procedural and substantive justice, democratic participation of relevant stakeholders, containment of any negative externalities (social and environmental) and environmental sustainability. It is axiomatic that such an approach would prevent any individual stakeholder from achieving its objectives fully – which is exactly the goal of conventional stakeholder theory. Rather, the survivability (and, where appropriate, expansion) of the organizational field would be optimized as a whole, with any zero-sum issues resolved through a process of negotiated settlements in which the exercise of power would be regulated by democratic institutions.

THE CASE OF GLOBAL CAPITALISM AND ITS CONTRADICTIONS

A good deal of mainstream stakeholder theory contextualizes the approach in the globalizing world of international business. Many of the examples and cases that illustrate the apparent efficacy of this method of 'ethical management' maintain that we might see its most positive outcomes when business processes cross national borders in terms of outsourcing, supply chains, foreign investment and managing the influence of NGOs and protest groups. This is not that surprising. The international economy and the activities of large multinational firms, such as BP, Tesco, Nike, Gap and so forth, have been subject to increased scrutiny and criticism for the way they conduct their businesses abroad. In a global business world where cheap labour, lax environmental standards and an openness to corruption are considered positive variables for setting up business, it is no wonder that stakeholder analysis is considered important for securing human rights, open participation and ethical standards apropos the environment and less powerful groups.

For example, the activities of Shell Nigeria in 1995 have often been seen as a case in which stakeholder theory *would have* resulted in a much more democratic outcome. A token consultation process was in place, but was obviously nothing more than a public relations exercise. Boele et al. (2001) document the complete failure of Shell to communicate substantively with the Ogoni people on the Delta – the authors outline the measures that could have been enacted to avoid the immense reputational disaster that transpired. Indeed, the facts of the case frequently shock students and teachers alike, especially pertaining to Shell's alleged use of thuggery to silence pro-testors through torture, abuse and violence (culminating in the state execution of the poet, Ken Saro-Wiwa). As Boele et al. point out, 'Shell admitted to importing arms and was accused of paying the Nigerian military to conduct operations in Ogoni, for example providing logistical support to armed units of the Nigerian police and military who were known to have shot at protesters' (2001: 130). They suggest that an engaged stakeholder-rights-based approach would have avoided the calamitous consequences that placed Shell in Nigeria at the centre of an international incident. Ironically, when Shell did begin to make headway addressing some its more flagrant disregard for human rights, it only exacerbated the tension given the broader context of exploitation that the firm represented:

> Stakeholders who feel oppressed are unlikely to enter genuine constructive dialogue unless the more obvious sources of denial of rights are first addressed. Thus, ironically, many of Shell's community development projects have become even greater sources for tension and conflict within the communities. (Boele et al., 2001: 130)

Cases like this are often used to exemplify the importance of globalization as a back-drop for understanding CSR and stakeholder management, especially when attempt-ing to produce fairer and more ethical business practices (of course, one must keep in mind that such business-led violence was around long before Shell Corporation, as the colonial and imperialist exploits of European expansion attests). But by the same token, we argue that it is in the area of global business that conventional stakeholder analysis is especially weak. It is at the international level that we see some of the most blatant and stark power inequities at play – inequities that are systemic, structural and irreconcilable with a truly just and democratic social economy (Levy, 2008). That is to say, nowhere do we find deeper and more unjust forms of asymmetrical power relations than in the context of multinational capitalism. The idea that stakeholder theory could exist within such a domain both undermines the conceptual creditabil-ity of the approach *and* reinforces a pro-business view of the global economy (that it is, deep down, a humanitarian social system).

THE GLOBALIZED STAKEHOLDER NETWORK

Conventional appeals to stakeholder management in this context appear not only infeasible, but downright misleading (along the lines of the liberal mantra, 'just be nice to each other'). Indeed, when stakeholder theory is practically evoked in this context, as Banerjee (2007) rightly observes, it becomes more a tool of containment, risk management and simple domination. We will argue in this section that a critical approach to stakeholder analysis (as discussed above) will provide a more realistic overview of how firms operate in the international area in relation to workers, the environment and so forth. Our CSA approach is particularly useful for revealing three important contradictions at the heart of the debates around globalization and the practices of internationalized business itself. An analysis of such contradictions, in turn, casts doubt on whether one can realistically remain true to the democratic ideals of stakeholder analysis without fundamentally rearranging the capitalist form (private ownership, profit-seeking behaviour, exploitation, etc.) as well as the global capitalist economic order.

But first, what exactly do we mean by globalization? For sure, it is a ubiquitous yet highly elusive term. It is usually used to describe increasing economic, political and socio-cultural integration driven by recent technological developments in information processing, communications and transportation worldwide as well as institutional permutations related to international regulation and governance (Dicken, 2010). The debate on the content and meaning of globalization is still conducted largely in binary terms; for example, globalization is understood either as increasing standardization or as increasing difference. More complex and nuanced studies exist (e.g. Held and McGrew, 2003), but these are mostly developed in areas such as cultural studies and have yet to affect the more mainstream areas of business or public policy.

Using our CSA framework as developed above, we will argue that the effects of globalization are best understood in terms of the following three sets of simultaneous contradictions: convergence and divergence, inclusion and exclusion, and centralization and decentralization. It is further argued that these contradictions can be effectively conceptualized and unpacked through CSA, a technique that focuses on broader structural (versus transient) commonalities and differences among key stakeholder groups apropos resource base, class positionality, access to decision-making opportunities, power asymmetries and so forth. These differentials are often omitted in mainstream or managerial stakeholder theory, CSR and other related fields.

It is important to note that the following analysis of the three central contradictions of globalization is not symmetrical as each contradiction involves different primary stakeholder groups and affects those groups in different ways. The focal level of analysis also changes across the three contradictions in the current international context dominated by the Western corporation, but increasingly those in China and beyond. This is consistent with the situation- or context-specific thrust of stakeholder theory, which is not invalidated by the assumption that the contradictions themselves and the underlying relationships between stakeholder groups are structural in nature.

CONTRADICTION 1: CONVERGENCE AND DIVERGENCE

The first contradiction of globalization that can be unpacked by CSA is that between convergence and divergence. This refers to the empirically observable mix of developments that homogenize cultural economic and social institutions on the one hand, and those on the other hand that maintain – and sometimes even increase – differences. Proponents of convergence focus on the increasing tendency for economic and social activity to fall within a range defined by Anglo-Saxon and Western European capitalist systems, a range including the form of government macroeconomic policy; general business practices; organizational strategies, structures and processes; and cultural orientation, particularly with respect to work and consumption (Hardt and Negri, 2009). For example, in travelling across the wealthier nations and through most of the newly industrializing countries, one navigates landscapes constituted by similarly designed airports and transportation systems, hotels, restaurants, and shopping and business centres, all operating according to broadly common international standards of etiquette and efficiency.

Although this convergence process is neither uniform nor irreversible in particular localities, it serves to standardize the rules of the game adequately for transacting business across national borders (e.g. see Friedman's (2005) concept of the 'flat world'). Observers argue that cultural diversity, as expressed in terms of widely divergent consumer demand preferences, is also receding as globalization unfolds. From a CSA perspective, several catalysts can be identified as being at work here. They include the global media and their associated demonstration effects – first to local elite stakeholders and then downwards to the middle classes (Stiglitz, 2003). Also significant is the work of various develop-ment institutions during the past several decades, which has resulted in many developing countries cultivating institutional and material infrastructures that are well articulated with those of the advanced countries (Held et al., 2010). Finally, the activities of MNCs themselves are increasingly prominent as these firms have brought their ways of doing business (e.g. quality standards, supplier networks, marketing techniques and human resource management approaches) with them into host countries, establishing standards for local best practice and generally moulding local business environments according to their needs (see Sassen, 2008).

Critics of the convergence thesis, however, maintain that the proliferation of con-sumer societies and lifestyle models and the associated convergence of consumer preferences should not be understood as a totalizing homogenization of stakeholder networks (Ritzer, 2009). This point is illustrated by Appadurai (2001), who argued that the globalization process transforms the consumer through commodity flows into a symbol, with global advertising assuming the role of key technology in the dis-semination of normative cultural models. Thus, although these models are globally standardized, globalization is not synonymous with homogenization. Rather, global-ization uses the instruments of standardization (e.g. clothing and fashion, enter-tainment, food and aesthetic experience) to create heterodox markets; that is, to serve and service local markets with global universal signs (see Giulianotti and Robertson (2007) in relation to the globalization of sport). In this formulation, transnational cultural ideology serves the global capitalist system through the perpetuation of the economic order by influencing the cultural order (Lash and Lury, 2007). From the perspective of capital, the key is to foster diffusion of the institutional apparatus of consumer society; how consumer preferences specifically manifest in a given society is a secondary matter – as is the manner in which global signs are interpreted by local stakeholders.

Following Lash and Lury's (2007) wide-spanning study of global flows of the (Western) sign via brands and images, we can see how the global–local conflict relates to the backlash against aspects of globalization associated with cultural impe-rialism (sometimes also referred to as Americanization; see Amin, 2010). From a normative CSA point of view, it is easy to sympathize with critics arguing that the constant barrage of foreign images through electronic media undermines notions of national identity (and the link between nation and state), substituting an intense but shallow pastiche of symbols that have no coherent meaning in local contexts. Observers such as Lem and Barber (2010) argue that the shock of this inundation by global media culture can cause community stakeholders to revert to primary iden-tity sources tied to very local affiliations with place, ethnicity and religion – which combine to forge coherent, meaning-laden, deep identity structures – as substitutes for undermined national identity. Yet these 'backlash' situations can also – perhaps somewhat perversely – present marketing opportunities for MNCs. For example, customized ethnic- and/or nostalgia-oriented products are increasingly targeted at alienated stakeholders whose consumption of such goods simultaneously reinforces their primary identity structures and increases their integration into the global eco-nomic system.

Jones (2009b) presents an interesting example of micromarketing from New Zealand. Lion Nathan Ltd, a transnational brewing company, produces a wide range of beers. Several of Lion's brands are targeted at specific localities and marketed to articulate with the embedded cultural identity of consumers in regionally defined markets. These brands are marketed in terms of their local and nostalgia-invoking aspects, thus fostering a powerful semiotic response from consumers longing for an idealized past.

This case is interesting from a CSA perspective because it illustrates some of the complex linkages and ironies generated by globalization: the site of production has gone from small, locally owned breweries to highly centralized corporate facilities owned largely by foreign interests; consumption of these products transfers income from local stakeholders to international investors; and consumption increases buyers' integration into consumer society (versus home brewing, a relatively popular pursuit in New Zealand). Yet, consumption also enhances the consumers' identification with their local *habitus* as a source of identity. In this case the local effect is a result of commercial decisions taken at the global level, but that does not diminish the fact that the products (although 'inauthentic') take their place among constellations of local signifiers, adding their semiotic power to those constellations and fuelling a factually false but experientially true and 'real' component of local stakeholder identities.

CONTRADICTION 2: INCLUSION AND EXCLUSION

The second contradiction of globalization that can be unpacked by CSA is that between inclusion and exclusion. This contrasts those stakeholders who are empowered (and enriched) by the globalization process with others who are relatively – sometimes even absolutely – disempowered and pauperized by that same process. Globalization has been framed in terms of a gravitational field emanating from a core source (Wallerstein, 1979). Those stakeholders closest to the centre of the field are ever more tightly integrated economically, politically and culturally. Yet, those further out in the 'system' are increasingly left behind. Their 'standing in place' is equivalent in practice to losing ground and to being increasingly excluded from the value- and wealth-generating processes happening at the core of the system. This dynamic manifests both across and within countries. In the former, we see substantial regions in Latin America, Central Asia and most of Africa simply bypassed as globalization unfolds (see Frieden, 2007; United Nations Conference on Trade and Development, 2010a), inspiring the phrase *global south* to describe the economic apartheid that accompanies the uneven diffusion of capital investment and job opportunities (Davis and Monk, 2008). In the latter, we see increasing socio-economic and spatial stratification within even advanced countries, something exacerbated by the recent global financial crisis (Marazzi, 2010).

The inclusion–exclusion dynamic affects company, worker and consumer stakeholders all in different ways. At the firm level, it has been driven by the massive industrial restructuring of the past two decades, itself generated by a historically unprecedented level of technologically induced 'time–space compression' (Harvey, 1990b) as well as changes in government policies. New technologies have facilitated the convergence of formally discrete industries such as communications, information processing and news and entertainment, creating a huge multimedia sector operating partly in 'electronic space' (Bard and Soderqvist, 2002). Meanwhile, changes in government regulations have fostered the intersection of banking, insurance and financial services within and across national markets (Harvey, 2007).

In many areas, these developments have changed the underlying economics of competition from 'big beats small' to 'fast beats slow' (Marazzi, 2010). Centres of value creation are almost uniformly dominated by MNCs (see United Nations Conference on Trade and Development, 2010a; 2010b). Meanwhile, less powerful stakeholders either are excluded from the value creation process altogether or (at best) partake in that process as subordinated network partners subject to the central co-ordination and control of dominant firms (Stiglitz, 2010). Relatedly and perhaps most importantly, in these core sectors, the generation of goods and services has become decoupled from employment. That is, the relative number of 'good' jobs that the contemporary economy generates is far less than in the previous Fordist era (see Amin and Membrez, 2008). High-skill workers (so-called symbolic analysts (Reich, 1991) or no-collar workers (Ross, 2004)) face greater opportunities as employers compete for their services, whereas low-skill workers are increasingly threatened by automated systems, a lack of union protection, relocation of their jobs to off-shore sites where labour costs are lower, and a general lowering of the social wage (Mohun, 2009).

This dual economic system of those who are 'inside' and those who are 'outside' seems to be growing not only within nation-states, but also across countries in an unprecedented manner. The International Labour Organization (ILO) (2010) report on the growth in the Global South indicates that the global financial crisis has made precarious or 'slack' employment the norm. However, the global job crisis is not simply a 'natural' feature of a fluctuating economy. It is related to the way in which capital twists and turns to increase profitability and reduce costs. Castells (2007) suggests that in Western economies we have finally witnessed the end of good work for the average worker. From a normative CSA framework, we would add that 'good work' is increasingly being supplanted by so-called 'shit work' – some combination of unsatisfying, insecure and poorly paying employment usually in the service sector and often performed by female and/or immigrant labour (see Fleming, 2009b). Certainly, the increasing polarization of labour markets and the consequent effects in a variety of spheres are at the very heart of the globalization debate and are of crucial significance to a CSA of international economic activity. The erosion of the welfare state has also been an important driver of the inclusion–exclusion dynamic. Faced with increasing capital mobility from the 1970s onward, most states supported regressive measures to lower wages and production costs – and even more fundamentally, to lower middle- and working-class expectations (see Stiglitz, 2010).

In many of the leading economies of the West, these developments have fundamentally changed the class structure of society, with a dramatic effect on less powerful stakeholders (Chang, 2010). The deepening of the neo-liberal agenda has created a 'captive state' in which austerity measures (for the public at least) have concentrated wealth in the upper percentiles of the ruling elite (see Harvey, 2007). In many countries, as mentioned earlier, this has served to shift socio-economic patterns of income, wealth and life chances from a diamond shape (with a bulge in the middle signifying a large middle class) towards an hourglass shape (representing growing segments of haves and have-nots and a shrinking middle class) (Lavelle, 2008). As a result, wealth and income have become polarized in both developed and developing countries (Chang, 2010). Even the historic economic boom in the United States during the 1990s did not reverse this trend (Mohun, 2009). Rather, it appears to have been an integral part of the process through which polarization of stakeholder groups was generated and exacerbated (Sassen, 2008).

These developments interact with each other through feedback loops in political, economic, technological and socio-cultural processes, leading to cumulative causation (Sassen, 2008). These interactions foster systematic and systemic processes of exclusion, separating stakeholders into winners and losers in categorical and seemingly intractable ways. Again, it is important not simply to put these trends down to the post-crisis world – as a cyclical economic aberration. It is more a product of the deepening of the capitalist logic of production via the intensification of neo-liberalism and employment policies over the last 20 years.

Importantly, social and geographic spaces (and the stakeholders who populate them) that have no value as markets, production platforms or sources of raw materials are beyond the purview of the key agents of advanced capitalism, MNCs, and will be bypassed (Davis, 2007). The rise of the 'planet of slums' and the cartographic nightmare of a globalized 'extreme neo-liberalism', as Harney (2009) calls it, has created a vast stratum of wasted lives. Castells (1996) referred to this emergent socio-spatial zone of vast and pure exclusion as constituting a kind of Fourth World. As such, structural irrelevance might be considered a fate much worse than dependency. The current dynamics of multinational capitalism do not create new forms of wealth, but polarize access opportunities and distribution in increasingly extreme ways (see Chang, 2010). It is interesting that even the World Bank has begun explicitly to use the term 'two-tiered global economy' to describe current patterns of economic development. From a CSA perspective, an additional insight with respect to the interactive nature of these developments is that the inclusion–exclusion dynamic also constitutes a dialectical process that eventually culminates in some form of systemic crisis – the recent privatization of debt via the sub-prime collapse only being the most recent (Harvey, 2010). Moreover, a cascading political crisis is likely following the collapse of financial and industrial markets, driven by the breakdown of social cohesion and institutional legitimacy as national stakeholders fracture along stark socio-economic lines. In Europe, following the 'at arm's length' governmental policies characterizing the early 2000s, many governments are now intervening in coercive ways to 'maintain order' and 'the rule of law' by criminalizing poverty, increasing their surveillance capabilities and redefining citizenship rights and responsibilities – and the very discourse of democracy itself (Dean, 2007; Galbraith, 2008).

CONTRADICTION 3: CENTRALIZATION AND DECENTRALIZATION

The third contradiction of globalization to be analysed via the CSA framework is that between centralization and decentralization. Here, the most salient level of analysis is the organizational one, and within the spectrum of organizational forms, attention necessarily centres on the MNC. The expansion of these firms from their home countries to a global scale has been widely chronicled (cf. Dicken, 2010). What is new with contemporary globalization is that the technologies exist today for MNCs to be spatially decentralized, with research and development, manufacturing and/or distribution operations literally placed planet-wide yet linked with each other and with headquarters and centrally co-ordinated in real time. Increasingly, the span of control of these firms is extending beyond their own organizational boundaries to encompass complex stakeholder networks that they construct, maintain and dominate as an alternative to high levels of vertical integration. Such firms are thus simultaneously centralized and decentralized along different dimensions.

The centralization–decentralization dynamic creates tremendous challenges for other stakeholders such as more localized firms that try to compete with MNCs as well as for governments, labour unions and other groups that vie with MNCs in some way for resources. This is due to the sheer power of this institutional form. For example, local firms have trouble accessing the locational advantages that MNCs are able to draw on by configuring their value chains in a manner that allows them to pursue absolute (not comparative) advantage at the company level (Pierre et al., 2009). Even very large domestic firms are thus usually unable to compete on cost against MNCs; they are also presented with disadvantages in areas such as learning, cost of capital and the ability to raise new capital, personnel recruitment and tax exposure (Ghoshal and Westney, 2005). The ability of MNCs to centralize and decentralize simultaneously also maximizes their leverage against workers (or their unions) and governments. This increase in bargaining power is achieved most simply by placing multiple groups of workers located in different nations in competition with each other for the jobs that MNCs generate and, similarly, putting states in competition with each other for the jobs, capital, technology and tax revenue with which MNC investment is associated (Korten, 2001).

The financial sector has been especially good at facilitating this process through the rapid movement of capital, centred around the United States in particular (Davis, 2009). This enables manufacturing or pharmaceutical MNCs, for example, to set up operations that are usually organized on a regional basis and have a substantial amount of excess capacity in most value-chain activities. MNCs can shift or relocate their operations relatively quickly should tax-hungry governments or militant labour unions press for a greater share of their income streams. In fact, the very threat of relocation is usually sufficient to provide a disciplining power against new wage claims or moves to increase corporate taxes. As Dicken (2010) points out, it is important that major economic, political, technological and socio-cultural developments since the 1970s have reduced the transaction costs of leveraging (or divide-and-conquer) strategies substantially for MNCs.

A related development of much significance has been the growing tendency for MNCs to replace hierarchically governed, vertically integrated production systems with network systems – groups of interdependent, vertically linked suppliers and/or distributors co-ordinated by focal (core) MNCs to produce goods or services in a manner that maximizes flexibility and minimizes risk for the primary stakeholder firm (Gereffi, 2008). The hierarchical network form of organization allows MNCs to reduce their transaction costs and increase their flexibility by delegating non-essential activities to subcontractors that bear most of the risks associated with uncertain market conditions (Jones and Haigh, 2007). These subcontractors are locked in MNC-centred value chains in which they have little power and in which the intermediate goods they produce have little trading value outside of the chain in which they are located. MNCs can then focus on high-value-added activities based on proprietary knowledge, technological intensity and scalar economies (Sassen, 2008). MNCs are thus able to have their cake and eat it too by enjoying the benefits of control and centralization without the liabilities of ownership.

Anticipating these events some years ago, Cowling and Sugden (1987) argue that the traditional definition of the firm (based on ownership) is in need of revision. That definition, founded as it is on an assumed identity between ownership and control, is largely obsolete in light of contemporary organizational arrangements. Increasingly, control extends widely beyond the boundaries of ownership as vertically integrated forms (in which ownership and control were commensurate) give way to nominally independent production networks organized around a primary stakeholder firm (in which ownership and control are nominally separate). Cowling and Sugden, therefore, suggest that a broadened definition of the firm based on effective strategic control rather than ownership is warranted. In the contemporary context, an important implication of this conceptualization is that official data on industrial concentration rates seriously underestimate the increasing level of control that MNCs exert in the international economy (Harvey, 2010). This point needs to be considered together with other developments, such as the unprecedented merger and acquisition activity occurring in industries such as automobiles, air travel, and banking and finance during the past decade and the proliferation of (anti-competitive) strategic alliances in technology-intensive, scale-sensitive industries (Stiglitz, 2010). From a CSA perspective, these trends towards market consolidation clearly foster serious concerns for both long-term consumer welfare and democratic accountability in both developed and developing countries (Lavelle, 2008).

THE IDEOLOGY OF STAKEHOLDER THEORY AND CONCLUDING REMARKS

Our inspection of the three central contradictions of globalization through CSA acknowledges that each contradiction interacts (or overlaps) in complex associations of mutual causality driven by the actions of key stakeholders and structural processes. As we can see, mainstream stakeholder analysis assumes that dialogue and consultation often occur on a level playing field, especially in the context of managing global networks and parties. Missing the broad flows of power and domination – centred about MNCs, finance markets and a capitalist state – allows scholars and practitioners to proceed as if the approach might create an ethical business world. For us, this is the ideological component of stakeholder analysis. Our alternative CSA approach, on the other hand, echoes the critical theory of Marx and Weber, underlining the structural processes of capital accumulation and institutional rationalization that constitute the core drivers of globalization (and also the main targets of anti-globalization forces) (Held and McGrew, 2003). More generally, we might distinguish our critical approach from typical, orthodox theories of stakeholder analysis along the dimensions outlined in Table 3.1.

Most importantly, given that globalization features so prominently in conventional stakeholder analysis, we feel that a detailed analysis of the political economy of international business forces one to take a more sobering outlook. In this context, as Banerjee also argues, the MNC's practical approach to 'stakeholder management' looks less rosy than usually depicted in business ethics textbooks:

> despite all the strident rhetoric about the 'stakeholder corporation' the reality is that stakeholders who do not toe the corporate line are either co-opted or marginalized. The stakeholder theory of the firm represents a form of stakeholder colonialism that serves to regulate the behavior of stakeholders. The (perceived) integration of stakeholder needs might be an effective tool for a firm to enhance its image is probably true. However, for a critical understanding of stakeholder theory, this approach is unsatisfactory. Effective practices for 'managing' stakeholders and research aimed at generating 'knowledge' about stakeholders are less systems of truth than products of power applied by corporations, governments and business schools. (2007: 72)

We fully concur and would add that the inclusion/exclusion dynamic can be seen as a driver of the other contradictions under certain circumstances, as when increasing

Table 3.1   Differentiating orthodox and critical stakeholder theory

	Orthodox stakeholder management theory	Critical stakeholder management theory
Assumptions about business and society	Pluralism in which the corporation is one player among many	Powerful institutions like the corporation dominate/exploit other groups for their own gain
Analytical focus	The corporation first and then consideration of groups that may benefit or harm it	The broader political economy that embeds groups exploited by the firm
Purpose of analysis	Corporate risk analysis and instrumental advance of business concerns	Voicing concerns of weaker parties to highlight and end corporate hegemony
Practical outcomes	Assumes win–win outcome among all stakeholders	Predicts dissent as weaker stakeholders bow to the interests of large corporations
Example 1: Shell in Nigeria (Crane and Matten, 2010)	Consultative dialogue with the Ogoni locals to arrive at workable consensus and sustainable development	The token of 'consultation' used to silence and manage troublesome local activist groups, with little deviation from 'business as usual'
Example 2: Globalization and the multinational firm	International business and society work together to create sustainable solutions and wealth for all	Large corporations control the wealth of large geo-political blocs at the *expense* of populations, democracy, the environment and sustainability. Conflict inevitable

marginalization of geographic spaces or socio-economic groups impels MNCs to reconfigure their value-chains (affecting the centralization–decentralization contradiction) and/or prompts states to adjust their policies on social welfare or law and order in novel ways (affecting the convergence–divergence contradiction). But perhaps our CSA approach in the context of globalization combines some of the virtues of both international political economy and conventional stakeholder theory. From the former, it incorporates a structural analysis that reveals how underlying and persistent patterns of asymmetrical power dynamics drive the ongoing processes of capital accumulation and institutional rationalization, along with the resulting distributional outcomes with respect to classes and institutions. Thus exposed are the theoretical and empirical 'tectonic plates' upon which the more transient 'shifting sands' of conventional stakeholder relations unfold and indeed affect those underlying structures in accordance with Giddens' (1979) classic theory of structuration.

CSA is not intended to be a management tool in the sense that it enhances the ability of a focal organization to pursue its own instrumental rationality on a unilateral basis. Rather, we would maintain that CSA promotes an increased awareness that the gains and pains of contemporary economic relations need to be distributed through negotiated structures rather than imposed from above through political fiat or market forces if institutional stability is to be maintained. In this sense, CSA eschews the managerialist tendency in the literature to define the legitimacy of the stakeholder network in terms that privilege dominant parties. Our estimations of 'who counts' are rendered more complex by analysing the contradictions of globalization because we discover that the benefits and costs of the overall process are distributed quite disproportionately. Put simply, CSA holds that 'everybody counts'. From a CSA perspective, transnational managers should approach the stakeholder networks in which their firms are key participants in a manner that is sensitized to the asymmetrical power relations of the international economic system and the consequent imperative of ensuring that outcomes are (at least) acceptable to all affected parties. It is likely that such a change in behaviour will require public policy intervention rather than arise voluntarily.

Following the rise to prominence of anti-globalization protest movements over the last 15 years (from Seattle in 1999 to the current protests at the G8 summits), debate continues as to whether there has been a move beyond rhetoric to a real change in behaviour on the part of the aggressive MNC. CSA would demand that change in rhetoric be followed by change in process and structure. The impact of globalization depends on who you are and where you are – defined in terms of both socio-economic and geographic space.

The claim that globalization will indeed benefit all stakeholders in the long run through superior global resource allocation has emanated from many quarters over the past few decades, most particularly from those corporate and investor groups currently benefiting from the process. However, as Keynes duly noted many years ago, 'In the long run we are all dead.' It is the short- and medium-term effects of globalization that merit urgent attention and action. If we are to take stakeholder theory seriously, it is vitally important to set it against the backdrop of international business. Otherwise, it becomes just another tool to extend the chains of exploitation and domination that define so much of what globalization means today. To this end, it is hoped that our critical approach might prove useful in terms of both conceptualizing the globalization problematic and supporting the formulation of effective strategies by all relevant stakeholder groups.

The employee is a central feature of much stakeholder theory and CSR research and practice. It tends to be so in a manner that treats the employee as a salient stakeholder who has rights that ought to be observed by the firm. For example, health and safety, a fair wage, avoiding child labour within international commodity chains, and so forth are central here (see Jones and Fleming, 2003). Indeed, as Crane and Matten (2010) have recently pointed out, when it comes to social reporting and social accounting, the treatment of workers in terms of upholding labour standards is often primary – as is the perception of being deemed 'a good employer'. Underemphasized in the literature, however, is the internal role of CSR and business ethics programmes – how it serves to deal with tensions between the values of workers and the unabashed pursuit of profit. This chapter serves to initiate a discussion in this area and will propose that CSR initiatives not only are driven by external stakeholders or a concern with labour standards and rights, but may also serve a cultural or even *ideological* purpose: to align employees' political and personal values with an aggressive business model, especially in industries that might be considered controversial.

Building on the previous chapters that posit a political understanding of CSR, linking it closely to the reproduction of the capitalist enterprise, this chapter argues that CSR plays an important internal ideological role in the corporation. Just as Marx once said that religion was the opiate of the masses (blinding us to the very worldly causes of the poor's misery), Žižek (2009) has argued that today it is a particular kind of environmentalism or eco-friendliness that serves this ideological role. Similarly, we will argue that CSR functions to incorporate workers especially when there is a breach between their progressive personal beliefs and their ongoing participation in an unsustainable institutional environment. The possible disconnect and subsequent attempt to realign the personal/political concerns of working stakeholders with the principles of commercialism represent a new terrain of stakeholder and CSR research. From this perspective, CSR not only becomes a vehicle for reconnecting the critical or conscientious worker with the for-profit firm, but, as we shall argue below, might also be used as a tool for capturing new ideas, products and skills. The ironic result could be the commercialization of ideas that employees developed to overcome the limits of commercialization in the first place.

In order to unpack these propositions the chapter is organized in four parts. First, we begin with a short vignette to provide an empirical flavour of the phenomenon that stakeholder theory tends to downplay when considering the role of the worker. Second, we will survey the mainstream management and consultancy literature to show how CSR is deemed a central instrument for attracting, motivating and retaining the working stakeholder. Third, a link will be made to the changing cultural politics of work in which a 'holistic' human resource framework appears to be of crucial importance. This is typified by the firm inviting workers to 'just be themselves' and express ostensibly non-work-related values and lifestyle indicators while on the job. The fourth section will argue that cultural or ideological integration is foremost here. How does a politically progressive, reflexive and socially sensitive individual reconcile him- or herself to a world of work that they feel at odds with? The discourse of CSR (e.g. consultancy firms supporting fair trade, tobacco multinationals giving lip-service to bio-diversity, etc.) may provide working stakeholders with a useful emotional safety valve to continue to labour in the 'heart of the beast'.

THE CURIOUS ENVELOPE

One of the authors had not previously given much thought to the way CSR might resonate with emergent problems relating to motivating, retaining and engaging employees. That was until the CSR Officer of a leading telecommunications firm approached him. Mary (a pseudonym) entered his university office, beaming with a happy and cheerful demeanour. The official reason for the meeting was to share ideas about the changing nature of business ethics and social responsibility in the telecommunications sector and perhaps to arrange a research project around achieving a sustainable business model. 'So, what are some of the CSR issues that you are facing at the moment?' he asked. She replied swiftly and not with a little apprehension. Her story is fascinating and rather disturbing.

The telecommunications firm – which we shall call Reen Corp – is a market leader in mobile phone technology in Europe. The UK national headquarters are based in a medium-sized city and employ a substantial workforce consisting of marketing, technical and service workers. The key issue for Reen Corp was its association with the placement of mobile phone masts in urban and suburban areas. As Mary said, 'We are extremely unpopular in some parts of the country because of the perceived controversy around mobile phone masts and radiation levels.' The author had vaguely heard about these concerns raised by scientists and neighbourhood activists and probed for further information. She responded:

> What these people do not understand is that the evidence concerning the risk of radiation exposure is pretty conclusive. It's a myth. What's more, they complain about putting a mast in a schoolyard or whatever, and then go home to use that very mast as if nothing was wrong. They're just complainers who have nothing better to do.

Mary shocked us regarding the lengths to which some concerned citizens went in order to convey the message that it was inappropriate to place mobile phone masts near schools, kindergartens and retirement homes. 'Oh, we get all sorts of hate mail, crank phone calls, and abuse,' she said. Apparently Reen Corp is now the target of such strong vitriol that it removed its company sign from its office building because a period of anonymity was thought to be best. Matters came to a head one day when a secretary received a large brown envelope with official markings and a stamp reading 'URGENT' on the front. On opening the envelope, the secretary smelt an awful odour, threw the envelope to one side and called security. Covering their faces with large handkerchiefs and using two chopsticks seconded from the canteen, the security guards emptied the contents. Someone had sent human excrement wrapped in clingfilm, with a message: 'this is how you treat our kids'.

The incident Mary relayed was indeed shocking and not a little disgusting. But in a surprising turn, Mary smiled and said: 'Oh, don't worry, we laughed about it in the end. It got sent to the glass cabinet, with all of the other crap that people send us. We use it to make fun of the weirdos out there.' In the author's mind, the connection with CSR was quite obvious. The controversy about radiation posed a major brand-reputation problem. One of Reen Corp's key assets is its brand and, as any corporate reputation expert would tell us, brands gain their value not only through recognition, but also through *positive* recognition. And if Reen Corp is perceived by the consumer to be putting the health of children at risk and flagrantly disregarding the concerns of the community, then it might decide to question the legitimacy of that product or, even worse, boycott it. As the author prefaced the discussion with this brief summary of the issues, Mary quickly interjected with a look of confusion:

> No, it's not consumer confidence we have in mind with all this CSR stuff. Our focus is really about employee engagement. We need to worry about *what they think* and make sure they feel that they can work hard in a company, and be sure we do not go against their personal values.

As a result, Reen Corp spent a good deal of time and money on CSR initiatives that were driven not only by external stakeholders such as consumers, the government or concerned citizens, but by workers' values, of both existing and potential future employees. CSR for them – involving philanthropy, sabbaticals to design more ecologically sound technological platforms, investment in bio-diversity and various think-tanks that generate discussion and dialogue pertaining to sustainable business models – was largely driven by how the firm relates to its workforce and vice versa.

THE WORKING STAKEHOLDER

While most scholarly investigations of CSR focus on external stakeholders, there is a modest but growing stream of research that attempts to understand the internal impact of various types of business ethics initiatives (see Bhattacharya et al., 2009; Gond et al., 2010). Key concerns, for example, have been attracting new employees (Greening and Turban, 2000; Turban and Greening, 1996) linking CSR to commitment and motivation (Peterson, 2004; Preuss et al., 2009) and analysing the role of human resource management in promoting CSR policies (Rupp et al., 2006; Wittenberg et al., 2007). This research, however, does tend to be very functionalist in orientation. CSR is deemed an instrumental variable that may or may not enhance employee performance in the managerialist sense of the term. 'Business as usual' or capitalism more generally (with all of its controversial social outcomes) is largely deemed unproblematic, and CSR is couched as something that might simply add value via higher employee productivity.

As might be expected, this functionalism is no more evident than in the consultancy industry as it proclaims the importance of CSR for managing the employer/worker cultural interface. Even a brief survey of these companies and their services on the Internet – using search terms such as 'CSR and employee' – throws up a variety of consultancies that are on hand to fine-tune this aspect of an organization's business ethics investment. The dominant discourse here centres on attracting, retaining and engaging staff. There are a number of administered surveys of varying quality and robustness that suggest employees are more willing to work for an organization that has a high-standing ethical record. One states, for example in relation to a global survey, that 'we found that CSR is the third most important driver of employee engagement overall. For companies in the US, an organization's stature in the community is the second most important driver of employee engagement, and a company's reputation for responsibility is also among the top 10 drivers' (Towers Watson, 2008). Besides attracting high-calibre new talent, for staff already part of the firm, maintaining an ethical presence is considered by some to be crucial if the enterprise is not to lose them to competitors (Bhattacharya et al., 2009).

It must be said that the rationale used by many of these consultancies regarding the efficacy of this internal role of CSR programmes does tend to be based on kitchen-sink psychology rather than substantive empirical observation. However, the key words evoked are nevertheless important. We propose that this interconnection of CSR and stakeholder management slots into a broader shift in the cultural politics of work. As a number of commentators have noted, employees are now demanding to express and develop aspects of self and identity that were once barred in the traditional workplace (Fleming and Sturdy, 2009). Rather than political views, self-ideals and lifestyle signifiers being prohibited at work, the 'humane' post-industrial enterprise is often replete with people who are different, authentic and even idiosyncratic (Kuhn, 2006). Indeed, the cultural makeup of the worker today makes for a tricky balancing act between corporate profit-seeking and personal principles. This is especially so among the emergent and inscrutable Generation-Y employees who think that work 'sucks' and is generally destructive, but nevertheless want to enjoy a healthy salary (Fleming, 2009a).

As opposed to the more mainstream functionalist literature and the consultancy proclamations outlined above, we suggest that a critical approach to understanding this facet of CSR would place the perennial contradiction between employees and employers or capital and labour at the heart of the analysis. In a cultural climate where workers tend to be cynical and even distrustful of business (while still feeling the necessity to participate), CSR could serve as a kind of ideological lure that allows doubting employees – who think capitalism and the corporation stand for everything wrong with the world – to continue working in the 'heart of the beast'. Let us now examine how this might be so.

CSR AND A CHANGING MANAGEMENT/WORKER INTERFACE

At one level, it is not too surprising that a firm like Reen Corp and others involved in so-called controversial industries might tailor well-wrought CSR policies to soften the emotional impact for conscientious workers. These scripted intimations to business ethics and environmentalism may pertain to the core competencies of the business (e.g. a petroleum company's views on sustainable energy) or may include broader statements that fall outside the core focus of the firm. The tobacco industry, for example, has long since given up on defending the serious health consequences of cigarettes. That battle was lost years ago and given the indomitable medical evidence coupled with immense governmental pressure (via taxes), the industry has changed tack. The key focus of its CSR policy is on the attitudes of its workers through investments in charities, bio-diversity and so forth. Moreover, in an industry like this, which has a fortress-like culture, it offers the typical inducements to workers that any other 'controversial' industry might (guaranteed life-time employment, higher-than-average salaries, etc.).

Employee-focused CSR initiatives in such industries are an important area of research that deserves more attention. But we would argue that this trend extends to companies in a diverse range of industries and sectors in which CSR is utilized to align the worker with the idea of business and corporate life more generally. This is not about the stigma of products that kill or harm, but *the stigma of work itself*. In the context of a bank-led financial crisis, a post-Enron incredulity towards big business and a cultural industry that hardly ever portrays work in a favourable light (think of *The Office*, *Office Space* and the innumerable documentaries reporting on the shockingly gratuitous greed of large corporations), many workers now view 'the job' with disrepute. Even pro-business commentators now openly acknowledge that 'the legitimacy of business has fallen to levels not seen in recent history' (Porter and Kramer, 2011: 4). In this context, we think that concerns with the disengaged employee and the potential palliative effects of CSR resonate with some significant changes in the character of post-industrial employment and its attendant cultural politics.

THE 'LIFESTYLE FIRM'

While the nature of work and the firm is still centred on profit maximization (via chains of exploitation, hierarchy and so forth), the ways in which this is achieved have undergone significant transformations. The emergence of knowledge work, the service sector and the creative industries, for example, is illustrative of this. But what concerns us here are the major changes around the meaning of work and the implications this has for employee identity and understandings of self both inside and outside the corporation. Indeed, shifts in the work–life balance, the increasing importance of diversity, and difference pertaining to ethnicity and sexuality correlate with a growing class of workers who are reflective, politically engaged and ever so cynical about the value of old-fashioned business (especially in the post-Enron and post-crisis period in Western economies). This has meant that the cultural codes for interfacing the employee with work itself have also undergone some major changes. Put in this larger context, CSR might be seen as a human resource tool designed to align an otherwise apprehensive and conscientious workforce with an unsustainable corporate world.

In the past, it was the staid 'organizational man' (Whyte, 1956) that prevailed in the large corporations of the Anglo-Saxon world. He or she was stripped of any uniqueness or idiosyncrasies that may have defined him or her outside of the office, and tended towards a homogeneous grey obedience to the rules of the corporation. As Weber famously stated, the office is marked by a strict abnegation of all that might interrupt the smooth and impartial 'machine' of the rational bureau.

In the last few years, however, as many commentators have observed, there has been something of a sea change in the corporate world regarding what it means to be at work. What has been called the rise of a more 'holistic' approach to human resource management (Fleming, 2009a) and the 'lifestyle firm' (Kuhn, 2006) has seen attempts to engage workers by allowing them to *just be themselves*, sometimes warts and all. The idea is that employees might be more engaged and motivated if they feel comfortable expressing, say, their gay identities or alternative political views at work, rather than hiding them from view for fear of chastisement. A good number of studies have noted how more 'life' (that is to say, those features of us that were deemed more appropriate to be expressed outside of work) have become integrated into the corporate cultures of a diverse range of firms (Land and Taylor, 2010). Consumer tastes, political sensibilities, sexuality, and ethnicity and lifestyle associatives are (up to a point at least) now welcomed into the once impersonal offices of the enterprise. Moreover, the converse trend of expecting more from work apropos life outside of employment has deepened this process. As Hochschild (1997) has noted, for example, a kind of 'time bind' operates here where (mostly female) employees often find the space of employment somewhere to escape from the hierarchies of the home.

We see a connection here between the more general emergence of 'holistic' management techniques in post-industrial workplaces (that both recognize and encourage the expression of the 'whole person') and firm-level CSR policies that aim to align working stakeholders with something they would otherwise find problematic (work itself, business, the corporation, etc.). Blowfield and Murray's reading of CSR briefly touches upon this theme in a manner that may help us take the analysis further:

> [Some commentators] argue the commercial imperative is only part of effective corporate responsibility management and that it should also be linked to the personal values of individual managers. They point out that individual discretion allows personnel to introduce their values into corporate responsibility policies, whether through officially sanctioned actions, the unintended consequences of an individual resolving a problem by drawing on personal beliefs, or an individual's entrepreneurship in bringing values into the workplace. (2008: 110)

This is certainly true. But what if these values the employee holds are distrustful or critical of corporate life, a disposition that is conveyed in innumerable films from the last decade including *Office Space*, *American Psycho* and so on? For sure, cynical society has not looked kindly upon the world of corporatized work, as the abundance of cultural references to anti-work attests (Svendsen, 2008). From the workers' perspective at least, it seems that the overall default view of business is one of: (1) profound distrust following the post-Enron revelation that a whole generation of employees had been hoodwinked by overpaid corporate liars and governmental lackeys; and (2) a feeling of unerring compulsion, the dull force of economic rationality whereby one feels little choice but to participate and make a living, especially in the expensive metropolises of the West. This critical and reflexive persona – especially among the unfathomable Generation Y demographic – both hates the world of work and is all the same driven by the individualistic, self-serving goal of getting the most out of it.

CSR AND THE DISENGAGED WORKER

In light of this pervasive culture of cynicism and disenchantment in the workforce, we might see CSR as an enterprise-led response to such concerns; for sure, concerns that for the most part are probably not vocally articulated, but are nevertheless shared by human resource managers, corporate executives and others in positions of authority who are certainly by no means immune to this economy of malaise. Indeed, in an article describing the new workplace as 'feel good factories', Brammer touches upon this important driver of CSR, which we want to discuss in a critical manner below:

> The overriding question, then, must be, why are employees beginning to care more about CSR? Its increasing importance to workers is part of a shift in wider social attitudes to the relationship between businesses and the societies they operate in. Employees are happiest when they associate themselves with organizations that

behave ethically and have positive reputations, association with these organizations is consistent with their personal values and enhances their self-image. (2006: 1)

True, but what is *not said* in this statement is of more importance. Why would working stakeholders feel unhappy *without* CSR? Where does this preceding sentiment of dissonance originate that prompts CSR in this manner? In the creative industries, for example, there is an unstated recognition that one is selling one's soul and becoming someone *one is not* as soon as one's labour of love becomes a commodity to be exchanged on the market like a bar of soap or can of baked beans. In Ross's (2004) excellent analysis of life in an IT firm in Boston, we see a new culture of business at play in a context where even the boss thinks work sucks. Razorfish, the firm that was studied, carefully cultivated a climate of counter-cultural chic so as to retain a sense of amateurism and slacker underground cool. This in turn gave the job a sense of authenticity and integrity. Management manufactured this culture because many workers in the industry are driven by a passion for software development and even non-corporate values of shareware, hacking private property and an 'IT communism' most notably summarized in the infamous *Hacker Manifesto*. As such, the company constructed a code that appealed to these creative, anti-commercial values. Strangely enough, left-wing and critical views of business and society were integrated into the official corporate discourse. As Ross puts it, 'giving the finger to corporate America … was a big boost for recruitment and employee morale' (2004: 110).

Similarly, we propose that the language of business ethics can recuperate the otherwise disaffected post-industrial employee. Workers with values at odds with or contrary to conventional understandings of business can be motivated nevertheless through what we might call a *discourse of the social* and it seems reasonable to suggest that CSR would be useful here. Obviously, this might especially be so among firms in industries generally associated with counter-cultural or even counter-commercial values including the arts, journalism and so forth. One only has to think of the creative industries to identify this peculiar dynamic (also see Frank (1998) in relation to the use of subversive motifs in the advertising world).

But it is not only in the crypto-subversive creative industries that we find this 'discourse of the social' being activated as a human resource management tool. Reporting on a study of two large international consultancy firms, Costas and Fleming (2009) found an analogous use of CSR, this time to realign the disengaged employee with the objectives of humdrum office work and an aggressive business model. They observed a raft of CSR initiatives that had little to do with outside stakeholders or clients. Fair trade branding in the cafeteria and *pro bono* sabbaticals were favourites in one firm, 'Y-International' (a pseudonym), an enterprise well known in the industry for being exceedingly masculinist, culturally abrasive and sporting an impressive burnout rate. With many of its employees recruited from the humanities and some even proclaiming to be 'communist', the firm's CSR programme provided staff with an emotional bridge that partially sutured the disconnect between their critical views of business and their practical participation in the enterprise.

THE IDEOLOGY OF CSR AND THE UNHAPPY WORKER

We can now unpack in more detail the various ways that CSR ideologically sutures these widespread anti-corporate values present among the workforce to the world of productivity, thus cultivating consent and reconciliation with the axiomatic principles of business. A central driver of this ideological moment is an interesting trend in contemporary management more generally. One of the more counter-intuitive developments in business organizations has been the appropriation of non-corporate or even anti-business rhetoric to motivate workers. Indeed, there has recently emerged a new discourse of management that is (prima facie at least) as 'anti-management' as the radicals who deride the excesses of accumulation and consumerism. This peculiar co-optation of criticality has been studied by Boltanski and Chiapello (2005). They argue that the radical humanist critique of capitalism popular in the 1960s and culminating with the May 68 revolt in Paris and elsewhere is now a key feature in the parlance of the modern corporation. As employees demanded to express their authentic feelings on the job and no longer accepted their dehumanization, disenchantment and alienation as a matter of course, management responded by evoking the imagery of 'spiritual freedom' to placate the workforce. In other words, the new spirit of business, as opposed to the 'old' Protestant work ethic of mental self-flagellation and the denial of pleasure, has been replaced with an ultra-liberal set of values under the rubric of 'liberation management' and free self-expression. Of course, this was all in the name of saving and extending an exploitative corporate form. To do so, Boltanski and Chiapello suggest, management began to borrow and turn to its own use the very discourse of radicalism that it once deemed dangerously subversive.

And might not CSR and its petition to non-capitalist principles also function as a kind of emotional alibi that inevitably serves to extend unsustainable corporate activity? Might not the discourse of business ethics allow one to taste the 'spirit' of a more moral world while becoming evermore enmeshed in an institutional environment that clashes with our moral values? For those working stakeholders who personally identify with the ethos of sharing, the environment, fair trade and egalitarianism, perhaps CSR helps quell the ethical anxieties that would otherwise arise from our participation in the commercial enterprise. In order to develop this argument further, we propose that there are two important ways that CSR may wed the anti-business values of the working stakeholder with the modern corporation.

AUTHENTICITY

Authenticity has seen a recent revival in the world of work (Fleming, 2009a). With the growing popularity of the aforementioned management approach in which employees both demand and are invited to 'just be themselves' (express what makes them different and unique in the workplace) the concept of authenticity becomes very significant. In relation to marketing and the CSR-branding process, for example, the quest for authentic products and service encounters has become big business (Potter, 2010). The 'authenticity marketing' movement is also popular in which consulting firms and various branding pundits aver that the corporation must avoid looking 'fake', 'superficial' or 'phoney' (Gilmore and Pine, 2007). Online consulting depositories like 'Authentic Business' and 'Authentic Marketing Services' and texts like *The Authentic Brand* (Rosica, 2007) attest to this new trend. As Trosclair (2007) argues in an online blurb regarding the virtues of branding authentically:

> The premise is simple: Today's consumers are 'longing' for authenticity because they find so many fakes and phonies in their lives. If people believe a company, product or service is authentic, they will buy and support it. If they think the company, its products and/or services are inauthentic, the firm is labelled a fake and is headed for failure. (http://suite101.com/article/authentic-marketing-strategy-a49260)

And the same sentiment might be said for the working stakeholder who enters the firm having been immersed in the critical consciousness of a post-Enron world of corporate crisis. In this cultural milieu the employee potentially finds him- or herself at odds with the world of work (Cremin, 2010; Sennett, 1998). Indeed, this tension can also lead to that nagging feeling we are inauthentic (or are not being ourselves) when on the job, and thus hypocritical because we do not 'practise what we preach'. An extended analysis of the exact meaning of inauthenticity and its causes is beyond the scope of this chapter, but most research agrees that it is defined by the feeling of not being true to oneself (Fleming, 2009a), that is to say, the lived contradiction between the personal values that we bring to the enterprise and the emotional and practical demands subsequently placed on us by this institution.

There are a number of examples in the literature to support this reading of CSR as a way of inspiring a sense of authenticity among employees with misgivings about the corporation (Michelli, 2007). Let us briefly discuss an 'ideal' case, that of Google, since it represents an exemplar of how authenticity and business ethics intersect. As is well known, the founders of Google placed much attention on Conway's law, which suggests that the technological systems so vital for flexible and innovative design will tend to reflect the organization's pre-existing structure. Hence the importance of allowing people to be themselves (in ways that are productive of course) and the predominance of the ideology of authenticity in the enterprise. Here we see the discourse of the 'new age' firm in its full glory, as stated on its website regarding the Google philosophy:

> We put great stock in our employees – energetic, passionate people from diverse backgrounds with creative approaches to work, play and life. Our atmosphere may be casual, but as new ideas emerge in a café line, at a team meeting or at the gym, they are traded, tested and put into practice with dizzying speed – and they may be the launch pad for a new project destined for worldwide use. (www.google.com/about/company/philosophy/)

As Vise (2005) has demonstrated, Google already had many of the cultural ingredients that would see a particular type of flexi-techno system emerge: youth, adherence to political autonomy, a do-it-yourself ethic and so forth. Crucial in the impressive array of progressive employment practices is the CSR policy that underpinned the founding of the firm, transforming it into a kind of social movement 'for good'. The Google philosophy relentlessly reminds workers (and users alike) that it intends to design a search engine that rebuffs the heavy and exploitative advertising of rivals such as Yahoo and AOL, as well as the predatory competitive tactics of the giant Microsoft. While this policy was geared to impress customers, Google blurred its customers and employees into one image, following the principle that most IT workers are usually attracted to the firms they purchase products from (and vice versa):

> Engineers who once longed to work for Microsoft came to see it as the Darth Vader of software, the dark force, the one who didn't play fairly. By contrast, Google presented itself as a fresh new enterprise with a halo, the motto Don't Be Evil, and a pair of youthful founders with reputations as nice guys. (Vise, 2005: 96)

In a very similar manner as described by Ross (2004) earlier in relation to Razorfish, perhaps the CSR campaign at Google is geared not only to customers, but to working stakeholders themselves. Again, the typical rationale given by consultants is that this attracts, retains and engages staff – this might be true. But if we place such terms against a broader *political* backdrop of a worry around being authentic (or true to oneself), the integrative aspect of the internally focused CSR project becomes evident. For in reality, Google is a capitalist firm that many of its IT workers realize is anathema to the beloved notions of open sourcing and hacker communism. The charge that it supported China's strict censorship policies, for example, flies in the face of open net-democracy. So, what does the company do to allay any trepidation among its workforce? The answer is *food*. The demographic of the typical Google employee is someone that would buy organic foodstuffs, support issues around bio-diversity and place much importance on a healthy lifestyle: something that sitting in front of a computer all day is not conducive to (the negative association between overwork in the office and being overweight among employees has been explored by Costas, 2010). So Google hired the Grateful Dead chef, Charlie Ayers, to cook healthy meals for the workers. The negative experience of corporate life triggered by fast food and being overweight was short-circuited through this 'responsible employment' practice (also see Cederström (2011) on the importance of the discourse of 'health' in this context).

ENTER THE CORPORATE REBEL

The second way in which this dimension of CSR might culturally integrate the values of the working stakeholder (especially in a climate of anti-business sentiment) is via the discourse of resistance. Of course, resistance has strong connotations of labour fighting the powerful corporation to gain autonomy, fairer working conditions and so forth. We propose that CSR too conveys a level of criticality about the 'greedy corporation', but more in a manner that resonates with Boltanski and Chiapello's (2005) 'new spirit of capitalism' discussed earlier. The themes of anti-exploitation and 'being against the establishment' or 'for the common good' are substituted by the CSR credo, thus redirecting a feeling of recalcitrance in a direction that achieves key business objectives. Think here of the way in which Starbucks has recently attempted to convey a sense of social responsibility among working stakeholders by 'embracing resistance'.

On this count, we remind the reader that the motifs of radicalism such as emancipation, freedom, liberation and anti-authoritarianism are now key features of a new management discourse emerging in the wake of widespread cynicism about the corporate world. Rather than radicalism (in this abbreviated form at least) being barred as dangerous or illegitimate, it now enters the official rhetoric of management as an ally of exploitation. Take this humorous statement by Frank when describing how anti-establishment radicalism and the pro-corporate ethos strangely joined forces to invent 'liberation management':

> Beginning in 1991–1992 (when *Nevermind* ascended the Billboard charts and Tom Peters' *Liberation Management* appeared), American popular culture and corporate culture veered off together on a spree of radical sounding bluster that mirrored the events of the 1960s so closely as to make them seem almost unremarkable in retrospect. Caught up in what appeared to be an unprecedented prosperity driven by the 'revolutionary' forces of globalization and cyber-culture, the nation became obsessed with youth culture and the march of generations … . In business literature, dreams of chaos and ceaseless undulation routed the 1980s dreams of order and 'excellence'. (1998: ix–x)

As also suggested by Brooks in his discussion of Bobos (or the bohemian bourgeoisie), management itself is taking on anarchic ideals, at least in a cardboard cutout fashion:

If you want to find a place where the Age of Aquarius radicalism is in full force, you have to go higher up the corporate ladder into the realm of companies listed on the New York Stock Exchange. Thirty years after Woodstock and all the peace rallies, the people who talk most relentlessly about smashing the status quo and crushing the establishment are management gurus and corporate executives. (2001: 110)

In a similar manner, we argue, many senior human resource executives are now worried about how to deal with the army of nonchalant and sulky Generation-Y employees joining their ranks; here, CSR plays a fundamental role in repackaging this sentiment of dissent in a way that is both manageable and potentially valuable for the firm (inspiring innovation, creativity and so forth) (Fleming, 2009a). Unlike earlier generations, employees today are less willing to suspend their counter-cultural values in the workplace. Moreover, the 'liberal organization' is marked by the transposition of liberalist morals into the sphere of work: life, liberty and happiness are to be found in the formal rituals of the enterprise too and not just on the weekends or when one finally escapes into the leisure industry. Moreover, the pervasive scepticism about the legitimacy of the Anglo-US model of the corporate form must feature in this managerial shift as well. We all know that the modern corporation has suffered a legitimation crisis in relation to its politically regressive impact on the environment, employees in the Third World and so forth (Parker, 2002).

So how does CSR and the working stakeholder fit into this? At a basic level, one is tempted to follow Žižek's (2008) characterization of the 'liberal communist' when he identifies a crucial moment when critics are able to reconcile their putatively anti-establishment ethics with a business-as-usual attitude. Take for example his description of George Soros and Bob Geldof (who, incidentally, is currently planning a £1 billion private equity venture in Africa):

some of them, at least, went to Davos. What increasingly gives a predominant tone to Davos meetings is the group of entrepreneurs, some of whom refer to themselves as 'liberal communists', who no longer accept the opposition between Davos (global capitalism) and Porto Alegre (the new social movements' alternative to global capitalism). Their claim is that we can have the global capitalist cake, i.e. thrive as profitable entrepreneurs, and eat it too, endorse the anti-capitalist causes of social responsibility and ecological concern. (Žižek, 2008: 14)

There is much truth to this. But looking a little closer, a more subtle psychological suturing operation is occurring. Like the question of authenticity mentioned above, CSR provides a medium for people to express their values (that reflect the broader societal concern about the effects of big business) and remain employed in the firm with minimum emotional dissonance. A good example can be found in the theories of Meyerson (2003) as she explores the 'tempered radical' in large US corporations. Meyerson celebrates these everyday 'radicals' who make quiet inroads into corporate domination through micro-ethical campaigns, without rocking the boat too much. God forbid challenging the supremacy of the corporation too stridently. The tempered radical is defined in the following way:

Tempered radicals are people who want to succeed in their organizations yet want to live by their values or identities, even if they are somehow at odds with the dominant culture of their organizations. Tempered radicals want to fit in and they want to retain what makes them different. They want to rock the boat, and they want to stay in it. (Meyerson, 2003: xi)

For all intents and purposes the tempered radical reflects a moment of reconciliation. Through acts of micro-resistance that do little to challenge corporate hegemony in any meaningful manner, workers can nevertheless enjoy a 'feel good' afterglow within an institutional setting that they know is largely unethical. Indeed, the activities of the tempered radical were further framed by Meyerson as employees 'resisting quietly and staying true to one's self, which includes acts that quietly express people's different selves' (2003: 8). Subsequently, the working stakeholder who feels personally uncomfortable in a cutthroat business world is able to – via the discourse of business ethics and CSR – express his or her identities (even if *against the firm*) and continue to work very hard.

CONCLUSIONS

Even though the 'employee as stakeholder' is much discussed in terms of labour rights and standards, the *ideological* function of CSR as an integrative tool requires more investigation. The practitioner literature suggests that CSR is important for attracting 'talent', retaining staff and creating more engaged workers. And this chapter has aimed to extend this investigation in a *critical* manner by suggesting that we need to delve further into the changing cultural makeup of the working stakeholder and societal values more generally. Given that many employees feel that they are often 'not themselves' when at work (a feeling exacerbated with the rising tide of cynicism and disappointment regarding business in a post-Enron and post-crisis corporate landscape), the CSR presence in a firm might operate as a political tool to smooth over the divide between capital and labour, employer and employee. This is especially so when the worker feels deeply at odds with his or her job and the business world more generally. That is to say, when one thinks that the worker is compromising an important part of his or her integrity when participating in the corporation. Here, CSR may help employees 'get by' while in the 'heart of the beast'.

Of course, not all workers feel alienated in their jobs or are cynical about big business. Moreover, not all CSR policies aim to integrate anti-work motifs in order to inspire staff. But evidence has suggested a broader shift with respect to 'liberation management' and the 'new spirit of capitalism' that seems to resonate with the culture of criticism that is pervasive today. The working stakeholders today demand more from their places of employment, to express their personal values and political views that are often contrary to the world of unbridled free enterprise. And in the extreme case, firms in controversial industries may rely upon CSR to insulate employees from the ethical anxieties they might experience. Because of the novelty of this research area, the ideas posited in this chapter have largely been built from theorizing and evidence from other studies. So, more direct empirical research is required to corroborate (or disprove) these claims. This could be done by analysing the way CSR features in the answers to the question: so if you hate capitalism, how do you cope with working here?

The final aspect of this new perspective concerning CSR at work pertains to its more predatory nature (see Hanlon and Fleming (2009) for an initial analysis in this regard). As we have seen above, pertaining to the blending of the 'lifestyle' human resource approach ('just be yourself') with the utility of the CSR discourse as an ameliorative buffer, the personal becomes an important commercial resource. Indeed, much of the practitioner literature argues that CSR campaigns are particularly engaging if initiated by workers themselves. This appeal to self-authored projects could be a way where firms actively capture and enclose innovations generated by workers as they seek solutions beyond the confines of commercialism. For example, a CSR project might serve as a 'key' for unlocking the personal skills, aptitudes and creativity of the worker. This is what Land and Taylor (2010) found in their study of an ethical clothing company trading in organic (but high-priced) products. In order to give the job and products a veneer of authenticity, it captured the personal values and anti-business ethos of its employees (related to tattoos, surfing, skating, etc.) and fed them back into the branding process. As the authors point out:

> The company manufactured the Ethico brand by producing catalogues, a website, and other marketing communications. In order to establish the authenticity of the brand, this immaterial labour of brand management drew upon the recreational activities of employees. This inscription of employees' lives into the brand created the economic value of the company's products, situating their 'lives' as a form of productive labour or 'work'. (Land and Taylor, 2010: 408).

In other words, CSR might be conceptualized not only as a cultural suture, but also as an instrumental foray into the social aptitudes of the workforce. Indeed, Blowfield and Murray's argument supports this when they suggest that CSR unlocks the value-adding skills of the worker: 'individual discretion allows personnel to introduce their values into corporate responsibility policies, whether through officially sanctioned actions, the unintended consequences of an individual resolving a problem by drawing on personal beliefs, or an individual's entrepreneurship in bringing values into the workplace' (2008: 110). Again, more empirical research is required to clarify the exact nature of this kind of corporate capture of the personal among working stakeholders and its connection to productivity (or otherwise). Another way of putting it might be to suggest that CSR is not only the corporate commodification of the very crisis it precipitated, but also the valorization of a personal crisis at the psychic level of the workers' inescapable sense of alienation. In addition to CSR being an ideological smokescreen to deepen capitalism and psychologically bind the worker to the corporation, it may also be an instrument for capitalizing on its own crisis and prospecting new forms of value created by consumers, workers and their respective social awareness. It is this facet of CSR that we turn to next.

One of the more interesting websites documenting the wide range of corporate scandals of recent years is hosted by Wikipedia. It lists each firm's industry and the incident that sparked an investigation, prosecution or allegation of unlawfulness. Unsurprisingly, the list is long and extensive – and all of the usual suspects are present including banks, airlines, pharmaceutical multinationals, security firms and petroleum companies. But other, less known firms also appear, those that operate outside the limelight of consumer visibility including transportation firms, health and safety agencies and animal-testing laboratories. The interminable inventory of corrupt firms (defined here in the conventional sense of breeching some law or regulation pertaining to the nature of the enterprise's business activity – bribery, health and safety, etc.) is fascinating not because it reveals in a somewhat sensationalist manner the bad behaviour of a large group of corporations. What we find interesting is that if one visits the official websites of these organizations, the most prominent feature is the self-proclaimed commitment to business ethics and social responsibility. Organizations that have compromised the safety of consumers, killed employees through lax health and safety practices, polluted large parts of the environment, and devastated local communities in search of lucrative raw materials are at the leading edge of CSR discourse and practice today.

When it comes to the websites, all manner of ethical activities are expounded from employee rights to environmental protection and preservation. These commitments are conveyed with vivid, colourful tones that frequently involve images of rainforests, hands embracing a globe and smiling children of African descent playing in lush green fields. Judging from the social accounting reports and independent monitoring, genuine resources are expended on responsibility activities beyond the core business. But is this all simply just smoke and mirrors? (Researchers have even hinted (Jones and Pollitt, 2002) that there is probably a correlation between the extent and magnitude of a firm's CSR campaign and the size and magnitude of its unethical undertakings!) And what is the political relationship between the tendency towards unsocial (or even unlawful) activities and a business's proclamations about ethics? There are plenty of critics who dismiss the ethical blustering of Shell, BAE Systems and Tesco as blatant window dressing, but what is the connection between the way capitalism functions today and what we earlier termed a 'discourse of the social'?

We all know the official replies from CEOs and boards of directors when they are accused of being hypocrites. And such responses are emblematic of the attempt to draw attention away from the axiomatic principles of business that are inherently contrary to the proclamations of even the most rudimentary CSR objectives. It reads something like this: 'We know that the company has had problems in the past and this is exactly why we have a CSR policy, to tackle these potential weaknesses and provide guidelines for future best practice.' Of course, this official rationale aims (1) to condone the hypocritical jam caused when a CSR policy sits alongside patently amoral business ventures, (2) to draw attention away from the intrinsic incompatibility of business *ethics* and business *itself*, and (3) to portray the company as something of a 'battler' which might fail once in a while, but ultimately has its heart in the right place (we might call this attempt to glean kudos from failure the 'George W. Bush syndrome'). Important here is the way in which many corporations always seem to be lagging behind their CSR objectives, always trying to catch up, to the point where we must wonder if there ever will (*or can*) be an organization that is not contravening the basic ethical expectations of society.

In this chapter, we want to build upon the arguments made in the book so far by attempting to develop a more nuanced and *critical* understanding of what Banerjee (2008) has called a 'political economy of CSR'. This is necessary since we must now move to the societal level and understand CSR as something that develops alongside permutations in neo-capitalism itself. And 'critical' in the sense that we do not take the discourse and practice of 'business of ethics' at face value but inscribe them within a larger structural economy of capitalism in crisis. We will survey the existing approaches available in the literature, and then extend them to include a new and less obvious understanding of CSR.

The first two perspectives we discuss are popular in the critical literature explicating CSR, but derive from substantially different theoretical grounds. The first treats CSR as a kind of *panacea* that may one day cure the ills of corporate capitalism if applied ardently. The second perspective to be explored, and one that we are more sympathetic to, views CSR as an instance of *propaganda*. The corporation was intentionally designed to adhere to the myopic search for profits, and the notion that it might also be something that delivers social goods beyond this remit (especially in controversial sectors of the economy such as the petroleum and arms industries) is simply a case of 'missing the forest for the trees'.

The third approach that we want to extend substantially builds on the insights of the propaganda perspective, and we think it harbours a good deal of insight for future analysis. It sees CSR as a kind of *parasitical* foray into the community, counter-corporate social movements and the widespread feeling of dissatisfaction prevalent today. What do we mean by this? Building on the work of Hanlon (2007) and Hanlon and Fleming (2009), it could be argued that CSR might represent not only a passive 'reaction' to claims of ethical impropriety (a kind of smokescreen), but also a more predatory excursion into the non-corporate social world (volunteer groups, mutual aid collectives, counter-consumption initiatives), capturing ideas and ways of life in order to make money from them. Extending the political view of CSR that sees it as mere corporate propaganda, we argue that it is also a way that organizations prospect for new ideas, legitimacy and ultimately profit.

To make these arguments the chapter will first establish a general backdrop regarding the nature of the firm that we feel any critical analysis of CSR must start with. This involves two important conceptual steps: the first sketches out the datum of the corporation as a utility-maximizing institutional form first and foremost (all other considerations within its sphere are an afterthought). The second step abstracts from the individual firm level to the general systemic plane, allowing us to analyse the multinational capitalist landscape as an interconnected system that by and large follows a number of elementary economic codes (none of which are particularly conducive to sustainability, ethics or community). Then we discuss the three critical approaches to

CSR noted above. Our extension of these critical theories regarding the corporate/ethics interface via our 'CSR as parasite' framework is then outlined at length using a number of examples. We conclude by considering the future role that a critical political economy of CSR might play in the scholarly community and beyond.

BACK TO REALITY: THE 'NATURE' OF THE FIRM

One has only to run an eye quickly down the 'corporate scandals' list mentioned above to find simple examples of the essential disconnect between the unstated code of business and the ethical expectations we might hold. Take for example BP, one of the firms held responsible for one of the largest oil spills in the history of the industry. When the 'Deepwater Horizon' oil rig exploded during a methane gas leak in 2010 (killing a number of workers), the damage was so severe that oil gushed into the sea for three months, with some estimates putting the flow as high as 100,000 barrels a day.

What makes this environmental, social and economic catastrophe so depressing is not that it obviously could have been prevented (like most human-made disasters), but that one of the firms held accountable had invested a huge amount of resources crafting a 'green friendly' image. Of course, the 2010 oil spill is not the only dubious incident with which the company has been associated. In 1965, 13 men died when the Sea Gem rig collapsed off the coast of England. The Prudhoe Bay spill in Alaska in 2006 leaked 212,252 gallons into the pristine waters of the North Slope. The company has also been charged with manipulating propane prices (resulting in a US$125,000 civil settlement) and oil prices; supporting Columbian paramilitaries to subdue locals protesting about the obtrusive placement of an oil pipeline (local farmers consequently won a multimillion-pound settlement); criticized for its activities around the infamous Baku–Tbilisi–Ceyhan pipeline given some well-evidenced human rights, health and safety and environmental concerns; involved in questionable political donations in the United States; supported strident pro-oil lobby groups; and has large investments in Russia (a country that has consistently violated the Energy Charter Treaty). Fast-forwarding to the most recent incident – the oil spill in the Gulf of Mexico – a BP report blamed poor management decisions and negligent monitoring of safety tests by workers. Another report issued by the Oil Spill Commission claimed that management was compromised by a 'rush to completion' mentality, which was exacerbated by a lax culture of safety on the rig.

Running alongside all of this is BP's comprehensive CSR policy. A visit to the company's website finds a myriad of statements about the CSR friendliness of the firm, including sustainability initiatives, alternative energy investments, health and safety programmes, human rights campaigns, etc. But nothing could have been more surprising – and some would say comical – regarding this bold CSR stance than the attempted rebranding of the firm a few years back. The iconic green shield of yesteryear was replaced with a green and yellow sun-like flower, and BP Amoco even claimed that BP now also stood for 'Beyond Petroleum'. Claims of hypocrisy were quick to follow. Some argued that the continuing massive oil spills (like the one mentioned above) were enough to dismiss the idea once and for all that the firm had any commitment to the environment beyond the profit motive. The claim that the company was investing in bio-fuels and alternative energy sources has been received with similar scepticism, especially given that a large majority of its prospecting activity continued to be in fossil-based fuels.

Given these claims of hypocrisy, BP now define its 'Beyond Petroleum' brand in the following somewhat embarrassing way on their CSR webpage: 'Beyond petroleum' is shorthand for what we do: exploring, developing and producing more fossil fuel resources to meet growing demand ...' Fascinating. Perhaps they now mean 'beyond' in a very literal sense, speeding up the demise of its core business resource through rampant overuse! For many firms who cannot afford to be so brazenly cynical, however, CSR is about casting its business model in a manner that makes it appear congruent with the ethical norms and expectations we would expect from, say, a visitor in our home or a neighbour. Hence the charge of hypocrisy when it consistently fails to abide by its own ethical declarations. But while the hypocrisy (and cynicism) is fairly obvious to most, the way we make socio-economic sense of such CSR tactics is important. What are the drivers, political contours and overall nature of this sudden foray of a large multinational into the realm of ethics?

CAPITALIST REALISM

To be critical of CSR is to observe that all is not what it seems (surface appearances belying a more ruthless reality principle) and to set the discourse of ethics within the power relations of late capitalism. That is to say, before we can really understand 'the truth' of CSR we must grasp the social and institutional logic of the for-profit firm, something we have iterated throughout the book. BP, like any multinational firm of its kind, is driven mainly by profits: that is its overarching *raison d'être*. Its fundamental operating principle is to make money for its owners and this is its driving criteria for success. In an unsustainable industry like this one and many others, therefore, the firm's very existence is at odds with some key ethics criteria relating to the environment and so forth. Moreover, even if it was not producing oil, a firm motivated purely by the pursuit of profits and higher returns to shareholders always runs the risk of cutting corners or what was euphemistically termed by the Oil Spill Commission in its report on the Gulf of Mexico crisis as a 'rush to completion' mentality. The quest for profits, control and returns on investments frequently rubs up against the principles of socially ethical behaviour. Indeed, who can forget the startling Ford Pinto case in which a defective automobile causing fatalities across the United States was left on the road given that it made perfect business sense to do so? (Ford managers did what every manager is trained to do in business school – a cost/benefit analysis – and it was calculated to be less expensive to pay litigation to the families of future dead consumers than to recall and modify the automobile; see Gioia, 1992.)

The first step, therefore, in developing a truly critical (or in our minds, *realistic*) political economy of the CSR is to place such initiatives in the context of an overwhelming institutional logic of capitalist expansion, crisis and control. And this context frequently means that institutions will by nature run up against some basic ethical objections. Another way to think about it would be to imagine a company like Tesco or whatever *taking CSR seriously*, and actually integrating those socio-political aspirations into the very logic of the business. We venture that if a firm did this, it would simply cease to exist. It is not that Shell or Tesco *will not* take CSR seriously, but simply *cannot* (e.g. BP would not exist in the low carbon future it celebrates in its CSR campaign). This kind of reasoning provides a more sober understanding of the political economy of the firm today.

Moreover, this mode of analysis has little to do with 'unethical' people, since we are analysing an institutional logic that in a Frankensteinian-like fashion has run out of control. One of the reasons why it is often difficult to bring the analysis to this point in popular and academic discussions about capitalism is the sheer embeddedness of what we might call the ideology of the corporation: if we did not have this institutional model, the rationale goes, then society would fall apart (we would have no roads, gas, electricity, DVDs, etc.). But we now really need to turn this kind of thinking around by demonstrating that it is *because* we have the corporation that the world is falling apart (it is because of the corporation, for example, that cheap generic drugs that could cure millions of African children of life-threatening diseases do not get shipped to where they are needed). Again, one might retort, but those drugs would have never been developed in the first place if not for private enterprise! Wrong. Perelman (2002) shows that the large majority of so-called corporate innovations are actually derived from publically funded or volunteer sources (public health care, universities and so forth). He calls this the corporate confiscation of creativity (usually through intellectual property law). In this sense, then, the corporate form is an extreme and unprecedented institutional matrix, and ought never to be equated with the norm (no matter how much the reference point for understanding 'the norm' is manipulated by ideology).

CSR AND THE FETISH OF CAPITAL

A second and crucial step for developing a critical political economy of CSR is to raise the analysis to the structural and more abstract level. This involves a premeditated circumspection focusing on individual firms that stand out for their hypocritical flirtation with CSR or who are implicated in some sordid scandal. A certain degree of abstraction is required to avoid what we might call the 'fetish of capital' (Marx used the notion of 'commodity fetish' to describe the perception of the commodity that sees it as the author of its own value and thus hiding the social structures that really brought it into existence – social labour). What do we mean by this in relation to our current study? To begin with, and returning to the arguments sustained in Chapter 1, we can always find an example of a business enterprise that is simultaneously ethical and profitable. These companies (the Body Shop or Whole Foods are often cited here) are then used to suggest that capitalism may potentially become an ethical totality, a rationality which we feel is clearly refuted by any informed understanding of the global market system. But another problem arises too when we become bogged down in individual cases, especially with firms like BP that are frequently rebuked for hypocrisy. An analogy can be found in the popular (and sometimes scholarly) treatment of corporate corruption. When yet another case of corporate fraud, laundering, bribery or pilfering is in the newspapers, we realize that this company has no doubt 'broken the rules' and for whatever reason delved into the seedy world of corporate crime. The Enron and WorldCom cases are salient here, as are the more recent examples of Siemens and BAE Systems. In isolating these firms as wrongdoers, a certain ideological trick can potentially emerge that gives the broader political economy an unwarranted degree of legitimacy (see Fleming and Zyglidopoulos, 2009).

And is there not a similar danger of perpetuating this 'fetish of capital' when we investigate the alleged business ethics transgressions vis-à-vis the CSR policies of various firms? For example, when exploring the possibility that a petroleum enterprise might be practising double standards in relation to its business ethics claims, it is easy to identify how it fails to live up to its own hype. And mainstream corporate ideology itself, as we mentioned earlier, has a robust response to this credibility gap between its wrought brand image and the murky reality in some faraway land or the lax safety protocols on semi-submergible rigs far out to sea. But as with the scholarship on corporate corruption, it would be tempting to indict BP for breaking the rules of the game. However, as Banerjee rightly points out in this regard:

> Focusing on the individual corporation as the unit of analysis can only produce limited results and serves to create an organization enclosure around corporate social responsibility. For any radical revision to occur, a more critical approach to organization theory is required and new questions need to be raised not only about the ecological and social sustainability about business corporations but the political economy itself. (2007: 73)

It is these two conceptual steps that we must take to proceed building a tenable critical political economy of CSR. The first places the discourse of CSR in the context of a powerful institutional logic (economic growth, control, profits, return on investment) that inherently takes priority over other competing social logics. Indeed, if a good number of our corporations sincerely practised CSR as they preach it, then they would cease to exist since they could not survive. And second, we must abstract away from single-firm analyses to the systemic level of multinational capitalism itself. Let us now explore three critical political economy theories of CSR that might be of use, the last of which we develop afresh from the most recent political investigations regarding the emergent nature of contemporary capitalism.

CSR: PANACEA, PROPAGANDA OR PARASITE?

Three perspectives appear to be salient when linking the discourse and practice of CSR to the general principles of the multinational capitalist economy in the literature. They might be termed CSR as *panacea*, *propaganda* or *parasite*. Let us explore each now in turn.

CSR AS PANACEA

There is a growing body of literature in the CSR field that is dissatisfied with the way in which it has become largely co-opted by the area of strategic management and by an instrumental concern regarding its value-added properties. This approach aims to rediscover the critical kernel of CSR that has been distorted or stripped by its appropriation by economic instrumental interests. How can CSR repoliticize late capitalism and how might it be deployed in corporate practice to change the way business and society interact so that we can finally arrive at a just and democratic solution? If the corporation and free market are not to run amok and destroy society and themselves, then a fuller commitment to CSR-associated concepts must be practised so that the unbridled features of the multinational economy can be reined in.

We have already discussed one sub-sector of this when we critically analysed 'new corporate citizenship' theory in Chapter 2. We can recall that this area of research was concerned with the receding nation-state and the vacuum that results in the protection and delivery of social, political and citizenship rights (Matten and Crane, 2005). Indeed, following the mutation of multinational capital and the widening influence of neo-liberal free market ideology, it has become incumbent on the firm to provide citizenship needs in areas outside of the traditional business model, especially given that these firms now constitute a hegemonic force in the new global order (Scherer and Palazzo, 2007).

According to this argument, of course, much work ought to be done to reform the nature of the firm, but this can be achieved, thereby allowing the MNC to come to the rescue and act as a political institutional force for 'good'. We will not repeat the serious doubts we have about this understanding of CSR, the corporation and the notion of corporate citizenship. Suffice to say that the corporation always was a political actor, and the state is now more prevalent in society than it ever has been. Following Harney (2009), it would be more accurate to say that the state has been reconfigured into an *extreme* neo-liberal entity to support the interests of business rather than those of 'the 99 per cent'. Moreover, this approach appears to be labouring under the questionable idea that the transnational firm might be able to fashion itself into an institutional force which is contrary to its inherent purpose. (Besides the ideological fantasy that celebrated predatory capitalism, Friedman (1970) was largely correct about what the nature of the firm entailed.)

Other research has tried to use CSR to politicize the enterprise in a progressive manner by using political science/theory concepts. The work of Scherer and Palazzo (2007; 2010), for example, draws upon a Habermasian theoretical framework in order to politicize organizations and generate new modalities of communication within and between organizations. They too suggest that CSR scholarship tends to pander to the instrumental concerns of the corporation, which diminishes its criticality (also see Marens, 2010). But again, the trouble begins with how realistic the normative part of the argument is. For them, the utilization of a more youthful Habermasian approach to render the firm accountable to its various stakeholders is too utopian. They therefore opt for the later Habermas or 'Habermas$_2$' and his notion of deliberative democracy as the panacea that will reform liberal capitalist societies. As opposed to liberal democratic accountability of the corporation, Habermas's concept of deliberative democracy integrates the social fabric of the firm into civil society, creating a more politically accountable managerial mentality. As Scherer and Palazzo argue:

> We propose a deliberative concept of CSR that mirrors the discursive link between civil society and the state. This concept aims at the democratic integration of the corporate use of power, especially in the transnational context of incomplete legal and moral regulation. Our interpretation of CSR shifts the focus from an analysis of corporate reaction to stakeholder pressure to an analysis of the corporation's role in the overarching processes of (national and transnational) public will formation and these processes' contribution to solving global environmental and social challenges. Corporate responsibilities are analyzed as resulting from the corporation's embeddedness in a context of changing societal institutions ... and the corporation is understood as a political actor. (2007: 1107)

Again, this perspective is laudable but still trades in a misunderstanding about the nature of capitalism and the corporation, as well as its relationship to democracy. The perspective continues to adhere to the liberal political assumption that the corporation might be a vehicle for free participatory democracy and that the otherwise highly undemocratic structure of business might be transformed by becoming re-embedded in the societal functions once conducted by governments. The problem is two-fold yet again; first, the state has not disappeared but is stronger now than ever, with a role of setting the rules and utilizing force to maintain an extreme brand of capitalism. This is why commentators often use the phrase 'capitalist state' to connote the thoroughgoing capture of this institution (see Hardt and Negri, 2009). And second, if this deliberative democratic approach was truly instigated – and clearly it would take a social revolution to do that – then we would no longer be dealing with the capitalist enterprise, but with a kind of socialist post-profit paradigm. But one cannot have capitalism and deliberative democracy simultaneously since they cancel each other out given the mutually exclusive institutional logics that, in essence, constitute them.

CSR AS PROPAGANDA

A more promising line of enquiry for placing CSR in the context of global capitalism might be found in the thoroughgoing criticism that defines it as a smokescreen to allow an unsustainable business model to appear sustainable. As the terminology indicates, this method of analysis is interested in the contradictions, disconnections and tensions between the ideological expression of the so-called *ethical firm* and its underlying reliance on economic exploitation, control and anti-social practices. Moreover, it is built squarely on the capitalist realism precept that we outlined above. Capitalism and its institutional forms involve certain axiomatic principles that are well understood: anything that might detract from a return on investment and economic efficiency will not survive in the corporate realm. This is why in big corporations CSR must always be justified with a 'business case'. The key question in the boardroom when the case is pitched is: *How will CSR make us money (either in the long run or short term) or at least explain how it will not be a revenue drain?*

Again it is at the systemic level that the propaganda model is most convincing because it is here we gain the best view of the unsustainable nature of the totality of global capital. The complex financial sector is prone to crisis and deeply unstable; the institutional momentum of vested interests could not even agree to a modest reduction in spiralling greenhouse gases, as the failure of the Copenhagen Climate Summit revealed (and what Greenpeace International Executive Director Kumi Naidoo called a 'failure of epic proportions' regarding the 2012 Rio+20 Earth Summit). As we write, energy agencies are debating who will be first to plunder the fossil fuel reserves soon to be exposed once the polar ice caps have melted sufficiently from global warming. While we can always find isolated cases of ethicality within the totality – something that perhaps functions in the same fetishistic manner that we discussed above in relation to the 'fetish of capital' – it is at the global level that the true extent of the systemic crisis is disclosed.

Claims that firms might adhere to a 'triple bottom line', sustainable business practices, and all other manner of CSR interventions in the context of an unrelenting global capital inevitably appear rather flaccid and even disingenuous. In this sense, CSR might be considered more a public relations gimmick. Banerjee (2007) demonstrates this powerfully with a startling example when he cites the CSR policy of a well-known firm. It claimed to adhere to the codes of:

Respect:	We will foster mutual respect with communities and stakeholders who are affected by our operations
Integrity:	We will examine the impacts, positive and negative, of our business on the environment, and on society, and will integrate human, health, social and environmental considerations into our internal management and value system
Communication:	We will strive to foster understanding and support our stakeholders and communities, as well as measure and communicate our performance. (Cited in Banerjee, 2007: 63)

Of course, the firm is Enron. The point is that CSR is often so removed from the business-as-usual reality of global capitalism that it is difficult to take many of the declarations around social responsibility very seriously. As Roberts nicely puts it:

> My fear is that all this talk of ethics is just that – talk; new forms of corporate self-presentation that have no reference to or influence on what is practiced in the name of the corporation, beyond those associated with good public relations. In this form, corporate social responsibility is cheap and easy; a sort of prosthesis, readily attached to the corporate body, that repairs its appearance but in no way changes its actual conduct. (2003: 250)

The way in which the propaganda of CSR functions will differ in each business observed. But we can identify two important elements. The first consists of *dissimulation*. This is where a CSR policy is geared towards covering up or softening a core business practice in the firm. Take for example the way in which airlines claim to be taking a responsible stance towards the reduction of greenhouse gases through carbon offsetting (also see Böhm and Dabhi, 2009). The image of a green and environmentally friendly firm functions to obscure its underlying operating principle that is blatantly unsustainable. The question of consumer consciousness is interesting in this context because we all know that the image is false and we can easily see through the CSR discourse at this level. But, as Žižek (1989) argues, regarding the way ideology functions today in the context of 'enlightened false consciousness', it is not our direct beliefs that are ideologically controlled but the gap between what we believe to be true and the truth of our actions. We know very well that when we book yet another budget airline ticket online that the environmentally friendly messages are but a silly marketing ploy. We know that the CSR discourse is untrue, *but we act as if it is true*. We know that the large supermarket we frequent is exploitative to its underpaid suppliers (who in turn are forced to damage the environment to make a living), but with the help of a few well-placed 'we are helping the environment' posters above the endless bank of deep-freezers, we act *as if* we do not know.

The second way that CSR might function as propaganda is through *detraction* – to draw attention away from the more damaging features of a firm. Detraction, we would suggest, is a key feature of CSR from this perspective, simply because it is so difficult to directly legitimate some of the nastier elements of the corporate world presently. With the rise of a pervasive (if only latent) critical awareness in popular culture, firms that are unable to candidly justify their activities (or even their existence in the case of tobacco companies) require a more diversionary stratagem. For tobacco companies, the question is about bio-diversity (and not the thousands of consumers killed by the health-damaging effects of their products). For clothing firms, it is about retail-store employee rights (and not the exploitative value chains that stretch around the world to some of the most poorest countries in the Global South). For arms and security companies, it is about philanthropy (and not the thousands of torture victims who are on the receiving end of their products in some long-forgotten prison cell). And the list goes on.

The propaganda approach is very useful for critically linking CSR to the global violence of corporate capitalism – that is, for developing a critical political economy of CSR. But if all of this talk is merely window dressing, simply false verbiage that no one really believes in, then why do firms go to such lengths to create the impression that capitalism might have an ethical side? One weakness with assuming that CSR is simply an ideological reaction to external pressures (of the state, the consumer and so forth) is that it tends to equate it with a certain degree of passivity. Indeed, we now need to place CSR initiatives within the context of a proactive mode of capitalism, whereby new sources of legitimacy and value are actively sought outside the traditional realm of business. This often entails firms parasitically prospecting not only conventionally non-business chains of social value, but also social movements that have arisen to counter the negative effects of those selfsame firms (which is, in effect, capitalism capitalizing on its own crisis). Social criticism needs to take this development more seriously than the propaganda view, as CSR is now an important predatory arm of this neo-corporate tendency.

CSR AS PARASITE

The conventional drivers of CSR are often seen to be pressures from consumers, workers, NGOs and the state. The result is usually the vast machinery of corporate branding, reputation management and colourful social accounting reports that we have discussed above. However, according to Hanlon (2007), Shamir (2008) and Hanlon and Fleming (2009), CSR might be seen not only as a useless piece of ideology that is designed to hide the inconvenient truth, but as something even more sinister: a predatory extension of corporate power under the crisis conditions of late capitalism. This perspective positions CSR in the context of a changing capitalist social structure of accumulation, in which the Fordist social compact on the 1970s between capital, labour and the state breaks down and a new cartography of corporate power is born – that of post-Fordism in which the boundaries between the corporation and the state, labour and life, work and non-work become increasingly blurred (Aglietta, 2000). As a result, as Hanlon and Fleming suggest:

> more and more areas of social life are opened up to the market place, e.g. education, health, childcare, care for the elderly, biodiversity, genes, etc. It is within this heightened exposure of the social processes that legitimacy must be considered. (2009: 948)

With the failure (in terms of diminishing returns for capital) of the tripartite Fordist compact between labour, the state, and capital, not only does the corporation become international to source cheaper labour and extend markets, but the logic of capitalism becomes more deeply embedded in society as the state reconfigures into a neo-liberal form (also see Shamir, 2008). It might appear that the concomitant privatization, commercialization and the deepening of markets precipitate the retraction of the state from social life (and up to a point this is true), but also it is more accurate to see this as a reconstitution: so-called free markets need a strong state, but also a neo-liberal one that is primarily an enforcer of the corporate hegemony (Stiglitz, 2010). As a result, this:

> is where CSR, HRM, and ethical marketing emerged to fill the void. If one accepts them then corporations will be responsible (no need to regulate or to task the state with tasks); HRM will ensure that the corporation will look after the individual employee who works hard so we do not need collective solutions; ethical marketing means that our consumption, wants, desires, dreams are safe in the hands of our long term partner – the corporation. (Hanlon and Fleming, 2009: 944)

But this shift simultaneously gives rise to another transformation, the increasing trend of seeing more and more areas of previously non-commodified and non-commercialized spheres of life become objects of capitalist valorization. This is what some have called 'bio-power' (Foucault, 2008) in which life itself (or *bios*) – lifestyle, tastes, the body, sexual relations and underground trends of social innovation occurring outside the dictates of the business life – is opened up to commercial capture and profit-seeking activity (Hardt and Negri, 2009; Rose, 2007).

One only has to glance at the many popular business books to see the bio-political firm at work – whereby it prospects and captures non-commercial sociality and sells it back to its creators for a profit. This is the basic business model of much academic publishing and web-based businesses like Google and Facebook. Another recent exemplar is Tapscott and Williams' (2008) international bestseller *Wikinomics*. They argue that a new trend in capitalism is the growing importance of collaboration, open source innovation, peering and sharing on a major scale. Many innovations occurring in business are originally sourced from outside the strictures of private property – including intellectual property – as consumers, amateurs and enthusiasts attempt to invent creative solutions and novel connections. Like the website that we mentioned in the opening pages of this chapter, modern culture is said to increasingly resemble Wikipedia, in which no one owns anything, producers collaborate and social value is derived from more communist principles. For Tapscott and Williams (2008), all of this (ironically) represents a great opportunity to make money out of the efforts of others. This example pertains to the exploitation of customer know-how, especially in relation to creative goods such as gaming platforms:

> For individuals and small businesses, the creative and entrepreneurial opportunities to build on these modern-day infrastructures have never been greater. By tapping open platforms you can leverage world-class infrastructures for a fraction of the cost of developing them yourself. (Tapscott and Williams, 2008: 147)

For Hanlon (2007) and Hanlon and Fleming (2009) this parasitical and even predatory extension of market reason into the social sphere might also be one way that CSR operates. Hanlon (2007) considers the proclamations from writers propounding the business case for CSR in relation to its benefits for corporate innovation:

> this [CSR] spending may well be a source of growth, since many of today's most exciting opportunities lie in the controversial areas such as gene therapy, the private provision of pensions, and products and services targeted at low income consumers in poor countries. These opportunities are large and mostly untapped, and many companies want to open them up. (Cogman and Oppenheim, 2002: 1)

In a similar vein, the *McKinsey Quarterly* has recently suggested that the next big markets for corporations are based in the developing world, new technologies, especially bio-technologies, and through privatizing the welfare states of the major economies (Cogman and Oppenheim 2002; Cook, 2008; Davis, 2005). Hanlon (2007) argues that in an attempt to open up these markets, the corporation have to be seen to be as legitimate, ethical and responsible. In effect, CSR is an instrument for capital to commodify its own crisis. Since it extends the critical view of CSR by placing it within a proactive political economy of the firm, let us unpack its dimensions (with examples) in a more thorough manner.

COMMODIFYING THE CRISIS

The emergence of bio-political forms of control renders redundant the old divisions between capital and labour, work and non-work, and production and reproduction as the 'society of control' penetrates the totality of community relations. As we have argued above, CSR is a crucial element to this process. This conceptualization of CSR is a far cry from the view that it represents: (1) a corporate world finally finding its ethical compass, reining in its more excessive and damaging elements to come into line with the values of society; or (2) an easily dismissed piece of reactive corporate ideology. As Hanlon notes:

> CSR represents a further embedding of capitalist social relations and a deeper opening up of social life to the dictates of the marketplace ... CSR is not a driving force for change but the result of a shift from a Fordist to a post-Fordist regime of accumulation at the heart of which is both an expansion and a deepening of wage relations. (2007: 157)

What makes this aspect of CSR more serious and perhaps even perverse is that it represents the firm seeing an opportunity to make money apropos its own crisis or dysfunctional externalities. What do we mean by this? If the raw material of CSR was once born out of a critical view of the negative effects that large corporations have on the social, economic and natural life of the planet, then its co-optation as an official discourse of capitalism represents something of a tragedy (since it then becomes merely an empty gesture designed to dissimulate or deflect attention away from the ills caused by the corporate form). However, when this ideological appropriation then becomes a vehicle to capitalize on social initiatives designed to counter the damaging consequences of corporate hegemony, we move from tragedy to perversity. Let us look at just a few of the ways that this parasitical strategy of CSR functions in today's society.

BRANDING AND CONSUMPTION

A typical way CSR endeavours to gain some kudos and added value from social movements that have sprung up to deal with the unfair outcomes of corporate hegemony is through brand appropriation. The production of environmentally friendly and organic goods has been a growing industry as consumption patterns become sensitized to environmental degradation. But the foray of large and otherwise exploitative firms into the sphere of green and equitable products has always been a major concern. From a corporate perspective, the idea is to glean some much needed legitimacy and positive association for an otherwise neutral or even negative brand if the company is able to place one of its products in the organic or environmentally friendly section of the supermarket.

There are many examples of this occurring, some of which we have already touched upon, but let us take an obvious one, namely fair trade. Crane and Matten define fair trade as a system aimed at offering the 'most disadvantaged producers in developing countries the opportunity to move out of poverty through creating market access under beneficial rather than exploitative terms. The objective is to empower producers to develop their open businesses and wider communities through international trade' (2010: 424). In relation to coffee and other such goods, fair trade might be seen as a step forward given the gross exploitation perpetuated by large multinational food companies.

Enter Nestlé. With fair trade sales close to US$4.08 billion in 2008, it made economic sense for Nestlé to get in on the action. The company's excursion into fair trade with its coffee brand Partners' Blend was considered to be an attempt to cash in on the value chains created by a social movement directly opposed to the core business model of firms like, well, Nestlé. With fair trade certification, it now was able to place this product in the 'ethical section' of the supermarket and have its brand exposed alongside other, less-cynical fair trade companies. Meanwhile, for the rest of its product line, it was business as usual, involving highly exploitative supplier chains that led to environmentally destructive farming techniques and exploited producers. Of course, the Fair Trade Foundation was caught between a rock and a hard place. It could not deny Nestlé certification since it met the rigorous criteria. Then again, it was obviously ludicrous to allow Nestlé to become associated with fair trade in light of its otherwise questionable trading practices (Crane and Matten, 2010).

SOCIAL ENTREPRENEURSHIP

Another way in which CSR might be considered a vehicle to capture value outside of the traditional operating mechanisms of the firm is through social entrepreneurship or the social entrepreneur. This refers to those activities initiated by an employee or some other actor in or around the corporation to surface and harness opportunities for ethical business practices (Elkington and Hartigan, 2008). The idea is that some individuals – driven by personal values regarding the ethicality of their organizational surroundings – may be entrepreneurial by spotting an interventional opportunity that could improve business and society.

There are two aspects of social entrepreneurship and its intersection with CSR that we might consider to represent a kind of extra-corporate capture of the social in the manner that we have described above. The first concerns that which occurs *inside* the firm. We have already touched on this dimension of capture at the end of Chapter 4 when we discussed how CSR might be more than just an instrument to meld the disengaged attitudes of employees with their work, but also a pathway into their much needed social competence – especially in the context of cognitive labour where discretion, virtuosity and social aptitude are key skills required by the worker in the post-Fordist firm. Indeed, recall that one of the main justifications for endorsing employee-led CSR initiatives is to allow employees to express themselves, but more importantly, to tap the social competencies of workers that the corporation finds difficult to yield from the work-task alone. As Blowfield and Murray noted, 'individual discretion allows personnel to introduce their values into corporate responsibility policies, whether through officially sanctioned actions, the unintended consequences of an individual resolving a problem by drawing people beliefs, or an individual's entrepreneurship in bringing values into the workplace' (2008: 110). In this sense, CSR can be a key to 'unlock' innovation (around product development, for example), enhance reputation (via community participation, for example) and exploit general social competencies by forming a resonance chamber between non-work sociability and the labour process itself.

And then we have social entrepreneurship *outside* the firm, all of those ways in which CSR creates a pathway between the ossified structure of the formal enterprise and the myriad of profit-making opportunities in the communities that have grown in the shadowy wasteland of late capitalism. Take this example from a business ethics consultant regarding the way in which a CSR youth empowerment programme might also be leveraged as a marketing opportunity:

> Generation-Y are the future consumers and employers across the private and public sectors. The need to create an authentic experience to this market is paramount .... The authenticity of your CSR initiatives depends ultimately on the people you choose to leverage. In the areas of youth and ethnic diversity – you must engage those who have strong reputations in their communities and who have the ability to connect to these audiences. (Dockery, 2008: 2)

Here, impoverished youth who are outside the basic principles of economic rationality (in conventional corporate terms at least) are seen as an opportunity to enhance brand value. Finding local youth leaders and prospecting/capturing their social networks is the first step in launching a strategic marketing campaign.

What we find fascinating about social entrepreneurship and the bio-political turn in the capitalist accumulation process is the reliance on some 'outside' to garner value, ideas and innovation. It is almost as if the firm needs the non-financial to reproduce itself and fuel economic growth – even Google's famous Innovation Ecosystem centres, along with its own workers, draw upon a range of external and 'free' sources of labour, including 'mashup creators, independent software vendors [and the] open source community' (Iyer, 2008: 60). There is reliance on enthusiasm, generosity and sharing that is key for the production of new ideas, notions that contradict the very axioms of private ownership and micro-regulation underscoring neo-liberal capitalism. As Hanlon nicely puts it:

> CSR is not simply a rough guide to unmet social needs which the corporation can then provide for us. It is actually a glimpse at how our sociality – our humanness – is developing. This 'thing' is beyond the corporation, beyond its control, and yet, without it the corporation has no function and no innovative potential – after all, how else does it know of need? (2007: 169)

COMMODIFYING RESISTANCE

Similarly, we might see corporations attempting to capitalize on the general malaise and dissent found in sub-communities or counter-movement groups opposed to the rule of the market or 'the establishment'. Hanlon (2007) notes a very interesting example of this from Davis (2005) writing in the *McKinsey Quarterly*. Being a strident proponent for CSR, Davis makes some very surprising comments about how to approach popular dissent. The comments are prefaced with the typical stance we might expect: 'From a defensive point of view, companies that ignore public sentiment make themselves vulnerable to attack' (Davis, 2005). But Davis then goes further, seeing this unease with capitalism not as a threat but a market opportunity. He comments, 'Social pressures often indicate the existence of unmet social needs or consumer preferences. Businesses can gain advantage by spotting and supplying these before their competitors do' (Davis, 2005).

An additional example of this strategic approach might be found in one of Starbuck's leading philosophical principles: *Embrace Existence*. Of course, as is well known, this company has been the target of severe criticism, from exploiting coffee farmers, to predatory anti-competitive location strategies, to wage-slavery in its stores. Indeed, whenever there is an anti-capitalism or alternative-globalization protest in town the police are automatically posted to Starbucks since it is assumed that a brick will be thrown through its window. But why, then, would Starbucks 'embrace resistance'? Of course, it does not, but it does see social entrepreneurial opportunities to bring in more customers. In one example recounted by Michelli (2007), Starbucks planned to open a store in a bohemian café district in San Fernando, in the United States. There was fervent resistance among the community since to them it signalled the demise of the edgy and locally owned café culture in the district. Michelli relays the comments of the district manager in charge of the operation:

> As Leanne explains, 'There were similar coffee shops in the San Fernando area, and nobody really wanted us to go there. There was a lot of resistance from some members of the council, but also from the community.' Leanne grew up in the San Fernando Valley. 'It was really important for me to give back to the community. I wanted to embrace its very artistic nature.' Upon opening the store, Leanne contacted a local artist. 'I asked him to bring some of his artwork into my location. He was more than happy to do so. So, for a three-month period, we took down Starbucks artwork and placed his amazing murals on our walls …. People appreciated that we would involve someone from their community.' (2007: 131)

Here we see a classic example of pre-corporate sociality being captured to yield value and enhance an inherently anti-community institutional logic. The quote is so rich with corporate discourse draped in the language of 'community good'. Of course, there was no question of *not* opening the store. Why call it 'my location' (rather than the communal 'our') and why is the artist suddenly someone from '*their* community'? The objectifying logic of the corporate gaze is struggling to remain hidden here since something that is meant to look like 'giving back' is actually a manoeuvre of capture (the artist, the bohemian anti-instrumental aura of the artist, etc.) in order to enhance value. Hanlon well describes this aspect of CSR when he notes, 'In short CSR will help make money from the problems businesses have helped to create, thereby shareholder value' (2007: 169).

CONCLUSION

This chapter has surveyed the variety of approaches available to us to place CSR in the context of a political economy of the (globalized) firm: CSR as a panacea, a type of propaganda and as a parasitical instrument of commodification. We found the first approach problematic since it still assumes that capitalism might one day shed its more anti-social and regressive tendencies. This is difficult, however, once we recognize that these tendencies, tensions and contradictions form some of the basic building blocks of capitalism. To reform this would be to revolutionize business and society, the economy and politics, and so on.

We obviously have more sympathy with the propaganda approach as this is based upon a sound understanding of what some have called 'capitalist realism'. The fact that CSR is wheeled out in corporate reports, glossy social accounting documents and websites does not mean that companies do not spend huge amounts of resources on such activities: and no doubt some initiatives are genuine. But taking into consideration the larger context of the institutional logic of capitalism (and its close ally, the nation-state) casts doubt on the efficacy of CSR to tame capital.

The aim of the last part of this chapter, therefore, has been to extend conceptually the idea that CSR might have a parasitical facet. From this perspective CSR reflects shifts in the nature of late capitalism and understands it as a socio-economic phenomenon rather than simply as a business or management issue. Moreover, and not that dissimilar to the observations made as far back as the 1950s regarding business ethics and philanthropy, CSR ought to be considered part of a larger trend in the nature of business and society in which corporations are increasingly appropriating social life and using arguments about self-actualization, social responsibility, ethical behaviour, etc. to legitimate their activities. This means that we ought to not simply dismiss it as ideological mystification. On the contrary, we should take it very seriously since it appears to deepen the ideology of money and control into ever more aspects of the social body in post-Fordist societies. Critical perspectives on CSR might now view it as a key element of the corporate search for both legitimacy and new markets at the heart of its own crisis.

CONCLUSION: THE BEGINNING OF (NON) CORPORATE SOCIAL RESPONSIBILITY?

The end of CSR? Again, we state that it never really began – in the sense that the majority of its proponents claim to free us somehow from the excesses of a system that is itself excessive (i.e. neo-liberal capitalism). Indeed, if it really could, and given the pervasiveness of CSR discourse in business practice today, then we would not still be in such dark 'end days' (Žižek, 2010a). We have argued in this book that potential influences on the firm for integrative CSR practice have been and are likely to continue to be ignored for many of the reasons we have outlined in the preceding chapters. Legally backed economic pressures, perceived threats from competitors and the expectations of institutional investors restrict managerial responsibilities to a demonstration that known business opportunities have been exploited at the limit of regulatory compliance. Regulated social disclosures are shown as having little effect on the operating methods of institutional investors and industrial corporations (UvA, 2005), despite changes in the content of social reports and types of reports (Kolk, 2005). The privileging of the owner stakeholder group in Western jurisdictions affords corporations *de facto* impunity over many economic externalities, a vital requirement for the perpetuation of crisis-ridden capitalism. Considered along with private donations to states, and complexities introduced by state–private sector commercial activity, non-onerous corporate legislation can be expected to continue. The most visible promotion of corporate social reporting practices involving the third sector to date, the Global Reporting Initiative stands as a sad example of co-optation and legitimation. And in the wake of the 2008 financial crisis, and a new wave of austerity measures in the corporate and state sectors (but who can tell the difference these days?), we do not see CSR beginning earnestly bar some kind of radical intervention.

We suggest that the extant CSR-related management literature suggests a limited future for current conceptualizations of CSR (also see Marens, 2010). Initiatives leave historical organizational structures intact, are designed without genuine stakeholder consultation and are unlikely to lead to observable industry-wide outcomes. Organizational diffusion of sustainability is blocked by practitioner reluctance to move away from shareholder primacy; the same is true of researchers with respect to challenging the social performance of their subjects. As large portions of humanity face catastrophe from armed conflicts, widespread poverty and ecological degradation traceable to the unchecked pursuit of economic markets (Millennium Ecosystem Assessment, 2005), CSR research appears paralysed, unable to offer solutions. The insurmountable contradiction between sustainability (aiming to minimize ecological footprints) and the growth of capitalist organizations is obvious to any informed researcher (see Banerjee, 2007; Gray and Milne, 2002). Paradoxically, the timidity of mainstream research is co-extensive with an avowed aim of CSR researchers to engage with practice. Caught in a rudderless drift, this ostensibly critical line of research is taken up with atomistic analyses of corporate governance guidelines, immediate stakeholder relationships, descriptions of social problems in the language of finance, and compendiums of social disclosures. Acquiring 'the quiet force of the taken-for-granted' (Bourdieu, 2001: 80), such research uncritically defaults to an organization-centred perspective which provides neither a theoretical rudder nor a normative catalyst for social change. We have suggested in this book that such a perspective also precludes enquiry into the underlying dynamics of stakeholder relations overwhelmingly stacked in favour of the multinational enterprise and the corporatized state.

Ethicists are not unaware of these deficiencies. The inadequacies of the literature reflects 'the conceptual apparatus [stakeholder management] ... pushed beyond its limits' (Freeman and Gilbert, 1992: 12). Liberal democracies and 'free' capitalist enterprise rely for their continuing legitimation on the Smithian assumption that unceasing capital accumulation, consumption and market expansion will provide for the welfare of market participants. Business ethicists who do not question the social effects of capitalism nor refer to the moral injunctions that contextualized Smith's work (Jones, 1993) exclude themselves from 'rethinking the social agents capable of bringing about transformation [in the] dynamics of social reproduction' (Dowbor, 1997: x). Indeed, CSR as an ostensibly critical stance towards the corporation, in effect, ideologically shores up the status quo by giving us the impression that we are dealing with a few 'bad apples'. As Žižek puts it, the problem is not that there is no criticality in academia or popular culture; there is, but it functions in a surprisingly conservative manner:

> There is no lack of anti-capitalists today. We are even witnessing an over-load of critiques of capitalism's horrors: newspaper investigations, TV reports and best-selling books abound on companies polluting our environment, corrupt bankers who continue to get fat bonuses while their firms are saved by public money, sweatshops where children work overtime. There is, however, a catch to all this criticism, ruthless as it may appear: what is as a rule not questioned is the liberal-democratic framework within which these excesses should be fought. The goal, explicit or implied, is to regulate capitalism ... but never to question the liberal-democratic institutional mechanisms of the bourgeois state of law. (2010b: 87)

And is not a very similar kind of silence evident within much of the CSR accounts of the corporation, the state, the economy and global governance institutions? While the excesses are criticized, it is done in a way that covertly validates the rules of the game (private property, commodification, multinational corporate control) because it propagates the fantasy that, ultimately, a 'reasonable' or 'ethical' socio-economic condition might be salvaged from the founding principles of the present system. Moreover, the quote above by Žižek is not as anti-democratic as it may seem at first glance. The 'liberal-democratic' framework he is deriding (one that we also feel CSR too implicitly supports through its particular form of criticism) is the very ideological matrix that consolidates the 'capitalist realism' of the unfree and, ultimately, undemocratic way of life we all experience today. In this conclusion, building on the preceding chapters and their respective arguments, we want to summarize our criticisms of CSR discourse and practice. Then we will make some suggestions about how the field might move in a direction so as to confront some of the pressing socio-political issues that are so prominent today.

THE 'DEAFENING SILENCE' OF CSR

One of the major arguments we have made in the book concerns the almost 'deafening silence' of much CSR research regarding the inherent anti-social nature of the current socio-economic paradigm and the catastrophes that it seems to be tallying up without respite. What factors explain this generalized and long-standing unwillingness to question capitalism, the market (that never seems to work perfectly) and the role of CSR? We would argue that it is a direct consequence of the failure of much recent CSR scholarship to be grounded in either business history or political economy. This means that it must inevitably work within a narrow discursive context in which many ideological constructs (e.g. the sanctity of property rights, managerial prerogative) are taken for granted rather than openly debated.

By implicitly presupposing some kind of synergy between wider social justice (or the interests of 'the 99 per cent') and a world still governed by large corporations, mainstream CSR has served as a functional element of hegemony (in a Gramscian sense) and has thus been partially anti-democratic in its impact. That is, by laying the groundwork for an expanded role for the corporate sector, CSR has undermined the protests of stakeholders aligning themselves with countervailing institutions, as these are deemed unnecessary at the least, or even 'inefficient' obstructions to the ability of national economies to compete in a globalized world. This is not even considering the extent to which these (potentially) oppositional stakeholders and countervailing institutions have been subordinated to corporate hegemony through the discursive colonization of economic rationality (Gorz, 1989) and in a mediascape which is almost totally privatized to the point where 'the truth is where the money is' (Joseph, 2002).

The danger of such a situation as described above can briefly be captured by two recent events in the corporate sector, one generalized and the other particular. The first is a report on the executive development industry based on a large-scale sample of global corporations (Duke, 2009). The purpose of this research was to determine sample firms' intentions to bankroll training and development programmes, along with the key issues that were of highest and lowest interest in terms of including (or not) in the programme content. The findings were striking with respect to CSR and (environmental) sustainability-related issues, which were at or near the bottom of both CEOs' current 'strategic issues' and with respect to their importance in being included in executive development programmes. Interestingly, the researchers themselves were surprised at how quickly CSR and sustainability become irrelevant to CEOs as the economic crisis deepens, especially given perceptions during the 'good times' that these topics were 'core' strategic concerns as well as priority areas of development for future corporate initiatives.

The second event, a singular instance of the explicit subordination of CSR, concerns Danfoss, a Danish engineering firm producing heating and cooling systems along with motion controls, primarily for industrial applications. In a 2010 internal document, the firm abandoned the use of CSR in its mission statement, replacing it with language based around 'creating value for stakeholders', where the term 'value' assumes a clear economic connotation. Interestingly, the term 'sustainability', although retained in the mission statement, was reframed away from an environmental inflection to indicate instead the ability of the firm's business model to sustain *profitability*. Despite supposedly having CSR in its 'DNA' – and winning many awards for being a leading Danish corporation in the practice of CSR – the firm nevertheless responded to the downturn in its business environment by quickly dismissing approximately

6,000 employees, or about 25 per cent of its workforce. These twin acts, the symbolic change of language and the material decision to trigger massive redundancies, evidence the tentative or contingent nature of even the most 'progressive' corporation's commitment to CSR.

As these two examples attest, CSR is realistically a concern for corporations when they require legitimacy or seek opportunities in the marketplace, the substance of which might even be a negative by-product of the corporations' activities, as we argued in the last chapter pertaining to the parasitical aspect of the phenomenon. In many respects, that Shell or British American Tobacco remain 'silent' in the face of their core business activities is not too surprising. But silence about the inability for corporate capitalism to be sustainable in a good deal of the CSR literature – especially the large sector captured by strategic management – is perplexing. In the face of an impending ecological disaster, economic ruin and the obviously systemic nature of exploitation, corruption and the reduction of all issues to 'the bottom line', CSR scholarship needs to abandon the idea that business and ethics might someday be married. The evidence to the contrary is staggering, and therefore we need to rethink seriously the conceptual bases and modes of investigation that appear to 'blind' CSR to some fundamental facts about the current condition of business and society.

TOWARDS SOME SOLUTIONS?

In light of our critique of the CSR field's failure to come to grips with some of the most pressing developments in the global political economy, the obvious question is: *what is to be done?* We would suggest a course of action which addresses the background (training and education) and institutional location of CSR scholarship (i.e. *who* does CSR research, and *where* are they based?) as well as (re)defining a core research agenda in order to make the field more independent, rigorous and socially relevant. Initially, we would suggest that research scholars abandon the use of the term 'CSR' (and its surrogates or derivatives) in both theoretical and normative analysis, confining it to those empirical cases in which organizational actors themselves use the language of CSR to signify their motives or explain their actions. Our rationale here is two-fold. First, CSR has not and *cannot* – because of its contestability among various power configurations – be defined with either precision or consensus (see Jones, 2009a; van Oosterhout, 2005). Second, the CSR discourse has been implicated in performing a 'masking' function for corporate interests for many years (Reich, 2007). As was exhibited in our earlier discussion of the business activity impact matrix (or BAIM), CSR is neither necessary nor useful as a badge for (what we termed in Chapter 1) quadrant IV (Enlightened Self-interest) actions and outcomes. It is in fact rather redundant and, if anything, adds a layer of 'smoke and mirrors' to behaviours which are otherwise much more accurately signified by the term 'enlightened self-interest'.

WHO'S WATCHING THE DETECTIVES?

A similar point was made in a recent review of CSR by *The Economist* (2008: 22), which observes that large corporations are embarking on ever more CSR activities as reactions to disparate developments including corporate scandals like Enron, increasingly powerful NGOs, the so-called 'war for talent' and climate change. Most corporations adopt CSR in order to protect or enhance their reputations with respect to key stakeholder groups. As the article states, 'paying attention to CSR can amount to *enlightened self-interest*, something that over time will help to sustain profits for shareholders' [italics added]. This is consistent with Lee's (2008) point that CSR research is increasingly focused on the link between CSR and financial performance, to the exclusion of issues which pertain to the wider political economy as well as fundamental ethical concerns. We would go further, arguing that mainstream CSR scholarship has allowed itself to be the victim of discursive capture by the instrumental allure of the 'business case' perspective (Vogel, 2005). We would explain this development as analogous to the phenomenon of 'regulatory capture' often observed in studies of the symbiotic relationships that typically emerge between regulator and regulatee (Dal Bo, 2006). To paraphrase Marx, then, who is watching the detectives?

It might be suggested that many of the developments discussed in this concluding chapter cannot be effectively studied from within the institutional location of the business school owing to fundamental discursive constraints influencing research funded and conducted in this context. For example, the consideration of genuinely critical theories of the corporation and its institutional function in contemporary society is largely beyond the capacity of business school researchers to interrogate, due to the disciplinary composition of constituent faculties and the resource dependencies of business schools (Harney et al., 2008). This is particularly the case in US universities, which are increasingly influenced (in terms of senior-level appointments) by major corporate donors – for example, the now-notorious 'Kenneth Lay Chair' at the University of Missouri at Columbia. And in the United Kingdom, the infamous Research Excellence Framework tends to privilege publications in business journals that are well known to avoid anything relating to war, poverty, capitalism and so forth (Harney et al., 2008).

MAPPING THE SPACES OF CSR

To develop a realistic understanding of how research on CSR is linked to the activities in business and society let us return to an earlier argument. It might be useful to link our call for extricating the study of CSR from the institutional location of the business school to the BAIM developed earlier in the book.

This results in the following normative suggestions for the continuing scholarly investigation of phenomena in the domain of CSR, stakeholder management (as discussed in Chapter 3) and corporate citizenship (as discussed in Chapter 2). Note that we are not underestimating the importance of theoretical and empirical enquiry on

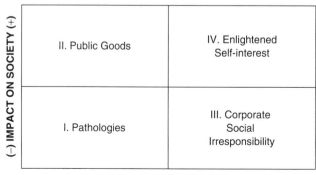

Figure 1.1

these topics; we are rather considering the institutional location and identity of those best placed to examine these phenomena from an *independent and critical* perspective. It could be that the business school is an appropriate home for the research of only a subset of the topic areas identified on the matrix, as there is little doubt that the 'relative autonomy' of scholars working from this base is minimal, and that their efforts must somehow be justified in instrumental terms.

First, we believe that quadrant IV (Enlightened Self-interest) is where most business school CSR research is located. Efforts in this area are often undertaken within the discipline of strategic management, since it is there that CSR and related topics are achieving visibility at the highest levels of management and increasingly being integrated into corporate and business-level strategies (McKinsey & Company, 2006; Porter and Kramer, 2006). Because the essence of strategic management is about finding new ways to create, capture and maintain (economic) value for the firm, and as instrumental CSR of both the risk mitigation and Porterian/differentiation varieties can provide means towards that end, it seems logical that this branch of CSR research should be subsumed within the strategic management field. This approach is consistent with Margolis and Walsh's (2003) observation that making CSR-oriented decisions contingent upon some form of investment return criteria effectively removes them from the realm of ethics and puts them squarely into that of economics.

Second, quadrant II (Public Goods) would be the proper domain of applied ethics and legal scholars, both based outside the institutional confines of the business school. Ethics scholars are equipped to grapple theoretically and normatively with altruism by individuals as well as (non-instrumental) corporate philanthropy. Meanwhile, legal scholars can critically examine corporate philanthropy from the perspective of circumstances generating dysfunctional governance mechanisms that enable management to spend 'other people's money' in pursuit of agendas incongruent with economic performance. We would invoke the same rationale to suggest that corporate governance scholars incorporate quadrant I (Pathologies) within their domain of enquiry.

Third, we believe that quadrant III (Corporate Social *Irresponsibility*) is the proper domain of organization theory scholars (dealing with organizational and inter-organizational phenomena) and political economy researchers (concerned with developments at the institutional level). This quadrant is where firms act in ways that generate benefits for a narrow group of proprietary stakeholders but trigger negative externalities for the wider society.

Consequently, we would argue that a critical political economy approach (as we developed in Chapter 5) is best placed to conceptualize externalities or crisis events as more than isolated phenomena. In fact, and as we have been proposing in relation to the ethically wayward firm, the current global crisis triggered by the meltdown of the US subprime mortgage market can best be understood not as a systemic dysfunction but rather a historically typical and emblematic example of the 'system' functioning normally. The channelling of public resources to subsidize the misadventures of financial capital by national governments (which are structurally dependent on their corporate sectors) is perfectly foreseeable from this theoretical perspective, with numerous historical precedents (see DuBoff, 1989; O'Conner, 1987). Moreover, we would suggest a research strategy which would deploy a synthetic, historically grounded, empirically oriented methodology acknowledging the fundamentally overdetermined (Resnick and Wolff, 1987) nature of complex social phenomena which took power, interests and distributional considerations seriously (see Jones and Fleming, 2003).

AND NOW THE BAD NEWS ...

As noted earlier, we are wasting time trying to gain consensus on an uncontested definition of CSR. However, decisions and the actions they trigger in the empirical world based on particular (and always contingent) notions of CSR held by diverse and often conflicting stakeholders *are* a valid and important subject of research. This is particularly true given that CSR will be inevitably implicated in the previously discussed gigatrends, just as instrumental constructs of CSR will become increasingly core elements of strategic management theory and corporate practice as public discontent increases. Proceeding to the matter of (re)defining the research agenda for the field, we would return to the BAIM and offer the following thoughts. Some important empirical questions relating to the matrix include determining the scope of each quadrant (which will vary depending on the geographical level of analysis and industry, among other factors); relevant trends going forward, particularly considering the impact of globalization and the activities of multinational corporations (MNCs); and the key agents, strategies and processes for expanding quadrant IV (Enlightened Self-interest) outcomes. We would argue that addressing such questions should be a focus of activity for positive CSR research, as well as the normative role of communicating opportunities and *responsibilities* to expand the scope of quadrant IV activities to corporate decision makers.

Of course, it might be tempting to prioritize the task of mapping the empirical contours of quadrant IV (Enlightened Self-interest) in order to identify additional opportunities for generating 'win–win' situations without having to alter fundamentally the nature of the corporate form or the dominance of economic rationality. The bad news is that we actually doubt that it would lead to anything looking like a systemic harmonizing of the current corporate form and an ethical social paradigm. But leveraging the same economic rationality, we would advocate major efforts to map quadrant III (Corporate Social Irresponsibility) because this is where a great deal of social and environmental 'fallout' is generated by corporate activity. In these efforts to map quadrants III and IV, we would further focus scholarly resources on environmental impacts, as climate change will be the biggest challenge confronting humanity for the foreseeable future.

One suggestion, which we ourselves are unsure about, would be to endeavour to rescript the economic rationality within firms today towards justice-sensitive outcomes. The primary challenge to advancing this agenda would be to extend corporate decision makers' time frames, as well as the cognitive maps they draw upon to develop strategy, in order to incorporate a broader range of stakeholders within expanded organizational fields. We would expect the likely methodology necessary to accomplish these objectives to involve action research and even consulting interventions. Working within corporations, CSR researchers would appeal to the instrumental terminology of 'risk management' or Porterian 'strategic' CSR. Collaborating with external stakeholders such as NGOs, critical researchers would catalyse these agents to stimulate corporations to move in the direction of promoting quadrant IV (Enlightened Self-interest) outcomes.

Again, the danger here is that this reformist methodology runs the risk of co-optation that we have alerted readers to throughout this book, yet we do grant the fact that practical relevance and impact must be both the *raison d'être* and benchmark for successful scholarly efforts. Realistically, some might argue, all we can do at best is enlarge the scope of quadrant IV (Enlightened Self-interest) and coax corporations to see the 'business case' for moving there from quadrant III (Corporate Social Irresponsibility). This will not prevent the coming catastrophic social and political upheavals linked to climate change and peak oil. But it could contribute to avoiding the worst climate change scenarios (Lynas, 2007).

If economic rationality, corporate control and the totality of the capitalist paradigm are as preponderant as we believe them to be, then the reformist approach outlined above might be too slight to exact a purposeful change. Whether the discourse of CSR is being practised in business schools, law or political science departments, in governmental agencies or in the corporation itself, some kind of rupture within current orthodoxy is required. One of our criticisms of CSR is that in examining its proclamations and aspirations – sustainability, ethicality, genuine democracy, respect for indigenous rights, free speech, etc. – a gross disconnect becomes apparent when we then turn to how business actually functions (often completely at odds with business ethics in its practical form). For example, a well-known military manufacturer claims that it is 'committed to becoming a recognized leader in responsible business conduct worldwide, we continue to strive for ways to improve our business and reputation. Maintaining high standards of business conduct is essential to enhance our overall business performance, build trust and maintain and improve our reputation with stakeholders' (BAE Systems, Responsible Business Conduct, Baesystems.com, 2012).

Apart from the bribery and corruption allegations against the 'defence' company, it and similar firms have long been criticized for their involvement in the war industry. As the group Campaign Against Arms Trading (or CAAT) points out:

> BAE's arms are sold indiscriminately around the world. It has military customers in over 100 countries. Its focus over the past few years has been on increasing sales to the US, specifically targeting equipment for the conflicts in Afghanistan and Iraq, and supplying Eurofighters to the Saudi Arabia regime. Other export deals include subsystems for Israeli F-16 fighter aircraft and sales to both India and Pakistan. (See www.caat.org.uk/issues/bae, 2009)

Companies like this, and those that produce torture weapons and other forms of instruments of violence, have been severely rebuked for 'making money out of death'. That they have a strident CSR policy (mainly focusing on their employees in the manner argued in Chapter 4) is unsurprising. As the critics of CSR have pointed out, this disconnect points to hypocrisy and ideological green-washing, but also the cynical distance that is often automatically built into many other discursive claims in the socio-political realm. In this sense, *CSR is not really meant to be taken seriously* or identified with too ardently. The same might also be said for corporate democracy, self-managing teams, a culture of caring and all manner of other liberal motifs in society today.

OVER-IDENTIFICATION AS RESISTANCE

But if CSR makes ambitious and radical claims about business and society that are not supposed to be taken seriously (and cannot be taken seriously without some radical change), then this is where its weakness lies too, a weakness that might be exploited to transform it into a politically progressive force. Critics of corporate domination (and the hypocrisy contained in its various tactics of legitimation) have long understood the power of *over-identification*. Taking an ideology *too seriously* and short-circuiting its inbuilt cynical distance by demanding its fullest enactment can have radically unsettling consequences. While there is always an excuse for permanently deferring the fullness of a discursive claim (here some have argued that liberal capitalism resembles a kind of permanent state of emergency in which democracy and justice never quite arrive), the political subversion of CSR might not be achieved by dismissing it as mere propaganda, but by identifying with it too much, and demanding its total realization.

A good illustration here is the communication guerrilla interventions against a number of European airlines who agreed to deport so-called 'illegal immigrants'. As autonome a.f.r.i.k.a gruppe (2002) report regarding the sabotage of Lufthansa by the German anti-racist collective 'kein mensch ist illegal', any form of criticism here would have to bypass the cynical liberalist distance we have noted above. 'Kein mensch ist illegal' therefore prepared overly *positive* leaflets with the company's colours/logos, claiming that the company was very concerned for its customer's comfort and safety, but simply could not restrain its 'prisoners' in handcuffs, gags and helmets. Therefore, the company regretfully declared that it also could not guarantee to protect its loyal customers from these criminals. The leaflets were in fact a glowing humanitarian portrayal of the company, but executed in a manner that immediately revealed the truthful 'hidden reverse' of such compassionate corporate behaviour and the company's seedy relations with a racist state. The critical kernel of the leaflets was its *consent* with the company's own caring image, but in a manner that completely undermined the usual suspension of criticism that we find in most forms of bourgeois ideology: 'the company found itself in a bind: it couldn't deny that it was carrying out the deportations, and that this inconvenienced customers, but it was offering them no compensation' (autonome a.f.r.i.k.a gruppe, 2002: 167–168). The company could not disagree with the leaflet unless it disagreed with itself. It had to buy into its own criticism and thus undermine itself, which reveals the productive element of these kinds of *détournement* that underwrite dissenting consenting.

If we take the claims, aspiration and social message of many CSR policies in the corporate and governmental sector too seriously, too far, as if they were actually genuine co-ordinates for reforming business and society, a powerful tool of criticism and practical change might emerge. For example, what if this statement by a large petroleum company was not taken 'with a grain of salt' or bracketed from actual everyday business, but adhered to, word for word?

> Contributing to sustainable development is integral to the way we do business. As we work to help meet the world's growing energy needs we aim to bring benefits to local communities and reduce impacts of our operations, including tackling greenhouse gas emissions. We look after our people and our core values of honesty, integrity and respect for people have been laid out in the Shell General Business Principles for over 30 years.

That companies themselves over-identify with their CSR claims, however, might seem unrealistic. It is not that employees and managers are naturally cynical, but that the psychological distance we mentioned above is an almost 'objective necessity' for getting things done. One has to be able to speak to power and feel secure in doing so before an exercise of over-identification or any other criticism of the firm can occur.

SPEAKING TO POWER

The tactic of over-identification outlined above requires one to speak the truth to power, but what kind of truth? And how do we speak when the logic of capitalism appears to be the only game in town? Reviving CSR – if that is at all possible given that its co-optation by the discourse of business seems fairly complete – would require a deeper resuscitation of its epistemic origins in a more genuinely *radical* agenda for social change (Tinker et al., 1991). Instead of endeavouring to *make sense* of the language of CSR (which is now the language of power), perhaps we now need to *not make sense of it*, and instead demand it justify itself on other grounds that are more critical. For it cannot be the case that all management discourses *deserve* being 'made sense of and given meaning to' (cf. Freeman and Gilbert, 1992: 16).

And this brings us, finally, back to the business school. If much CSR scholarship is about legitimating big business (by giving it a veneer of potential ethicality), then might the business school be able to turn the tables, and transform CSR into a platform for truly rethinking the corporate form? Could it become a space to expand quadrant III type of research? Could it speak the truth to power, take CSR too seriously and thus transform it into a radical platform for social change?

Perhaps. Business school academics are being called upon to comment more and more in times of crisis. As experts invited to speak, a new kind of 'responsible research' might utilize the media to make more strident claims about what is to be done. Like any kind of 'speaking the truth to power', this would come with certain risks and dangers, not least from an increasingly corporatized university hierarchy. In the United Kingdom, for example, universities are now expected to make positive contributions (or 'impact') to the economy. And this has become a stick to beat academics with in an increasingly managerial institution. A personal risk to business scholars is that by being associated with the activism of groups such as CorpWatch they put themselves at risk of being professionally marginalized in their business schools. Activism, however, takes many forms, some of which are more direct than others. The choice of research approach is demanded by its context. But rather than seeing this command to make a positive 'impact' as a regressive moment (of transforming universities into stupid handmaidens for big business or 'the 1 per cent'), might not this neo-liberal missive itself be subverted by taking it *too seriously*, remedying the ills of late capitalism by heralding its imminent demise, and thus to the betterment of 'the 99 per cent'?

In any case, before any of these alternative paths are pursued, CSR researchers need to complete three preliminary steps. First, interconnections between corporate and non-corporate forms of organization need examination. The extent to which lobby groups curtail the force of the state as a potential agent for corporate change cannot be ignored (Tinker and Carter, 2003). Second, researchers need to radicalize the 'dividing practice' (Bourdieu, 2001) of ranking business first, society second. The agendas of many CSR researchers, to judge from their published work, indicate a championing rather than a questioning of the corporate form and its economic interests. Third, CSR researchers must reconsider their own commitment to progressive research. Progress depends on mobilizing the 'organizational means to encourage all competent researchers to unite their efforts with those of … responsible activists' (Bourdieu, 2001: 15). For the committed CSR researcher, the co-opting forces of capitalism demand an unflinchingly critical epistemology.

CONCLUSIONS

In conclusion, we suggest that current CSR research needs to seriously change its course of action in both theory and practice. This would involve reinvigorating countervailing (to capital) institutions and discourses in order to 'rebalance' social formations and put corporations and markets in their place. In *The Lives of Animals* (1999), J.W. Coetzee makes the point that, having triumphed in the war for species supremacy, humanity had two postures to choose between with respect to how it apprehended the natural world: stewardship or predation. That the second course was almost always taken was, according to Coetzee, neither inevitable, necessary, nor morally defensible. Analogously, we would suggest that the corporation has undeservedly found itself at the top of the institutional 'food chain' and has wreaked havoc for too long. This has nothing (or very little) to do with bad people. Under the bizarre conditions of neo-liberal hegemony and existing governance arrangements there is really *no choice* the corporation can make other than to pursue profitable growth according to its 'hard-wiring'.

Polanyi (1944) seminally established the socially disruptive and destructive tendencies of an unrestrained market economy. Similarly, the corporation is the embodiment of the 'visible hand' (Chandler, 1977). The globalized corporation is a new leviathan (Chandler and Mazlish, 2005), running rampant through gaps in global regulation, arbitraging national differences to its narrow and private advantage. Moreover, the actions of these organizations for the most part *increase* these gaps rather than the opposite. It thus seems idealistic (or naive) at best to normatively sanction an expanded role for corporations in social and economic development. Rather, we should be looking for opportunities in theory and practice to roll back corporate hegemony, retrieve the non-marketized 'commons', de-privatize what remains of the public sphere, and put a reanimated and potentially more independent state to work, breaking up local, national and global oligopoly market structures.

We maintain that the critical tone of this conclusion should not be deemed extreme, as some might like to say. For it is the self-destructive status quo before our eyes that is extreme, resembling a runaway train. Returning to Walter Benjamin, we merely invite CSR researchers to pull on the emergency brake cord.

This can be done by making CSR discourse groan under the weight of its own impossibility. For example, the truly radical potential of the corporate citizenship concept can be found in efforts directed at theorizing an increased democratic accountability of the corporation along the lines of 'political CSR' as articulated by Scherer and Palazzo (2010). We were critical because we did not see it as a reality in today's hyper-capitalism, but in theory, the notion of a deliberative democracy would dislodge the current hegemony of self-serving corporatism. In other words, the gap between positive and normative elements of this line of enquiry remains to be closed to influence events 'on the ground'. If the MNC did actually guarantee citizenship rights (beyond its instrumental concerns) and was held accountable by all stakeholders, then it would quickly cease to look like the MNC as described above. Such a manoeuvre would contradict the basic principles of private ownership, the managerial prerogative, cost externalization and many other axioms of the capitalist firm. Under such conditions, the MNC would become a truly *revolutionary* institution in that it would supersede itself for common goals rather than those of a bemused and confused '1 per cent' (they don't even believe their luck).

CSR, then, is not about curbing or taming the free market of the corporation, but about saving an un-saveable social proposition. It represents the ideological justification for an unjustifiable constellation of social institutions: the enterprise, the market and an increasingly authoritarian and anti-democratic capitalist state (unjustifiable because it stands against everything that a progressive modern politics ought to be about – freedom, self-determination, democracy and civil liberties for 'the 99 per cent'). So, the end of CSR? Perhaps, since the concept no longer really enables us to understand the fuller political implications of why firms continue to avoid reforming the underlying principles that are the real cause of so such damage we see unfolding in the business world today. In this respect, CSR is better understood as an ideological practice that sustains corporate hegemony rather than attenuate or shift its axiomatic principles. For with the birth of CSR, the ills of global capitalism seem to have exponentially increased rather than waned. And more importantly, would we really need the notion of CSR if large corporations, markets and neo-liberal governments were to become truly accountable and democratic? Probably not.

REFERENCES

Abelson, P. (2002). *Lectures in Public Economics*, 4th edn. Sydney: Applied Economics.

Adams, C.A. (2002). 'Internal organizational factors influencing corporate social and ethical reporting: beyond current theorising', *Accounting, Auditing and Accountability Journal*, 15 (2): 223–250.

Aglietta, M. (2000). *A Theory of Capitalist Accumulation: The US Experience*. New York: Verso.

Aglietta, M. and Berribi, L. (2007). *Desordres dans le capitalisme mondial*. Paris: Odile Jacob.

Alford, R. and Friedland, R. (1985). *Powers of Theory: Capitalism, the State, and Democracy*. Cambridge: Cambridge University Press.

Althusser, L. (1969). *For Marx*. London: Penguin.

Amin, A. and Membrez, J. (2008). *The World We Wish to See: Revolutionary Objectives for the Twenty-First Century*. New York: Monthly Review Press.

Amin, S. (2010). *The Law of Worldwide Value*. New York: Monthly Review Press.

Anderson, P. (2010). 'Two revolutions', *New Left Review*, 61: 51–96.

Ansoff, I. (1965). *Corporate Strategy*. New York: McGraw-Hill.

Anyon, J. (2005). *Radical Possibilities*. New York: Routledge.

Appadurai, A. (2001). *Globalization*. Durham, NC: Duke University Press.

Armstrong, P., Glyn, A. and Harrison, J. (1985). *Capitalism Since 1945*. London: Blackwell.

Arrighi, G. (2007). *Adam Smith in Beijing: Lineages of the Twenty-first Century*. London: Verso.

Austin-American Statesman (2002). 'Offshoring American jobs', 21 October.

autonome a.f.r.i.k.a gruppe (2002). 'Communication guerrillas: using the language of power', in E. Lubbers (ed.), *Battling Big Business: Counter Greenwash, Infiltration and Other Forms of Corporate Bullying*. Monroe, ME: Common Courage Press.

Ayres, E. (1999). 'Why are we not astonished?', *World Watch*, 12 (May/June): 25–29.

Bacon, D. (2004). *The Children of NAFTA: Labour Wars on the U.S./Mexico Border*. Los Angeles: University of California Press.

Baer, W. and Montes-Rojas, G. (2008). 'From privatization to re-nationalization', *Oxford Development Studies*, 36 (3): 323–337.

Bakan, J. (2004). *The Corporation: The Pathological Pursuit of Profit and Power*. New York: Free Press.

Banerjee, S.B. (2007). 'Corporate social responsibility: the good, the bad and the ugly', *Critical Sociology*, 34 (1): 51–79.

Banerjee, S.B. (2008). 'The political economy of corporate social responsibility', in A. Scherer and G. Palazzo (eds), *Handbook of Research on Corporate Citizenship*. Cheltenham: Edward Elgar, pp. 706–740.

Banerjee, S.B. (2009). 'Necrocapitalism', *Organization Studies*, 29 (12): 1541–1563.

Bansal, P. and Clelland, I. (2004). 'Talking trash: legitimacy, impression management, and unsystematic risk in the context of the natural environment', *Academy of Management Journal*, 47 (1): 93–103.

Bansal, P. and Roth, K. (2000). 'Why companies go green: a model of ecological responsiveness', *Academy of Management Review*, 13 (4): 717–736.

Barber, F. and Goold, M. (2007). 'The strategic secret of private equity', *Harvard Business Review*, September.

Bard, A. and Soderqvist, J. (2002). *Netocracy: The New Power Elite and Life After Capitalism.* Englewood Cliffs, NJ: FT Press.

BBC News (2010). 'Shell should end Nigeria "abuse"', 11 April.

Becker, G. (1981). *A Treatise on the Family.* Cambridge, MA: Harvard University Press.

Benston, G.J. (1982). 'Accounting and corporate accountability', *Accounting, Organizations and Society*, 7 (2): 87–106.

Berardi, F. (2009). *The Soul at Work.* Los Angeles: Semiotext(e).

Bhattacharya, C. and Sankar, S. (2004). 'Doing better at doing good: when, why and how consumers respond to corporate social initiatives', *California Management Review*, 47 (1): 9–25.

Bhattacharya, C.B., Korshun, D. and Sen, S. (2009). 'Strengthening stakeholder company relationships through mutually beneficial corporate social responsibility initiatives', *Journal of Business Ethics*, 85 (2): 257–272.

Biddle, D. (2000). 'Recycling for profit', in *Harvard Business Review on Business and the Environment.* Boston, MA: Harvard Business School Press.

Blanchot, M. (1997). *Friendship.* Stanford, CA: Stanford University Press.

Blowfield, M. and Murray, A. (2008). *Corporate Social Responsibility: A Critical Introduction.* Oxford: Oxford University Press.

Boele, R., Fabig, H. and Wheeler, D. (2001). 'Shell, Nigeria and the Ogoni: a study in unsustainable development, corporate social responsibility and "stakeholder management" versus a rights-based approach to sustainable development', *Sustainable Development*, 9 (3): 121–135.

Böhm, S. and Dabhi, S. (eds) (2009). *Upsetting the Offset: The Political Economy of Carbon Markets.* London: Mayfly.

Boltanski, L. and Chiapello, E. (2005). *The New Spirit of Capitalism*, trans. G. Elliott. London: Verso.

Bourdieu, P. (2001). *Firing Back against the Tyranny of the Market.* New York: The New Press.

Brammer, S. (2006). 'The feel good factories', *Guardian*, 21 January.

Breman, J. (2009). 'Myth of the global safety net', *New Left Review*, 64: 97–108.

Brenner, N. (1998). 'Global cities, global states', *Review of International Political Economy*, 5 (1): 1–37.

Brenner, N. (1999). 'Globalisation as reterritorialisation', *Urban Studies*, 36 (3): 431–451.

Brooks, D. (2001). *Bobos in Paradise.* New York: Simon & Schuster.

Brooks, G. (2005). Personal interview, Macquarie University.

Brown, D., Dillard, J. and Marshall, S. (2005). 'Triple bottom line: a business metaphor for a social construct', *Critical Perspectives on Accounting Proceedings*, City University of New York.

Brown, L. (2005). *Outgrowing the Earth.* San Francisco: Earthscan.

Bruyn, S.T. (1987). *The Field of Social Investment.* Cambridge: Cambridge University Press.

Burawoy, M. (1979). *Manufacturing Consent.* Chicago: University of Chicago Press.

Burrell, G. and Morgan, G. (1979). *Sociological Paradigms in Organizational Analysis.* London: Heinemann.

Calton, J.M. and Kurland, N. (1996). 'A theory of stakeholder enabling: giving voice to an emerging postmodern praxis of organizational discourse', in D. Boje et al. (eds), *Postmodern Management and Organization.* Thousand Oaks, CA: Sage.

Carroll, A. (1998). 'The four faces of corporate citizenship', *Business and Society Review*, 100 (1): 1–7.

Castells, M. (1996). *The Rise of the Network Society.* Oxford: Blackwell.

Castells, M. (1997). *The Power of Identity.* Oxford: Blackwell.

Castells, M. (2007). *The Power of Identity: The Information Age: Economy, Society, and Culture*, Volume II. Oxford: Basil Blackwell.

Cecchetti, S., Mohanty, M. and Zampolli, F. (2010). 'The future of public debt', BIS Working Paper no. 300, March.

Cederström, C. (2011). 'Fit for everything: health and the ideology of authenticity', *ephemera*, 11 (1): 27–45.

Chandler, A. (1977). *The Visible Hand*. Cambridge, MA: Harvard University Press.

Chandler, A. and Mazlish, B. (2005). *Leviathans*. Cambridge: Cambridge University Press.

Chang, H.-J. (2010). *23 Things They Don't Tell You About Capitalism*. London: Allen Lane.

Charkiewicz, E. (2005). 'Corporations, the UN and neo-liberal bio-politics', *Development*, 48 (1): 35–43.

Chomsky, N. (1999). *Profit over People: Neoliberalism and Global Order*. New York: Seven Stories Press.

Clarkson, M. (1995). 'A stakeholder framework for analyzing and evaluating corporate social performance', *Academy of Management Review*, 20: 92–117.

Coase, R. (1937). 'The nature of the firm', *Economica*, 4: 386–405.

Coetzee, J.W. (1999). *The Lives of Animals*. Princeton, NJ: Princeton University Press.

Cogman, D. and Oppenheim, J. (2002). 'Controversy incorporated', *McKinsey Quarterly*, No. 4.

Cook, S. (2008). 'The contribution revolution: let volunteers build your business', *Harvard Business Review*, 86 (10): 60–69.

Costas, J. (2010). 'Work-ing out: an analysis of sport, culture and identity in two management consultancy firms', Paper presented at the Academy of Management Pre-conference Workshop on Bio-Power at Work, August 9, Montreal, Canada.

Costas, J. and Fleming, P. (2009). 'Beyond dis-identification: towards a discursive approach to self-alienation in contemporary organizations', *Human Relations*, 62 (3): 353–378.

Cowling, K. and Sugden, R. (1987). *Transnational Monopoly Capitalism*. Oxford: Oxford University Press.

Cowton, C. (2004). 'Managing financial performance at an ethical investment fund', *Accounting, Auditing & Accountability Journal*, 17 (2): 249–275.

Cox, R., Gill, S., Hettne, B., Rosenau, J. and Sakamoto, Y. (1995). *International Political Economy*. London: Zed Books.

Crane, A. (2001). 'Unpacking the ethical product', *Journal of Business Ethics*, 30 (4/2): 361–373.

Crane, A. and Matten, D. (2008). 'Incorporating the corporation into citizenship: a response to Néron and Norman', *Business Ethics Quarterly*, 18 (1): 27–33.

Crane, A. and Matten, D. (2010). *Business Ethics*. Oxford: Oxford University Press.

Cremin, C. (2010). 'Never employable enough: the (im)possibility of satisfying the boss's desire', *Organization*, 17 (2): 131–149.

Daboub, A.J. and Calton, J.M. (2002). 'Stakeholder learning dialogues: how to preserve ethical responsibility in networks', *Journal of Business Ethics*, 41 (1–2): 85–98.

Dacin, P.A. and Brown, T.J. (1997). 'The company and the product corporate associations and consumer responses', *Journal of Marketing*, 61 (1): 68–84.

Dal Bo, E. (2006). 'Regulatory capture: a review', *Oxford Review of Economic Policy*, 22 (2): 203–225.

Davis, G. (2009). *Managed by the Markets: How Finance Re-shaped America*. Oxford: Oxford University Press.

Davis, I. (2005). 'What is the business of business?', *McKinsey Quarterly*, No. 3.

Davis, J.J. (1994). 'Consumer response to corporate environmental advertising', *International Marketing Review*, 11 (2): 25–37.

Davis, M. (2006). *Planet of Slums*. London: Verso.

Davis, M. (2007). *In Praise of Barbarians*. Chicago: Haymarket Books.

Davis, M. and Monk, D. (eds) (2008). *Evil Paradises: Dream Worlds of Neo-liberalism*. New York: New Press.

de Grey, A. (2008). *Aux frontières de l'immortalité*, 16 November, Gerald Caillat, director.

de Medeiros, C. (2009). 'Asset-stripping the state', *New Left Review*, 55 (January/February): 109–134.

Dean, J. (2007). *Democracy and Other Neo-liberal Fantasies*. Durham, NC: Duke University Press.

Deetz, S. (1992). *Democracy in an Age of Corporate Colonization*. New York: SUNY Press.

Diamond, J. (2006). *Collapse*. London: Penguin.

Dicken, P. (2010). *Global Shift*. London: Sage.

Dick-Forde, E. (2005). 'Democracy matters in corporate accountability: a Caribbean case study', *Critical Perspectives on Accounting Proceedings*, City University of New York.

Dockery, R. (2008). 'Are companies' corporate social responsibility initiatives authentic?', *Epoch Times*, www.epochtimes.com. Assessed 9 December 2010.

Donaldson, T. and Preston, L.E. (1995). 'The stakeholder theory of the corporation: concepts, evidence, and implications', *Academy of Management Journal*, 20: 65–91.

Dowbor, L. (1997). 'Preface', in P. Freire, *Pedagogy of the Heart*. New York: Continuum.

Drumwright, M. (1994). 'Socially responsible organizational buying: environmental concern as a noneconomic buying criterion', *Journal of Marketing*, 58 (3): 1–19.

DuBoff, R. (1989). *Accumulation and Power*. Armonk, NY: M.E. Sharpe.

Dugger, W.M. (1989). *Corporate Hegemony*. New York: Greenwood Press.

Duke, C.E. (2009). *Learning and Development in 2011*. Durham, NC: Duke Corporate Education.

Dunne, S. (2007). 'What is corporate social responsibility now?', *ephemera*, 7 (2): 372–80.

Edward, P. and Willmott, H. (2008). 'Corporate citizenship', *Academy of Management Review*, 33: 771–773.

Electronic Engineering Times (2001). 'Study predicts core tech services boom in India', 3 July.

Elkington, J. (1994). 'Towards the sustainable corporation: win-win-win business strategies for sustainable development', *California Management Review*, 36 (2): 90–100.

Elkington, J. and Hartigan, P. (2008). *The Power of Unreasonable People: How Entrepreneurs Create Markets to Change the World*. Boston, MA: Harvard Business School Press.

Farzad, K.R. and Boje, D. (2008). 'Story-branding by empire entrepreneurs: Nike, chilled labour and Pakistan's soccer ball industry', *Journal of Small Business and Entrepreneurship*, 22 (1): 9–24.

Feyerabend, P. (1993). *Against Method*. London: Verso.

Financial Times (2010). 'East outmanoeuvres west over Africa', 2 June.

Fisher, M. (2009). *Capitalist Realism: Is There No Alternative?* London: Zero Books.

Fleming, P. (2009a). *Authenticity and the Cultural Politics of Work*. Oxford: Oxford University Press.

Fleming, P. (2009b). 'Shitty work', Paper presented at the European Group of Organization Studies, June, Barcelona.

Fleming, P. and Spicer, A. (2007). *Contesting the Corporation*. Cambridge: Cambridge University Press.

Fleming, P. and Sturdy, A. (2009). '"Just be yourself!" Towards neo-normative control in organizations?', *Employee Relations*, 31 (6): 569–583.

Fleming, P. and Zyglidopoulos, S. (2009). *Charting Corporate Corruption: Structure, Agency and Escalation*. London: Edward Elgar.

Fligstein, N. (1990). *The Transformation of Corporate Control*. Cambridge, MA: Harvard University Press.

Foreign Policy (2006). 'The world's megacities', 12 June.

Fortune (2004). 'Joining the march of jobs overseas', 17 May.

Foucault, M. (1979). *Discipline and Punish: The Birth of the Prison*. New York: Pantheon.

Foucault, M. (2008). *The Birth of Biopolitics*. Basingstoke: Palgrave Macmillan.

Fox, D. (2009). *Cold World*. London: Zero Books.

Frank, T. (1998). *The Conquest of Cool: Business Culture, Counterculture and the Rise of Hip Consumerism*. Chicago: University of Chicago Press.

Frederick, W.C. (2006). *Corporation Be Good! The Story of Corporate Social Responsibility*. Indianapolis: Dog Ear Publishing.

Freedman, M. and Stagliano, A.J. (1991). 'Differences in social-cost disclosures: a market test of investor reactions', *Accounting, Auditing and Accountability Journal*, 4 (1): 68–83.

Freeman, R.E. (1984). *Strategic Stakeholder Management*. Minneapolis: University of Minnesota Press.

Freeman, R.E. and Gilbert, D.R., Jr (1992). 'Business, ethics and society: a critical agenda', *Business and Society*, 31 (Spring): 9–17.

Freeman, R.E. and Phillips, R. (2002). 'Stakeholder theory: a Libertarian defense', *Business Ethics Quarterly*, 12: 331–349.

Freeman, R.E., Harrison, J. and Wicks, A. (2007). *Managing for Stakeholders*. New Haven, CT: Yale University Press.

Frieden, J. (2007). *Global Capitalism: Its Fall and Rise in the Twentieth Century*. New York: W.W. Norton.

Friedland, R. and Alford, R. (1991). 'Bringing society back in: symbols, practices, and institutional contradictions', in W. Powell and P. DiMaggio (eds), *The New Institutionalism in Organizational Analysis*. Chicago: University of Chicago Press.

Friedman, M. (1970). 'The social responsibility of business is to increase profits', *The New York Times Magazine*, September 13.

Friedman, T. (2005). *The World is Flat: A Brief History of the Twenty-First Century*. New York: Farrar, Straus & Giroux.

Fukuyama, F. (1992). *The End of History and the Last Man*. New York: Free Press.

Galbraith, J.K. (1958). *The Affluent Society*. New York: Free Press.

Galbraith, J.K. (1967). *The New Industrial State*. New York: Mentor.

Galbraith, J.K. (2008). *The Predator State*. New York: Free Press.

Gasland (2010). London: Dogwoof Pictures.

Gelb, D.S. and Strawser, J.A. (2001). 'Corporate social responsibility and financial disclosures: an alternative explanation for increased disclosure', *Journal of Business Ethics*, 33 (1): 1–13.

Gereffi, G. (2008). *The New Off-Shoring of Jobs and Global Development*. Geneva: International Labour Office.

Ghoshal, S. and Westney, D. (2005). *Organization Theory and the Multinational Corporation*. New York: Palgrave Macmillan.

Giddens, A. (1979). *Central Problems in Social Theory*. New York: Macmillan.

Gilmore, J. and Pine, B. (2007). *Authenticity: What Consumers Really Want*. Boston, MA: Harvard Business School Press.

Gioia, D. (1992). 'Pinto fires and personal ethics: a script analysis of missed opportunities', *Journal of Business Ethics*, 11: 379–389.

Gioia, D. (1999). 'Practicability, paradigms and problems in stakeholder theory', *Academy of Management Review*, 24 (2): 228–232.

Giulianotti, R. and Robertson, R. (2007). *Globalization and Football*. London: Sage.

Gond, J.-P., Palazzo, G. and Basu, K. (2009). 'Reconsidering instrumental corporate social responsibility through the Mafia metaphor', *Business Ethics Quarterly*, 19 (1): 55–84.

Gond, J.-P., El Akremi, A., Igalens, J. and Swaen, V. (2010). 'A corporate social performance – corporate financial performance behavioural model for employees', in C. Bhattacharya et al. (eds), *Corporate Responsibility and Global Business: Implications for Corporate and Marketing Strategy*. Cambridge: Cambridge University Press.

Goold, M., Campbell, A. and Alexander, M. (1998). 'Corporate strategy and parenting theory', *Long Range Planning*, 31 (2): 308–314.

Gore, A. (2006). *An Inconvenient Truth*. London: Bloomsbury.

Gorz, A. (1989). *Critique of Economic Reason*. London: Verso.

Gossett, W. (1957). *Corporate Citizenship*. Lexington, VA: Washington & Lee University Press.

Gowan, P. (2009). 'Crisis on Wall Street', *New Left Review*, 55: 5–29.

Gray, J. (1998). *False Dawn*. London: Polity.

Gray, R. (1992). 'Accounting and environmentalism: an exploration of the challenge of gently accounting for accountability, transparency and sustainability', *Accounting, Organizations and Society*, 17 (5): 399–425.

Gray, R. and Milne, M.J. (2002). 'Sustainability reporting: who's kidding whom?', *Chartered Accountants Journal of New Zealand*, 81 (6): 66–70.

Gray, R., Owen, D. and Maunders, K. (1988). 'Corporate social reporting: emerging trends in accountability and the social contract', *Accounting, Auditing, and Accountability Journal*, 1 (1): 6–20.

Greening, D.W. and Turban, D.B. (2000). 'Corporate social performance as a competitive advantage in attracting a quality workforce', *Business & Society*, 39: 254–280.

Greer, J. (2008). *The Long Descent*. Gabriola Island, BC: New Society Publishers.

Greer, J. (2009). *The Ecotechnic Future*. Gabriola Island, BC: New Society Publishers.

Guardian (2008). 'BA executives face charges of price-fixing', 26 July.

Guardian (2009a). 'The tropics on fire', 16 February.

Guardian (2009b). 'Peak oil could hit soon, report says', 8 October.

Guardian (2010a). 'Martin Amis in new row over "euthanasia booths"', 24 January.

Guardian (2010b). 'Human Genome Project leader warns against attempts to patent genes', 24 June.

Guardian (2010c). 'Tax evasion stifles poorest nations', 26 January.

Guardian (2010d). 'WikiLeaks cables: Shell's grip on Nigerian state revealed', 9 December.

Guardian (2012). 'Rio+20 Earth Summit: campaigners decry final document', 24 June.

Guillén, M. (2001). *The Limits of Convergence*. Princeton, NJ: Princeton University Press.

Habermas, J. (1973). *Legitimation Crisis*. Boston, MA: Beacon Press.

Hahn, J. (2010). 'Half a world from Gulf, a spill scourge 5 decades old', *New York Times*, June 16.

Haigh, M. and Hazelton, J. (2004). 'Financial markets: a tool for social responsibility?', *Journal of Business Ethics*, 52 (1): 59–71.

Haigh, M. and Jones, M. (2010). 'The institutional drivers of CSR', Working Paper, Ashridge Business School, Hertfordshire.

Hanlon, G. (2007). 'Rethinking corporate social responsibility and the role of the firm – on the denial of politics', in A. Crane et al. (eds), *Oxford Handbook of Corporate Social Responsibility*. Oxford: Oxford University Press.

Hanlon, G. and Fleming, P. (2009). 'Updating the critical perspectives on corporate social responsibility', *Sociology Compass*, 3: 937–948.

Hardt, M. and Negri, A. (1999). *Empire*. Cambridge, MA: Harvard University Press.

Hardt, M. and Negri. A. (2009). *Commonwealth*. Cambridge, MA: Harvard University Press.

Harney, S. (2009). 'Extreme neoliberalism', *Ephemera*, 9 (4): 318–329.

Harney, S., Parker, M. and Dunne, S. (2008). 'The responsibilities of management intellectuals: a survey', *Organization*, 15 (2): 271–282.

Harrison, B. and Bluestone, B. (1988). *The Great U-turn*. New York: Basic Books.

Harvey, D. (1990a). 'Critical theory', *Sociological Perspectives*, 33 (1): 1–10.

Harvey, D. (1990b). *The Condition of Postmodernity*. Oxford: Blackwell.

Harvey, D. (2007). *A Brief History of Neoliberalism*. Oxford: Oxford University Press.

Harvey, D. (2010). *The Enigma of Capital and the Crises of Capitalism*. New York: Oxford University Press.

Hay, C., Marsh, D. and Lister, M. (eds) (2005). *The State*. Basingstoke: Palgrave.

Heilbroner, R. (1985). *The Nature and Logic of Capitalism*. New York: Norton.

Heinberg, R. (2005). *The Party's Over*. Forest Row, East Sussex: Clairview Books.

Held, D. (1996). *Models of Democracy*. Cambridge: Polity.

Held, D. and McGrew, A. (2003). *Globalization/Anti-globalization*. Cambridge: Polity.

Held, D., McGrew, A., Goldblatt, D. and Perraton, J. (1999). *Global Transformations*. Cambridge: Polity.

Held, D., Kaldor, M. and Quah, D. (2010). 'The Hydra-headed crisis', London School of Economics, Global Governance Pamphlet.

Herman, E. (1981). *Corporate Control, Corporate Power*. Cambridge: Cambridge University Press.

Hindess, B. (1993). 'Citizenship in the modern West', in B. Turner (ed.), *Citizenship and Social Theory*. London: Sage.

Hochschild, A. (1997). *The Time Bind: When Work Becomes Home and Home Becomes Work*. New York: Henry Holt.

In Our Times (2010). 'The Frankfurt school'. BBC 4 Radio, 14 January.

Independent (2009). 'World on course for catastrophic six degree rise, reveal scientists', 18 November.

Intergovernmental Panel on Climate Change (2008). *Climate Change 2007*. Geneva: IPCC.

International Energy Agency (2011). *World Energy Outlook 2011*. Paris: IEA.

International Energy Agency (2012). *Tracking Clean Energy Progress*. Paris: IEA.

International Labour Organization (2010). 'ILO report for the G20 Summit in Seoul (11–12 November 2010)'. Geneva, Switzerland.

Invisible Committee (2009). *The Coming Insurrection*. Cambridge, MA: MIT Press.

Iyer, B. (2008). 'Reverse engineering Google's innovation machine', *Harvard Business Review*, April: 59–68.

Jacques, M. (2009). *When China Rules the World*. London: Penguin.

Jay, M. (1984). *Marxism and Totality*. Berkeley, CA: University of California Press.

Jensen, M. (2002). 'Value maximization, stakeholder theory, and the corporate objective function', *Business Ethics Quarterly*, 12 (2): 235–247.

Jensen, M.C. and Meckling, W.H. (1976). 'Theory of the firm: managerial behavior, agency costs and ownership structure', *Journal of Financial Economics*, 3 (4): 305–360.

John, A. and Klein, J. (2003). 'The boycott puzzle: consumer motivations for purchase sacrifice', *Management Science*, 49 (9): 1196–1209.

Johnson, H. (1958). 'The resolution of a dilemma', *Business Horizons*, 12 (5): 69–74.

Johnson, S. (2009). 'The quiet coup', *The Atlantic Online*, May.

Jones, C., ten Bos, R. and Parker, M. (2005). *For Business Ethics: A Critical Approach*. London: Routledge.

Jones, I.W. and Pollitt, M.G. (eds) (2002). *Understanding how Issues in Business Ethics Develop*. Basingstoke: Palgrave Macmillan.

Jones, M. (1993). 'Adam Smith and the ethics of contemporary democratic capitalism in New Zealand', *International Journal of Social Economics*, 20 (12): 3–13.

Jones, M. (1996). 'Missing the forest for the trees: a critique of the social responsibility concept and discourse', *Business and Society*, 35 (1): 7–41.

Jones, M. (1999). 'The competitive advantage of the TNC as an institutional form', *International Journal of Social Economics*, 24 (7): 943–958.

Jones, M. (2002). 'Globalization and organizational restructuring', *Thunderbird International Business Review*, 44 (3): 325–351.

Jones, M. (2003). 'Globalisation and the organisation(s) of exclusion', in S. Clegg and R. Westwood (eds), *Debating Organization Theory: Point-Counterpoint in Organization Studies*. London: Macmillan, pp. 252–270.

Jones, M. (2009a). 'Disrobing the emperor', *Management of Environmental Quality*, 20 (3): 335–346.

Jones, M. (2009b). 'Globalization and culture', Working Paper, Ashridge Business School.

Jones, M. and Fleming, P. (2003). 'Unpacking complexity through critical stakeholder analysis: the case of globalization', *Business and Society*, 42 (4): 430–454.

Jones, M. and Haigh, M. (2007). 'The transnational corporation and new corporate citizenship theory', *Journal of Corporate Citizenship*, 27: 51–69.

Jones, T. (1995). 'Instrumental stakeholder theory: a synthesis of ethics and economics', *Academy of Management Review*, 20: 404–437.

Joseph, M. (2002). *Against the Romance of Community*. Minneapolis: University of Minnesota Press.

Jowit, J. (2010). 'Corporate lobbying is blocking food reforms, senior UN official warns', *Guardian*, 22 August.

Kagan, R. (2009). *The Return of History and the End of Dreams*. New York: Atlantic Books.

King, A. and Lenox, M. (2001). 'Does it really pay to be green? An empirical study of firm environmental and financial performance', *Journal of Industrial Ecology*, 5 (1): 105–116.

Klare, M. (2002). *Resource Wars*. New York: Owl Books.

Klein, N. (2007). *Shock Doctrine: The Rise of Disaster Capitalism*. London: Penguin.

Kolk, A. (2005). 'Environmental reporting by multinationals from the Triad: convergence or divergence?', *Management International Review*, 45 (Special Issue/1): 145–166.

Korten, D. (2001). *When Corporations Rule the World*. San Francisco: Berrett-Koehler.

Kuhn, T. (2006). 'A "Demented Work Ethic" and a "Lifestyle Firm": discourse, identity, and workplace time commitments', *Organization Studies*, 27 (9): 1339–1358.

Kulkarni, S.K. (2000). 'Environmental ethics and information asymmetry among organizational stakeholders', *Journal of Business Ethics*, 28 (3): 215–228.

Lanchester, J. (2010). *I.O.U.: Why Everyone Owes Everyone and No-one Can Pay*. New York: Simon & Schuster.

Land, C. and Taylor, S. (2010). 'Surf's up: life, balance and brand in a new age capitalist organization', *Sociology*, 44 (3): 395–413.

Lasch, C. (1996). *The Revolt of the Elites*. New York: Pantheon.

Lash, S. and Lury, C. (2007). *The Global Culture Industry: The Mediation of Things*. Cambridge: Polity.

Lavelle, A. (2008). *The Death of Social Democracy*. Burlington, VT: Ashgate.

Leavitt, T. (1958). 'The dangers of social responsibility', *Harvard Business Review*, 36 (September–October): 41–50.

Lee, M. (2008). 'A review of the theories of corporate social responsibility', *International Journal of Management Reviews*, 10 (1): 53–73.

Lehman, G. (1999). 'Disclosing new worlds: a role for social and environmental accounting and auditing', *Accounting, Organizations and Society*, 24 (3): 217–241.

Lem, W. and Barber, P.G. (2010). *Class, Contention and a World in Motion*. New York: Berghahn Books.

Levy, D.L. (2008). 'Political contestation in global production networks', *Academy of Management Review*, 33 (4): 943–963.

Livesey, S.M. (2002). 'The discourse of the middle ground: citizen Shell commits to sustainable development', *Management Communication Quarterly*, 5 (3): 309–343.

Lustig, J. (1979). *Corporate Liberalism: The Origins of Modern American Political Theory, 1890–1920*. New York: Praeger.

Lynas, M. (2007). *Six Degrees*. London: Fourth Estate.

Lynas, M. (2010). 'How do I know China wrecked the Copenhagen deal?', *Guardian*, 22 December.

Mackenzie, C. and Lewis, A. (1999). 'Morals and markets: the case of ethical investing', *Business Ethics Quarterly*, 9 (3): 439–452.

Maignan, I., Ferrell, O.C. and Hult, G.T.M. (1999). 'Corporate citizenship: cultural antecedents and business benefits', *Journal of the Academy of Marketing Science*, 27 (4): 455–469.

Marazzi, C. (2010). *The Violence of Finance Capital*. Los Angeles: Semiotext(e).

Marcuse, H. (1964). *One-dimensional Man*. Boston, MA: Beacon Press.

Marens, R. (2010). 'Destroying the village to save it: corporate social responsibility, labour relations, and the rise and fall of American hegemony', *Organization*, 17: 743–766.

Margolis, J. and Walsh, J. (2003). 'Misery loves companies: whither social initiatives by business?', *Administrative Science Quarterly*, 48 (June): 268–305.

Marks, L.J. and Mayo, M.A. (1991). 'An empirical test of a model of consumer ethical dilemmas', *Advances in Consumer Research*, 18: 720–728.

Matten, D. and Crane, A. (2005). 'Corporate citizenship: towards an extended theoretical conceptualization', *Academy of Management Review*, 30 (1): 166–179.

Matten, D., Crane, A. and Chapple, W. (2003). 'Behind the mask', *Journal of Business Ethics*, 45 (1): 109–120.

McCarthy, C. (1985). *Blood Meridian*. New York: Random House.

McIntosh, M., Leipziger, D., Jones, K. and Coleman, G. (1998). *Corporate Citizenship: Successful Strategies for Responsible Companies*. London: Financial Times/Pitman.

McKinsey & Company (2006). 'Global survey of business executives', *McKinsey Quarterly*, January: 37–45.

McWilliams, A. and Siegel, D. (2001a). 'Corporate social responsibility and financial performance: correlations for misspecification', *Strategic Management Journal*, 21: 603–609.

McWilliams, A. and Siegel, D. (2001b). 'Corporate social responsibility: a theory of the firm perspective', *Academy of Management Review*, 26 (1): 117–127.

McWilliams, A., Siegel, D. and Wright, P. (2006). 'Corporate social responsibility: strategic implications', *Journal of Management Studies*, 43 (1): 1–18.

Meyerson, D. (2003). *Tempered Radicals: How Everyday Leaders Inspire Change at Work*. Cambridge, MA: Harvard University Press.

Michelli, J. (2007). *The Starbucks Experience: 5 Principles for Turning Ordinary into Extraordinary*. New York: McGraw-Hill.

Millennium Ecosystem Assessment (2005). *Millennium Ecosystem Assessment Synthesis Report*. Draft report. www.millenniumassessment.org/en/Products.Synthesis.aspx. Accessed April 2005.

Miller, P. and O'Leary, T. (1989). 'Hierarchies and American ideals, 1900–1940', *Academy of Management Review*, 1: 250–265.

Milne, M.J. and Chan, C.C. (1999). 'Narrative corporate social disclosures: how much of a difference do they make to investment decision-making?', *British Accounting Review*, 31: 439–457.

Mintz, B. and Schwartz, M. (1990). 'Financial flows and corporate hegemony', in S. Zukin and P. Dimaggio (eds), *Structures of Capital*, Cambridge: Cambridge University Press.

Mitchell, R.K., Agle, B.R. and Wood, D.J. (1997). 'Toward a theory of stakeholder identification and salience: defining the principle of who and what really counts', *Academy of Management Review*, 22 (4): 853–88.

Mittelman, J. (ed.) (1996). *Globalization*. Boulder, CO: Lynne Rienner.

Mohun, S. (2009). 'Boom and bust in the American economy', Inaugural Lecture, 6 February, Queen Mary College, University of London.

Moneva, M., Archel, P. and Correa, C. (2006). 'GRI and the camouflaging of corporate unsustainability', *Accounting Forum*, 30: 121–137.

Moon, J. and Vogel, D. (2008). 'Corporate social responsibility, government, and civil society', in A. Crane et al. (eds), *Oxford Handbook of Corporate Social Responsibility*. Oxford: Oxford University Press.

Moon, J., Crane, A. and Matten, D. (2005). 'Can corporations be citizens?', *Business Ethics Quarterly*, 15 (3): 429–453.

Moore, B. (1967). *Social Origins of Dictatorship and Democracy*. Boston, MA: Beacon Press.

Moyo, D. (2012). *Winner Take All*. London: Allen Lane.

Naisbitt, J. (1982). *Megatrends. Ten New Directions Transforming Our Lives*. New York: Warner Books.

Neimark, M.K. (1995). 'The selling of ethics: the ethics of business meets the business of ethics', *Accounting, Auditing and Accountability Journal*, 8 (3): 81–96.

New York Times (2005). 'Halliburton overcharged $108 million, report says', March 15.

Nolan, W.F. and Johnson, G.C. (1967). *Logan's Run*. New York: Dial Press.

O'Conner, J. (1987). *The Meaning of Crisis*. New York: Basil Blackwell.

O'Dwyer, B. (2003). 'Conceptions of corporate social responsibility: the nature of managerial capture', *Accounting, Auditing and Accountability Journal*, 16 (4): 523–557.

Ojeda, M. and Hennessy, R. (2006). *NAFTA From Below: Maquiladora Workers, Farmers, and Indigenous Communities Speak Out on the Impact of Free Trade in Mexico*. Los Angeles: Coalition for Justice in the Maquiladoras.

Panitch, L. and Konigs, M. (2009). 'Myths of neo-liberal deregulation', *New Left Review*, 57: 67–83.

Parker, M. (2002). *Against Management: Organization in the Age of Managerialism*. Cambridge: Polity.

Patten, D.M. (1990). 'The market reaction to social responsibility disclosures: the case of the Sullivan Principles Signings', *Accounting, Organizations and Society*, 15 (6): 575–587.

Perelman, M. (2002). *Steal this Idea: Intellectual Property Rights and the Corporate Confiscation of Creativity*. New York: Palgrave.

Perrow, C. (1986). *Complex Organizations*. New York: McGraw-Hill.

Peterson, D.K. (2004). 'The relationship between perceptions of corporate citizenship and organizational commitment', *Business and Society*, 43 (3): 269–319.

Pfeffer, J. and Salancik, G. (1979). *The External Control of Organizations*. New York: Harper & Row.

Pierre, G., Robertson, R., Brown, D. and Sanchez-Puerta, L. (2009). *Globalization, Wages and Quality of Jobs*. New York: World Bank.

Polanyi, K. (1944). *The Great Transformation*. Boston, MA: Beacon Press.

Porter, M. and Kramer, M. (2002). 'The competitive advantage of corporate philanthropy', *Harvard Business Review*, December: 36–52.

Porter, M. and Kramer, M. (2006). 'Strategy and society: the link between competitive advantage and corporate social responsibility', *Harvard Business Review*, December: 21–38.

Porter, M. and Kramer, M. (2011). 'Creating shared value', *Harvard Business Review*, 89 (1/2): 62–77.

Potter, A. (2010). *The Authenticity Hoax: How we get Lost Finding Ourselves*. New York: HarperCollins.

Preston, L. (1985). 'Freedom, markets, and voluntary exchange', *American Political Science Review*, 78: 959–970.

Preuss, L., Haunschild, A. and Matten, D. (2009). 'The rise of CSR: implications for HRM and employee representation', *International Journal of Human Resource Management*, 20 (4): 975–995.

Prothero, A. (1990). 'Green consumerism and the societal marketing concept: marketing strategies for the 1990s', *Journal of Marketing Management*, 6 (2): 87–103.

Reed, D. (1999). 'The realms of corporate responsibility', *Journal of Business Ethics*, 21: 23–36.

Reich, R. (1991). *The Work of Nations*. New York: Vintage.

Reich, R. (1997). 'The corporation as citizen', *California Management Review*, Fall: 61–73.

Reich, R. (2007). *Supercapitalism: The Transformation of Business, Democracy, and Everyday Life*. New York: Knopf.

Reinhardt, C. and Rogoff, K. (2009). *This Time it's Different: Eight Centuries of Financial Folly*. Princeton, NJ: Princeton University Press.

Resnick, S. and Wolff, R. (1987). *Knowledge and Class*. Chicago: University of Chicago Press.

Richardson, B.J. (2002). 'Ethical investment and the Commonwealth's Financial Services Reform Act 2001', *National Environmental Law Review*, 2: 47–60.

Rinehart, J. (2006). *The Tyranny of Work: Alienation and the Labour Process*. Toronto: Nelson.

Ritzer, G. (2009). *Globalization: A Basic Text*. New York: Wiley Blackwell.

Roberts, J. (2003). 'The manufacture of corporate social responsibility: constructing corporate sensibility', *Organization*, 10 (2): 249–265.

Ronit, K. and Schneider, V. (1999). 'Global governance through private organizations', *Governance*, 12: 243–266.

Rose, N. (2007). *The Politics of Life Itself: Biomedicine, Power and Subjectivity in the Twenty-First Century*. Princeton, NJ: Princeton University Press.

Rosica, C. (2007). *The Authentic Brand: How Today's Top Entrepreneurs Connect with Customers*. London: Noble Press.

Ross, A. (2004). *No-Collar: The Humane Workplace and Its Hidden Costs*. New York: Basic Books.

Rupp, D.E., Gananpathy, J., Aguilera, R.V. and Williams, C.A. (2006). 'Employees' reactions to corporate social responsibility: an organizational justice framework', *Journal of Organizational Behaviour*, 27: 537–543.

Sandel, M. (2009). *Justice*. London: Penguin.

Sassen, S. (1998). *Globalization and its Discontents*. New York: New Press.

Sassen, S. (2006). Interview. *The Possibility of Hope*. Alfonso Cuaron, director.

Sassen, S. (2008). *A Sociology of Globalization*. New York: W.W. Norton.

Scherer, A. and Palazzo, G. (2007). 'Towards a political conception of corporate responsibility: business and society seen from a Habermasian perspective', *Academy of Management Review*, 32 (4): 1096–1120.

Scherer, A. and Palazzo, G. (2008a). 'Corporate citizenship: rise or demise of a myth?', *Academy of Management Review*, 33 (3): 771–775.

Scherer, A. and Palazzo, G. (2008b). 'Globalization and corporate social responsibility', in A. Crane et al. (eds), *Oxford Handbook of Corporate Social Responsibility*. Oxford: Oxford University Press.

Scherer, A. and Palazzo, G. (eds) (2008c). *Handbook of Research on Global Corporate Citizenship*. Cheltenham: Edward Elgar.

Scherer, A. and Palazzo, G. (2010). 'The new political role of business in a globalized world? A review of a new perspective on CSR and its implications for the firm, governance and democracy', *Journal of Management Studies*, 48 (4): 899–931.

Scherer, A., Palazzo, G. and Baumann, D. (2006). 'Global rules and private actors', *Business Ethics Quarterly*, 16 (4): 505–532.

Schumacher, E. (1973). *Small Is Beautiful*. London: Blond & Briggs.

Schumpeter, J. (1945). *Capitalism, Socialism and Democracy*. New York: Harper.

Schwartz, M.S. (2003). 'The "ethics" of ethical investing', *Journal of Business Ethics*, 43: 195–213.

Schwartz, M. and Carroll, A. (2003). 'Corporate social responsibility: a three-domain approach', *Business Ethics Quarterly*, (13): 503–530.

Sennett, R. (1998). *The Corrosion of Character: The Personal Consequences of Work in the New Capitalism*. London: W.W. Norton.

Shamir, R. (2008). 'The age of resonsibilization: on market-embedded morality', *Economy and Society*, 37 (1): 1–19.

Smith, N.C. (1990). *Morality and the Market: Consumer Pressure for Corporate Accountability*. London: Routledge.

Statman, M. (2000). 'Socially responsible mutual funds', *Financial Analysts Journal*, 56 (3): 30–39.

Staudt, K. (2008). *Violence and Activism at the Border: Gender, Fear, and Everyday Life in Ciudad Juarez*. Austin, TX: University of Texas Press.

Stern, N. (2007). *The Economics of Climate Change*. Cambridge: Cambridge University Press.

Stieb, J. (2009). 'Assessing Freeman's stakeholder theory', *Journal of Business Ethics*, 87 (3): 401–414.

Stiglitz, J. (2003). *Globalization and its Discontents*. New York: Free Press.

Stiglitz, J. (2010). *Freefall: America, Free Markets, and the Sinking of the World Economy*. New York: W.W. Norton.

Svendsen, L. (2008). *Work*. Durham: Acumen.

Tapscott, D. and Williams, A. (2008). *Wikinomics: How Mass Collaboration Challenges Everything*. London: Atlantic Books.

Tatz, C. (1982). *Aborigines and Uranium and Other Essays*. Richmond, Victoria: Heinemann Educational Australia.

The Economist (2008). 'Special report on corporate social responsibility', 19 January.

Tichy, N., McGill, A. and St. Clair, L. (eds) (1997). *Corporate Citizenship*. San Francisco: New Lexington Press.

Tinker, T. (2005). 'The withering of criticism: a review of professional, Foucauldian, ethnographic, and epistemic studies in accounting', *Accounting, Auditing and Accountability Journal*, 18 (1): 100–135.

Tinker, T., Neimark, M. and Lehman, C. (1991). 'Falling down the hole in the middle of the road: quietism in corporate social reporting', *Accounting, Auditing and Accountability Journal*, 4 (2): 167–200.

Tinker, T. and Carter, C. (2003). 'Spectres of accounting: contradictions or conflicts of interest', *Organization*, 10 (3): 577–582.

Toffler, A. (1984). *Megatrends: Ten New Directions Transforming Our Lives*. New York: Warner Brothers Books.

Towers Watson (2008). 'Corporate social responsibility: no longer an option', www.towersperrin.com/tp/showdctmdoc.jsp?url=Master_Brand_2/USA/News/Spotlights/2008/2008_07_30_Spotlight_Corporate_Social_Responsibility.htm. Accessed 30 July 2008.

Trevino, L. and Weaver, G. (1999). 'Letter to AMR regarding convergence stakeholder theory', *Academy of Management Review*, 24: 621–626.

Trosclair, A. (2007). 'Authentic marketing strategies', www.advertising.suite101.com/article.cfm/authentic_marketing_strategy. Accessed 13 December 2010.

Turban, D.B. and Greening, D.W. (1996). 'Corporate social performance and organizational attractiveness to prospective employees', *Academy of Management Journal*, 40 (3): 658–672.

Tyran, J.-R. and Engelmann, D. (2005). 'To buy or not to buy? An experimental study of consumer boycotts in retail markets', *Economica*, 82 (285): 1–16.

UN-Habitat (2003). *The Challenge of Slums*. London: Earthscan.

United Nations Conference on Trade and Development (2010a). *Least Developed Countries Report*. Geneva: United Nations.

United Nations Conference on Trade and Development (2010b). *World Investment Report (WIR)*. Geneva: United Nations.

USA Today (2004). 'Reverse brain drain threatens U.S. economy', February 23.

UvA (2005). *KPMG International Survey of Corporate Responsibility Reporting 2005*. University of Amsterdam.

Van Buren, H.J. (2001). 'If fairness is the problem, is consent the solution? Integrating ISCT and stakeholder theory', *Business Ethics Quarterly*, 11: 481–499.

van Oosterhout, H. (2005). 'Corporate citizenship: an idea whose time has not yet come', *Academy of Management Review*, 30 (4): 677–682.

van Oosterhout, H. and Heugens, P. (2008). 'Much ado about nothing', in A. Crane et al. (eds), *Oxford Handbook of Corporate Social Responsibility*. Oxford: Oxford University Press.

Vise, D. (2005). *The Google Story*. New York: Pan Books.

Vogel, D. (2005). *The Market for Virtue: The Potential and Limits of Corporate Social Responsibility*. Washington, DC: Brookings Institution Press.

Wallerstein, I. (1979). *The Capitalist World Economy*. Cambridge: Cambridge University Press.

Watkins, S. (2010). 'Blue labour?', *New Left Review*, 63 (May/June): 5–15.

Weiss, L. (1998). *The Myth of the Powerless State*. London: Polity.

Welzer, H. (2012). *Climate Wars*. London: Polity Press.

Whitley, R. (1992). *Business Systems in East Asia*. London: Sage.

Whitley, R. (2007). *Business Systems and Organizational Capabilities*. Oxford: Oxford University Press.

Whyte, W. (1956). *The Organization Man*. New York: Simon & Schuster.

Wicks, A., Feeman, R.E., Werhane, P. and Martin, K. (2010). *Business Ethics*. Englewood Cliffs, NJ: Pearson Education.

Williamson, O. (1975). *Markets and Hierarchies*. New York: Free Press.

Wittenberg, J., Harmon, J., Russel, W.G. and Fairfield, K.D. (2007). 'HR's role in building a sustainable enterprise: insights from some of the world's best companies', *Human Resource Planning*, 30 (1): 10–20.

Wood, D. (1991). 'Corporate social performance revisited', *Academy of Management Review*, 16: 691–718.

Wood, D. and Logsdon, J. (2001). 'Theorising business citizenship', in J. Andriof and M. McIntosh (eds), *Perspectives on Corporate Citizenship*. Sheffield: Greenleaf, pp. 83–103.

Wood, T. (2009). 'Latin America tamed?', *New Left Review*, 58 (July–August): 135–150.

Žižek, S. (1989). *The Sublime Object of Ideology*. London: Verso.

Žižek, S. (2008). *On Violence*. London: Profile Books.

Žižek, S. (2009). *First as Tragedy, then as Farce*. London: Verso.

Žižek, S. (2010a). *Living in the End of Times*. London: Verso.

Žižek, S. (2010b). 'A permanent economic emergency', *New Left Review*, 64 (July/August): 85–96.

INDEX

Figures and Tables are indicated by page numbers in **bold**.

Academy of Management Review, 1
Africa, 60
  health, 84
  oil reserves, 27
  'race for', 24
  water supply, 16
ageing populations, 24–5
alternative energy sources, 24
Althussur, L., 40
Amis, Martin, 25
Amnesty International, 26, 30
anti-business rhetoric to motivate workers, 74
anti-globalization protests, 66
AOL, 75
Appadurai, A., 59
Argentina, 43
arms industry, 88, 103
Australia, 39
Australian Wilderness Society, 15
'Authentic Business', 74
'Authentic Marketing Services', 74
authenticity, 74–6
  and inauthenticity, 75
autonome a.f.r.i.k.a gruppe, 104
Ayers, Charlie, 76
Ayres, E., 30

BAE Systems, 84, 103
Baer, W. and Montes-Rojas, G., 43
Baku-Tbilisi-Ceyhan pipeline, 82
Banerjee, S.B., 4, 6, 51, 64, 85, 87
Bangalore, 46
Bangladesh, 46
banks
  reckless activities, 21
  rescue of, 38
Barret, Craig, 46
Bechtel Corporation, 43
benefits of CSR to firms, 5
Benjamin, Walter, 106
Bhattacharya, C. and Sankar, S., 13
bio-diversity, decline of, 23
bio-political firms, 90, 91
Blowfield, M. and Murray, A., 4, 72,
  79, 92
Body Shop, 1, 10, 84

Boele, R. et al., 57
Bolivia, 43
Boltanski and Chiapello, 74, 76
Bourdieu, P., 14
BP, 1, 56, 82–3
  CSR policy, 82–3
  oil spill, 1
  unethical behaviour, 82
Brammer, S., 72–3
brand appropriation, 91–2
branding, 1, 69, 74, 79
Brazil, 27
Brenner, N., 39
Breyer, James, 47
'BRIC' nations, 24
British Airways, 21
British American Tobacco, 1, 15, 99
Brooks, D., 76–7
Business Activity Impact Matrix (BAIM),
  20–2, **21**, 99, 102–3
  'Corporate Social Irresponsibility', 21–2
  'Enlightened Self-Interest', 22
  'pathologies', 21
  'Public Goods', 21
business firms, 40
  financialization of, 41
business ontology, 29
business schools, 105

Campaign Against Arms Trading (CAAT), 103
Canada, 39
capital accumulation process, 25–6
capitalism
  and deliberative democracy, 87
  eco-capitalism, 30–1
  as instrument of common good, 31
  overlap with ethics, 4
  'producing people', 12, 26
capitalist realism, 2–3, 51, 83–4
carbon emissions agreement, 2
Carroll, A., 20
Castells, M., 62
Central Asia, 60
centralization and decentralization, 62–4
child labour, 17, 67, 97
children's health, 84

Chile, 7
China, 24, 26, 47
    economic growth, 27
    and Google, 76
citizenship, 33, 85–6
    meanings of, 38
class structure, 61
clean energy, 24
climate change, 2, 10, 14, 23, 26, 102
clothing firms, 88
Coalition for Environmentally Responsible
    Economies, 15
Coetzee, J.W., 106
cognitive maps, 29
commodification of non-commercial spheres of
    life, 89–90, 93–4
'commodity fetish', 84
community good, 94
consumer boycotts, 13, 17
consumers
    favouring 'green' products, 12, 13, 17
    sovereignty of, 12
convergence and divergence, 58–60
Conway's law, 75
Copenhagen Climate Change Conference 2009, 2,
    14, 24, 87
corporate innovations, 84
corporate liberalism, 35
corporate social responsibility (CSR): definitions,
    4, 20
corporate–noncorporate interconnections, 105
Corporation, The (film), 43
CorpWatch, 105
Costas, J. and Fleming, P., 73
costs of regulation, 14
Cowling, K. and Sugden, R., 63
Crane, A. and Matten, D., 37, 52, 91
creative work, 73
critical stakeholder analysis (CSA), 51, 52, 54–6,
    65–6
critics of CSR, 5–6
critiques of CSR, 6–8
cultural diversity, 59

Danfoss, 98–9
Davis, I., 93
Davis, M., 25, 43
'Deepwater Horizon', 82
deliberative democracy, 86–7
    and capitalism, 87
demand for 'green' products, 12
democracy, 86
democratic capitalism, 27
deportation of 'illegal immigrants', 104
deregulation, 39
detraction in CSR policy, 88
developing countries, 24, 25, 28, 37, 91
    development institutions, 59
    fall in urban employment in, 43
Dick-Forde, E., 9

Dicken, P., 63
dissimulation in CSR policy, 88
Dockery, R., 93
Donaldson, T. and Preston, L.E., 53
double standards in CSR, 4
Dugger, W.M., 12

eco-consumerism, 12
    promoting social justice, 12
Economist, The, 99
economic rationality, 14, 38
education as business, 2
education, rights to, 37, 44
Edward, P. and Willmott, H., 36
electricity, 26–7
employees see workers
empowerment/disempowerment, 60
'end of history' thesis, 24
energy depletion, 23–4, 26–7, 29–30
enlightened self-interest, 100, 101
Enron, 21, 84, 87–8
environmentalism, 67
'ethical capitalism', 4
ethical consumer, 12–13
ethical marketing, 89
ethical standards
    and corporate scandals list, 80
    and hypocrisy, 80–1, 83
    in/compatibility with business, 81, 84
    and staff attraction, 69–70
ethicist arguments for CSR, 4–5
European Commission, 4
European Group for Organization Studies
    Conference 2009, 33
European Union environmental legislation, 13–14
extreme neo-liberalism, 14, 30, 39–40, 51, 62, 86

Facebook, 90
fair trade, 1, 91–2
'fetish of capital', 84–5
financial crisis, 18, 38, 51
financial hegemony, 41–2
financial market integration, 41
financialization of business ethics, 11–12
financialization of firms, 41
firms, definition of, 63
firms, ownership and control of, 63–4
Fisher, M., 2
Fligstein, N., 41–2
food security, 28
Ford Pinto, 83
Fordist compact, 89
Foreign Policy, 25
Fortune 500 corporations, 13
fossil fuel supplies, 24, 26, 29–30, 87
Fourth World, 62
Frank, T., 76
Frankfurt School of Critical Theory, 31
Freeman, R.E., 52, 54
Freeman, R.E. et al., 53

Freeman, R.E. and Phillips, R., 54
Friedman, Milton, 5, 50, 51
Friends of the Earth, 15

Gap, 17, 56
Gasland, 27
Geldof, Bob, 8, 77
General Electric, 41
General Motors, 41
Generation-Y employees, 70, 77, 92–3
generational conflict, 25
genome revolution, 7, 24–5, 28
Ghana, 46
'gigatrend capitalism', 23–5
Gioia, D., 20
global advertising, 59
Global Carbon Project, 23
global media, 59
Global Reporting Initiative (GRI), 15–16, 96
global south, 60, 61
global warming, 23, 26
globalization
    of agriculture, 28
    centralization and decentralization, 62–4
    convergence and divergence, 58–60
    and cultural diversity, 59
    empowering capital, 14
    expansion of sites for MNCs, 42
    inclusion and exclusion, 60–2
    meaning of, 58
Google, 75–6, 90, 93
Gowan, P., 41
greenhouse gases, 87, 88
Greenpeace, 26, 30
Greer, J., 27, 30
Guillén, M., 39
Gulf of Mexico oil spill, 1, 7, 82, 83

Habermas, J., 86
Hacker Manifesto, 73
Halliburton, 37
Hanlon, G., 6, 81, 90, 91, 93
Hanlon, G. and Fleming, P., 81, 89
Harney, S., 14, 62
Harvard Business Review, 1
Harvey, D., 19
health, 2, 28, 43, 76, 84
health and safety, 46, 53, 80
Heilbroner, R., 12, 26
Held, D., 38, 48
Held, D. et al., 39
Herman, E., 41
Hochschild, A., 72
HRM, 89
Human Genome Project, 28

ideology of corporation, 84–5
immanent critique, 19
inclusion and exclusion, 60–2
India, 45, 47

Indonesia, 44
industrial restructuring, 60
International Energy Agency (IEA), 24
innovations, 90
Intel, 46
Interfaith Center on Corporate
    Responsibility, 15
International Labour Organization (ILO), 61
Iran, 27

Jakarta, 28
Japan, 39
job creation, 61
    'good' work replaced by 'bad', 61
Johnson, S., 41
Jones, M., 60
Jones, T., 5

Kenneth Lay Chair, 100

labour markets, 61
Lagos, 28
Land, C. and Taylor, S., 79
Lasch, C., 38, 47–8
Lash, S. and Lury, C., 59
Latin America, 60
    water supply, 43
Lee, M., 20, 100
legitimation, 15–16
Lehman, G., 14
Lem, W. and Barber, P.G., 59
Levy, D.L., 54
liberal communism, 7–8, 77
'liberation management', 74, 76
life expectancy, 24–5
lifestyle firms, 71–2
limited liability, 34
limits of business, 31, 35
Lion Nathan Ltd., 60
lobby groups, 105
lobbying by businesses, 14
local identity, 60
Lufthansa, 104
Lustig, J., 35

McCarthy, Cormac, 106–7
McIntosh, M. et al., 34
Mackenzie, C. and Lewis, A., 11
McKinsey & Company, 22
McKinsey Quarterly, 90, 93
management
    new discourse of, 74
    and radicalism, 76–7
managers, responsibilities of, 50
manufacturing sectors
    de-industrializing, 38
maquiladoras, 56
Margolis, J. and Walsh, J., 101
'market of stakeholders', 10
marketing and branding for CSR, 8

marketing/branding exercise, CSR as, 1
marketization of CSR, 10
Marx, Karl, 67
material progress, 31–2
Matten, D. and Crane, A., 34, 36–7, 48
Matten, D. et al., 34
Medeiros, C. de, 43
megacities, growth of, 25, 28–9
Mexico, 27, 44, 56
Meyerson, D., 77
Michelli, J., 94
micromarketing, 60
Microsoft, 22, 75
migration from rural areas to cities, 28
Milne, M.J. and Chan, C.C., 11
Mintz, B. and Schwartz, M., 41
MNC *see* multinational corporations (MNCs)
modernization thesis, 27
monetarist policies, 12
Moneva, M. et al., 16
Moon, J. et al., 34, 44
Moon, J. and Vogel, D., 35–6
multinational corporations (MNCs), 25, 26, 27
    centralization/decentralization, 62–4
    and competing local firms, 62–3
    control in international economy, 64
    and convergence of business methods, 59
    filling institutional vacuums, 47–8
    globalization and, 42
    increased bargaining power, 42
    as political force for good, 86
    removal from politics, 35
    standing in for government services, 37
    twentieth century growth, 35
    and urban poverty, 43
    see also new corporate citizenship (NCC)

Naidoo, Kumi, 29, 87
neo-classical economics, 12
Nestlé, 17, 92
Netherlands, 13
network systems, 63
new corporate citizenship (NCC), 22, 33–49,
    85–6
    development, 33, 36
    and evolution of citizenship, 38
    maintaining workers' rights, 44–5
    and outsourcing, 45–8
New Right ideology, 39
new technologies, 60
New Zealand, 39, 60
NGOs, 15–16
    influence of, 29
    institutional capture of, 15
    sectional, promotional and anchored, 15
Nigeria, 29
    Shell, 37–8, 56–7
Nike, 17, 44, 56
North American Free Trade Agreement (NAFTA), 28
nostalgia oriented marketing, 59, 60

O'Dwyer, B., 9
oil spills, 1, 82, 83
oil supplies, 24, 26, 27, 29–30
Oosterhout, H. van and Heugens, P., 44
'organizational man', 71
outsourcing, 14, 45–8
    and citizenship, 46–7
    and spacial restructuring, 46, 47
    and stakeholders, 47
over-identification, 103–4

panacea of CSR, 85–7
parasitic nature of CSR, 89–90
Partners' Blend, 92
pension funds, 11
Perelman, M., 84
pharmaceutical firms, 63
Poland, 27
Polanyi, K., 106
polarized wealth, 61
political CSR, 44, 106
Porter, M. and Kramer, M., 22
poverty, 25, 43, 96
PricewaterhouseCoopers, 4
priorities of firms, 10
private equity funds, 41
privatization, 33, 37, 39, 43,
    89, 90
profit-seeking behaviour, CSR as, 9–10
profiteering, 17
profits
    compatibility with ethics, 84
    ethical manner of pursuit of, 2
    primary motive for corporations,
        5, 50, 83
    pursuit of as path to goodness, 53–4
    put 'before people and the planet', 29
propaganda, CSR as, 87–9
property rights, 5
Prothero, A., 12
Prudhoe Bay spill, 82
public relations departments, 9
public spending cuts, 43
public-private distinction, 34

radicalism, 76–8
Razorfish, 73
Reed, D., 53
Registration, Evaluation, Authorisation and of
    Chemicals Directive, 14
regulation, 60
regulatory capture, 100
Reich, R., 35
research
    Business Activity Impact Matrix (BAIM),
        20–2, **21**
    'business case' perspective, 100
    CSR and financial performance, 20
    on executive development
        industry, 98

research *cont.*
  focused on CSR and financial
    performance, 100
  legitimating profit-motive, 18
  link to business and society, **100**–1
  need for change, 105–6
  preliminary steps for researchers, 105
  progressive research, 107
  and use of term 'CSR', 99
  weakness of, 96–7
Research Excellence Framework, 100
resistance, 76–8, 93–4
Restriction of Hazardous Substances
  (ROHS), 13
revenues-costs gap, 10
Rio+20 Earth Summit 2012, 2, 14, 29
rise of corporations, 35
Roberts, J., 6, 50, 88
Rosica, C., 74
Ross, A., 73, 75
Royal Dutch Shell, 29–30
Russia, 82

Sao Paulo, 28
Sassen, S., 39
Scherer, A. et al., 34, 44
Scherer, A. and Palazzo, G., 45, 86
Sea Gem rig disaster, 82
self-regulation, 19, 45
separation of CSR from core operations, 9
Shamir, R., 6
shared values, 22
Shell, 1, 29–30, 99
  Nigeria, 37–8, 56–7
Siemens, 84
Singapore, 24, 27
slums, rise of, 25, 28–9
Smith, Adam, 31
Smith, N.C., 12, 15
social competencies, exploitation of, 92
social entrepreneurship, 22, 92–3
social funds, 11–12
Soros, George, 77
South Africa, 27
sovereign wealth funds, 41
spacial restructuring, 46, 47
stakeholder management, 50, 51, 53
  promoting enlightened behaviour, 54
stakeholder theory, 50–60
  and critical stakeholder analysis (CSA), 51, 52,
    54–6, **65**–6
  definitions, 52
  empowerment/disempowerment, 60
  failings of, 54–5
  and globalization, 56–64
  legal and moral obligations, 53
  orthodox and critical, **65**
  and power of stakeholders, 55
  stakeholder democracy, 51
Starbucks, 10, 76, 93–4

state
  and capital, 14
  and civil society, 86
  loss of powers to corporations, 39, 56
  reconfiguration of, 38–40, 89
  relationship with business, 35–6, 39–40, 86–7
  rescinding civil liberties post 9/11, 39
state regulation, 13–14, 33
Stieb, J., 54
'strategic corporate philanthropy', 22
structural adjustments programmes (SAPs), 43
Sulston, John, 28
surplus humanity, 25, 43
sustainability, 24, 26, 96, 98
  and capitalism, 26
sweatshops, 17, 97

Tapscott, D. and Williams, A., 90
tax liability, 38, 48
tax policy, 39
tempered radicals, 77–8
Tesco, 48, 56
tobacco industry, 70, 88
triple bottom line reports, 15
Trosclair, A., 74
tuberculosis, 43
'two-tiered global economy', 62

UN Conference on Trade and
  Development 2010, 60
UN Environment Programme Finance Initiative
  (UNEPFI), 16
UN Global Compact, 33
UN (United Nations), 1
UN-Habitat, 43
United Kingdom, 39
  universities, 40
United States, 24, 39, 56
  drivers of employee engagement, 70
  energy supplies, 27
  Environmental Protection Agency, 13
  financial crisis, 41
  outsourcing from, 46, 47
University of Missouri, 100
urban poverty, 25, 43
urbanization, 25, 28
USSR, 26

Van Buren, H.J., 54
Vise, D, 75
Vogel, D., 22

Washington Consensus, 24, 38, 43
Waste Electrical and Electronic Equipment
  Act, 13
water supply
  Africa, 16
  Latin America, 43
welfare, 89
welfare state, 61, 90

West, decline of, 24
Western development model, 24
Western liberal capitalism, 25
Whole Foods, 84
Wikipedia: inventory of corporate scandals, 80
Wood, D., 20, 43
workers
  and authenticity, 74–6
  child labour, 17, 67, 97
  and creativity, 73
  exploitation of, 88
  happy with CSR, 72–3
  and health discourse, 76
  and holistic management, 71–2
  initiating CSR, 78–9
  and meaning of work, 71
  reconciliation to business values, 73–4

workers *cont.*
  and resistance, 76–8
  self and identity, 70, 71
  social competencies of, 92
  values of, 67, 69
    at odds with business values, 73
    and drivers of engagement, 69–70
World Bank, 34, 62
world health, 28, 43, 84
World Trade Organization (WTO), 28
WorldCom, 84

'Y-International' (pseudonym), 73
Yahoo, 75
youth empowerment, 92–3

Žižek, S., 30–1, 43, 67, 77, 88, 97

CORPORATE SOCIAL RESPONSIBILITY

Edited by **Esben Rahbek Gjerdrum Pedersen**, *Copenhagen Business School*

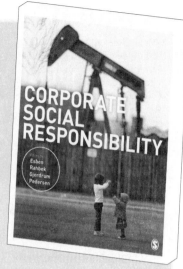

Why has CSR become part of the mainstream business and academic agenda in the 21st century? How can CSR be fully integrated in business strategy and day-to-day operations? Do companies become more vulnerable to criticism from stakeholders if they make public their commitment to CSR? These are just some of the questions and challenges explored in this exciting new textbook. Readers will not only gain comprehensive knowledge and understanding of the history of CSR, the key CSR drivers, the main theoretical CSR perspectives and the dominant CSR practices found in the business community, they will also, more crucially, learn how to implement CSR in practice. Written and edited by leading academics in the field, *Corporate Social Responsibility* is an engaging and accessible text designed for any student seeking an introduction to this complex and ambiguous subject.

CONTENTS

PART 1: INTRODUCTION \ Esben Rahbek Gjerdrum Pedersen Chapter 1: The Life and Times of CSR \ **PART 2**: THE INTERNAL ORGANISATION OF CSR \ Robert Strand Chapter 2: CSR and Leadership \ Esben Rahbek Gjerdrum Pedersen Chapter 3: CSR and Accounting \ **PART 3**: THE EXTERNAL ORGANISATION OF CSR \ Chapter 4: CSR and Suppliers \ Michael Carrington, Ben Neville Chapter 5: CSR and Consumers \ Celine Louche Chapter 6: CSR and Shareholders \ Reinhard Steurer Chapter 7: CSR and Government \ Arno Kouroula Chapter 8: CSR and Non-Governmental Organisations (NGOs) \ Esben Rahbek Pedersen **PART 4**: CONCLUSION AND PERSPECTIVES

READERSHIP

Students of corporate social responsibility

November 2013 • 432 pages
Cloth (978-0-85702-244-8) • £85.00
Paper (978-0-85702-245-5) • £29.99

ALSO FROM SAGE

CORPORATE GOVERNANCE

Principles and Issues

Donald Nordberg *Westminster Business School*

uk.sagepub.com//nordberg

Offering a fresh look at the commonly accepted view of what constitutes good governance, Donald Nordberg explores the contexts of board decisions and draws upon his academic research and years of business and financial journalism in Europe, North America and Asia to provide a distinctive and pertinent contribution to the literature on corporate governance.

The book:

- Features 21 detailed case studies, drawn from international examples, to prompt discussion and analysis
- Provides topical, up-to-date examples and evidence
- Gives attention to the important question 'What next for Corporate Governance?'

Supporting features include: case study questions; 'Agenda Point' boxes to provide further analysis and consideration on topical issues; further readings; and a companion website, featuring online resources.

CONTENTS

Introducing Corporate Governance \ The Problems of Corporate Governance \ **PART 1**: PRINCIPLES OF CORPORATE GOVERNANCE \ Theories of Corporate Governance \ Mechanisms of Corporate Governance \ Corporate Governance in a Global Economy \ Codes of Corporate Governance \ **PART 2**: ISSUES ON THE BOARD'S AGENDA \ Issues within the Board \ Issues between Boards and Management \ Issues between Boards and Owners \ Issues between Owners \ Issues between the Company and Its Publics \ **PART 3**: REPORTING, REBALANCING AND THE FUTURE \ Transparency: The Universal Antiseptic \ Governance beyond Corporations \ An Unsettled and Unsettling Future?

READERSHIP

Final-year undergraduate and postgraduate students of corporate governance; also students of corporate social responsibility and business ethics, and related topics

2010 • 288 pages

Cloth (978-1-84787-332-3) • £87.00
Paper (978-1-84787-333-0) • £28.99

ALSO FROM SAGE

THE SAGE HANDBOOK OF CORPORATE GOVERNANCE

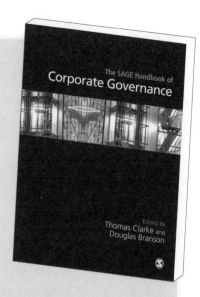

Edited by **Thomas Clarke** *University of Technology, Sydney* and **Douglas Branson** *University of Pittsburgh*

The urgent and sustained interest in corporate governance is unprecedented, with the connections between corporate governance and economic performance being emphasized by the World Bank, the IMF and others in the global economic community.

In this timely and definitive intellectual analysis of a key discipline, *The SAGE Handbook of Corporate Governance* offers a critical overview of the key themes, theoretical controversies, current research and emerging concepts that frame the field. Consisting of original substantive chapters by leading international scholars, and examining corporate governance from an inter-disciplinary basis, the text highlights how governance issues are critical to the formation, growth, financing, structural development, and strategic direction of companies and how corporate governance institutions in turn influence the innovation and development of industrial and economic systems globally.

Comprehensive, authoritative and presented in a highly-accessible framework, this Handbook is a significant resource to those with an interest in understanding this important emerging field.

READERSHIP
Postgraduate students, researchers and academics in corporate governance, business ethics and corporate social responsibility

April 2012 • 680 pages
Cloth (978-1-4129-2980-6) • £95.00

ALSO FROM SAGE